THE
WORLD'S
WILDEST CONS

ALSO BY DUNCAN McKENZIE

The World's Even Dumber Criminals

THE
WORLD'S
WILDEST
CONS

INCREDIBLE TRUE TALES OF HUSTLES, FRAUDS AND SWINDLES

DUNCAN McKENZIE

Collins

HarperCollins Publishers Ltd
Bay Adelaide Centre, East Tower
22 Adelaide Street West, 41st Floor
Toronto, Ontario, Canada
M5H 4E3

www.harpercollins.ca

Library and Archives Canada Cataloguing in Publication
information is available on request.

ISBN 978-1-4434-7195-4

Printed and bound in the United States of America
24 25 26 27 28 LBC 5 4 3 2 1

CONTENTS

Introduction   1

Author's Note   3

Chapter 1: Just Hand Me Your Money   5

Chapter 2: Princes and Prisoners   19

Chapter 3: Scamily Family   37

Chapter 4: Can You Cash a Cheque?   51

Chapter 5: It's Just a Game   69

Chapter 6: Winning the Lottery   85

Chapter 7: Gold and Jewels   95

Chapter 8: Trojan Horse Scams   115

Chapter 9: Con Artist Artists   123

Chapter 10: False Advertising   131

Chapter 11: A Miscellany of Miscreants   149

Chapter 12: And You Tell Two Friends . . .   159

Chapter 13: S.O.B. Stories   169

Chapter 14: We've Got You Covered   179

Chapter 15: Robbing Peter to Pay Ponzi   187

Chapter 16: High-Tech Cons   199

Chapter 17: Romance and Marriage Scams   209

Chapter 18: Too Good to Be False?   225

Chapter 19: The Imposters   247

Chapter 20: Chump Change   259

Chapter 21: Bad Company   267

Chapter 22: Animal Scams   275

Postscript   287

Acknowledgments   289

THE
WORLD'S
WILDEST CONS

INTRODUCTION

Cons, scams, swindles and frauds—the methods used in these crimes are intriguing, and their practitioners seem to earn a grudging respect not given to other criminals. It's right there in the job title. A crook who opens a safe is a safecracker. One who quietly lifts wallets is a pickpocket. But the criminal who uses trickery to win the confidence of a victim is a con *artist*. Artist! What other branch of crime gets such respect?

Part of the draw comes from the sheer audacity of the con artist's activity. It is a psychological game using deception and guile. The scammer may spin complex and appealing stories their victims want to believe. These criminals—part thief, part actor, part conjuror—frequently avoid force, and instead engage in a battle of wits with their targets, persuading, seducing, confusing and distracting. Like good magicians, their secret strategies are hard to detect, often surprising and sometimes genuinely creative.

When we hear about a successful con, we can't help wondering, *If that were me, would I be fooled?* And in some cases, if you don't know the method, you might well be.

It's been said that you can't con an honest person. It's not true. In fact, many of the cons we'll look at profit from the cruel exploitation of a person's genuine charity, compassion or love. But there are some scams—arguably the ones that make the best stories—which seem to

1

operate according to a twisted system of criminal honour, deliberately scamming those who hoped to scam others.

So, let's step warily into the realm of the con artist—it's a world of deception, duplicity and disguise. In the pages that follow, you'll learn the sneaky secrets that con artists have used to manipulate others, tricks that have earned criminals thousands and, in many cases, millions of dollars. Some come from the pages of ancient history, while others use the latest computer technology, but they have all been effective in separating people from their money, and many are still in use. A good con never dies.

We hope you will put this information to good use in protecting yourself from all sorts of cons. Of course, you could also put it to bad use, and use these schemes to con others, but we know you wouldn't do that, because ... well ... we have *confidence* in you.

AUTHOR'S NOTE

Pseudonyms have been used to protect the identities of various individuals mentioned in this book where warranted or deemed appropriate in the circumstances. Any name that's in quotation marks the first time it appears in this book is a pseudonym and not (as far as we know) the real name of the person so identified.

In some cases, details of a story have been amalgamated from different instances of the same widespread scam, but we have tried to ensure the example accurately portrays common details of the con.

CHAPTER 1

JUST HAND ME YOUR MONEY

Cons go back a long way. The animal kingdom is full of cheats and tricksters. It's likely been going on for hundreds of millions of years.

One species of firefly sends mating flashes resembling those of another species. When hopeful suitors from the other species approach, they are seized and eaten.

A fish called the fangblenny hangs out with the "cleaner fish" it resembles. The cleaners gently remove parasites from the scales of the big fish. The fangblenny looks like it will do the same, but instead of cleaning, it bites off a chunk of flesh.

Crows use predator alarm calls to scare away their relatives from newly discovered food, then the corvid con artist has time to move in and grab it.

Human cons are a sophisticated version of a very ancient pattern.

THE ORIGINAL CON ARTIST

Criminals who carry out scams have gone by many names: *swindlers, rogues, mountebanks, bamboozlers, grifters*. The origins of many of these terms are lost in time. But we can say exactly when the term *con artist* appeared. It was in nineteenth-century America.

In 1848, in New York City, a Baptist minister heard a knock at his door. The visitor was a well-dressed man who said his name was William Thompson. Without wasting too much time on preliminaries, Thompson asked if the minister was in any financial distress.

"Because if you are, I will be happy to give you money."

The clergyman was puzzled, but insisted that, no, he didn't need any money.

Thompson was relieved to hear it.

"But how about your church? If it should need money now, or in the future, I'll be there to help. That's the sort of confidence I have in you, my friend, even though you are a stranger to me."

"Well, thank you," said the minister.

"Yes, sir, the way I see it, not many people would have so much confidence in a stranger to make the sort of offer I have just made."

The pastor wasn't quite sure how to deal with this boast, but he agreed. Yes, that was probably true.

A thought seemed to enter Thompson's head. He wanted to explore the idea further.

"I have shown my confidence in you, but even though you are a man of the cloth, you probably wouldn't have the same confidence in me."

"Oh, I don't know about that," laughed the pastor. "I should hope I am just as capable of trusting an honest stranger."

"With respect, I find that hard to believe," said Thompson. "It's all very well to say it, but no, no, I don't think you could show your confidence in me."

The two men discussed the point, and finally the pastor was determined to prove it. He produced $30 in cash—the equivalent of about $1,000 today—and handed it to Thompson.

"Take it and bring it back tomorrow."

Thompson seemed overcome with emotion at this display of trust.

"You *do* have confidence in me." He walked to the door. "I am going to leave, for the present," he said. "But, rest assured, this is not the last you'll hear of me."

Thompson left with the money and never returned.

Of course, the minister had just been cheated out of $30. But Thompson's last words were true, even though he didn't yet know it. The minister would hear of him again, because Thompson was about to enter the history books as the original "Confidence Man."

Thompson had grown up in New York. As a youngster, he had picked pockets, carried out burglaries and committed other low-level crimes. He was a bold criminal, but not a very skilled one. In 1841, when he was twenty or so, he and his brother were caught robbing a lace store. He spent two years in prison.

While he was behind bars, Thompson wondered if there were better opportunities outside New York. He had heard that in Philadelphia, the head of law enforcement, a corrupt "high constable" named James Young, operated a well-organized network of criminals. Their connections to the police meant the gang could steal with less risk of prison time. He liked the sound of that.

When Thompson had served his time in New York, he headed for Pennsylvania and applied for work with Young and his criminal gang. Young accepted him into the organization, but Thompson didn't stay for long. The newcomer was careless and clumsy, and as his reputation spread, the more skilled thieves refused to work with him. He was kicked out of the criminal underworld.

Unable to support himself even as a common thief, Thompson decided on a different career path—he would be a swindler. Somewhere along the way, he had been told that the key to success in swindling was to establish trust and "build confidence." Thompson's hustling was as clumsy as his thieving and he took this idea very literally. Instead of doing something ingenious to build his mark's confidence, he just walked up to them and asked for it. He dared them to "show your confidence in me" by handing over money.

The approach was simple, bold and idiotic. It was so stupid that it sometimes worked. Once Thompson was gone with their belongings, his victims felt like idiots, but that worked in Thompson's favour: they were ashamed to tell the authorities about how they'd been so easily duped.

After he'd worked Philadelphia for a while, Thompson moved to other big cities, then returned to New York, where he used his unsophisticated tactics to steal the $30 from the Baptist minister. He used many aliases. Sometimes he was Samuel Thompson (the name used in many early newspaper reports about him). Sometimes he was James Thompson. He may also have been Samuel Thomas, Samuel Powel, Samuel Williams, William Evans, Samuel Willis, William Davis and William Brown.

Thompson didn't always make house calls. More often, he approached strangers on the street.

In May 1849, walking on William Street in New York, Thompson approached a ship's joiner named Hugh McDonald.

"How are you doing?" asked the criminal. He smiled as if he recognized McDonald.

"I've been well," said McDonald cautiously.

Thompson made some other friendly inquiries, and McDonald was puzzled. He figured this stranger must be someone he knew, but had forgotten.

"Could you lend me 50 cents?" asked Thompson.

"I don't have 50 cents to lend," said McDonald.

"If you don't have 50 cents, can you lend me $5?" Thompson asked.

If the man was trying to be playful, McDonald didn't appreciate it. He said no, he couldn't.

Thompson seemed amused. "You don't appear to know me," he said.

McDonald confessed he didn't and asked the man's name.

It was time for Thompson to play his confidence card. "That won't do you any good," he said. "The truth is, I don't want your 50 cents or your $5. I only wanted your confidence. I have plenty of money of my own. Look." Thompson pulled out bills from his pockets and showed the money to McDonald. "If you want help, I will give it to you. You can have $5,000 or $6,000 if you want, at any time."

McDonald was confused by this discussion. He hadn't asked for money. He glanced at his pocket watch and said he was in a hurry and needed to go.

"That's a handsome watch," said Thompson. He knew a thing or two about watches. This one was gold, and he guessed it to be worth more than $100. "Would you lend me that watch?"

"No!" said McDonald. "I wouldn't lend this watch to my father."

Thompson could see he had failed in his effort to win McDonald's confidence, so he switched to a different strategy. He grabbed the watch, yanked it from its chain, then ran off down the street.

McDonald was astonished and he stood for a few moments in a state of incomprehension. Why would a man who claimed to be his friend and wanted to give him thousands of dollars suddenly run off with his watch? Then McDonald realized that Thompson was a thief—and one who was getting away. McDonald tried chasing him, but Thompson gave him the slip.

It was the last time Hugh McDonald ever saw his pocket watch, but two months later, he spotted Thompson on a street just a few minutes' walk from his previous encounter. McDonald quickly found a policeman and had Thompson arrested.

Thompson gave a string of inconsistent excuses. He had never had the watch. And if he had had the watch, it was probably given to him. He offered to pay McDonald for the watch he'd never had. Then, once again, Thompson tried to run. This time, however, he failed to escape. The officer took Thompson to "the Tombs"—the jail in Manhattan's old Egyptian-style Halls of Justice—to await trial.

Others who had lost watches visited the jail. They identified Thompson as the man who had cheated them. They were small-time crimes in a city where such thefts occurred on a daily basis.

But while Thompson languished in jail, his exploits were reported in the *New York Herald*. The journalist who was covering local crimes embellished some of the facts to make more exciting copy. In a series of short articles, the writer gave Thompson the title "the Confidence Man." He exaggerated a little as he described the swindler's psychological attack—the way Thompson could use his persuasive powers to lull his victims into a false sense of security. The articles claimed criminals called this process "putting them to sleep."

It sounded as if Thompson could mesmerize any ordinary person and persuade them to hand over valuables. Readers were fascinated. They started following his case. Other newspapers picked up the story.

The truth is, the only thing extraordinary about Thompson's methods was how awkward they were. That's why, after his clumsy attempts at persuasion failed to work on Hugh McDonald, he resorted to grabbing the watch. At heart, Thompson was just a low-level thief. But in the public imagination, his powers seemed to reach almost supernatural levels—he was a supervillain who could take control of another person's mind.

Everyone in New York was talking about "the Confidence Man" and his powers. Within weeks of the articles appearing, an enterprising playwright had dashed off a farce titled *The Confidence Man*. The *New York Herald* said it was "one of the funniest things of the season," and it helped keep Thompson in the limelight. Thompson rapidly became a criminal celebrity. The newspapers had given him the label "the Confidence Man," but now he started using the label himself.

Herman Melville, the author of *Moby Dick*, followed the case. It became the inspiration for a book by Melville, also titled *The Confidence Man*.

A new term had entered the language. A *confidence man* (later *con man* and *con artist*) came to mean an ingenious and persuasive swindler. Thompson himself was not ingenious: he was a clumsy fool whose crimes would have been forgotten by history if a journalist hadn't invented the term to mesmerize the public, so they would hand over their money and buy more newspapers. You could say the creation of the new term *con* was itself a con.

THE PIGEON DROP

William Thompson's concept of how to win a person's confidence was simplistic, and he seems to have had far more failures than successes. Most people aren't fools—they won't usually hand over their valuables without a good reason. But the basic idea of winning a stranger's confidence is sound, and when that is combined with a convincing story, people might just hand over money—lots of money.

In summer 2015, an elderly Florida woman, "Clarisse," was shopping at her local supermarket and struck up a conversation with a well-dressed stranger. "Jim" was close to her own age, and she found they had plenty to talk about. As they chatted near the exit, a younger woman, "Vanessa," approached them carrying a black duffel bag. She seemed confused. Vanessa said she had just found the bag in the parking lot. It was full of money.

They all took a peek. Sure enough, the bag was stuffed with bills. They could find no identification inside, but they did find a note. It appeared to be a checklist for various weights of commodity. It seemed like the money was payment for a drug deal that had gone wrong.

Clarisse could hardly believe it. Imagine leaving so much money in a parking lot!

Of course, the money had to be turned in, they all agreed on that. But there was no harm in dreaming, and they talked about what they would do with so much money. Vanessa said she would move to a better apartment. Jim said he would take a vacation with his wife. Clarisse said she had two young grandchildren she'd like to help support.

As they talked, Jim wondered aloud if perhaps they could keep it. Come to think of it, he'd heard about some sort of "finders-keepers" law.

"I've heard about that, too," said Vanessa. In fact, she had a friend who was a lawyer and she thought she should ask his advice before they turned the bag in. It would be crazy not to.

Vanessa went off to phone her lawyer friend, while Clarisse and Jim waited.

"He will probably say we have to turn it in."

"Sure . . . sure."

But as they sat there with the bag, it was hard not to think about all that money.

Vanessa returned with surprising news. Her lawyer friend said, if they played their cards right, they would almost certainly be able to keep the money! But they shouldn't celebrate too soon—it would take several months to process it legally. To keep things above board, the lawyer had advised Vanessa that each of the three finders should demonstrate that they had the resources to support themselves during that time.

Clarisse was confused. Support themselves? Of course she could support herself!

Vanessa said it was some kind of legal thing. Her lawyer had told her that they might each make a good-faith deposit of, say, $20,000 in cash. When it was clear that they each had the funds, the money would be returned, and they could do a three-way split of the cash from the duffel bag.

Clarisse wasn't sure about all this. But if she had doubts, Jim certainly didn't. He wanted to get things settled, and right away. He went to his bank and returned with the money, which he placed in a white plastic grocery bag he had with him. Next, they went with Vanessa to her bank. She came out with her money and put it in the grocery bag with Jim's.

Now it was Clarisse's turn to make her good-faith deposit. She felt a little confused about all this legal talk, but she was excited at the prospect of imminent wealth, and the other two didn't seem to have a problem with it. So Jim and Vanessa cheerfully accompanied her as she went to her bank and withdrew $20,000 from her savings. The withdrawal almost drained the account, but, as Jim reminded her, it would soon be back, along with much more money. Jim put Clarisse's cash in the plastic grocery bag. He then placed the bag with the "good-faith" cash into the black duffel bag and zipped it up.

Vanessa was excited. She wanted to tell her boyfriend what had happened. He was working at a store across the street. She passed the duffel bag to Clarisse to look after while she was gone.

Jim and Clarisse waited for Vanessa, but she took a while to return. Clarisse hoped everything was all right. Jim was concerned. He went off to check on her.

Clarisse kept waiting, holding tight to the duffel bag and feeling nervous about guarding so much money. Neither of her partners returned. She eventually peeked inside the bag. There was the "good-faith" bag, and underneath it, the wads of cash. Although, on closer examination, the stacks of cash didn't look quite right. They were just prop money.

Clarisse felt a sudden sense of panic. She pulled out the white grocery bag containing all that "good-faith" money. It was stuffed with strips of newspaper. Where was the money her partners had put in it? More to the point, where was the money *she* had put in it?

The con that fooled Clarisse was a much more effective confidence trick than anything William Thompson ever practised, and she was well-played by the participants. Clarisse didn't merely hand over money she was carrying; she went to the bank to get everything she had.

This con is a classic, and it's known as the "Pigeon Drop." In its early form, in the 1930s, a stuffed wallet was dropped near the "pigeon" (the victim), who finds himself negotiating with two other people who pretend to be strangers to each other, but are actually working as a team.

Inflation has taken its toll on the scam: a wallet full of money has become a large bag. Still, the basic idea remains the same, and although it is an old con, it still finds many victims each year. The scheme usually involves at least two scammers, who sometimes pretend to distrust each other while both expressing trust in the victim.

Because each of the co-finders unhesitatingly places "good-faith money" in a bag, the victim feels more comfortable following suit. If these strangers can trust each other, they can trust them, too. Using a little sleight of hand, the criminals exchange the bag with the victim's money—usually the only real money involved—for worthless paper. The victim feels secure holding onto the whole bag, which they think contains a fortune, and by the time they think to check the contents, the thieves are far away.

Pigeon Drop scammers often target older women, usually in shopping malls or parking lots. Because the whole deal is shady—they are, after all, scheming to keep found money—the victims of this scam are often reluctant to go to the police afterwards. Some criminals deliberately play up the idea that the victim is participating in an illegal conspiracy.

In 1987, the *Shreveport Journal* reported on a duo who were carrying out the Pigeon Drop scam in Shreveport, Louisiana. The scam worked the same way it did with Clarisse, but with some interesting differences.

The victim was a young woman, "Tasha." She was in a store when she was first approached. She had a pleasant conversation with another woman around her own age, "Shaundra." As they talked, they were joined by a third woman, "Liz," who said she had found a bag of money in the store. The three women discussed what to do with it, and they eventually decided to divide it between the three of them.

Liz claimed that having the money would get them in trouble with the IRS. In order to spend it, they must launder it. Fortunately, she knew a bank official who she believed could help them.

It was necessary for each person to put in "good-faith money." Liz contributed. So did Shaundra. When Tasha didn't have enough money, the other women generously allowed her to contribute jewelry.

The situation ended like most pigeon drops: Tasha was left with a bag of worthless paper, and the other women disappeared with her money and jewelry.

The story surrounding Tasha's pigeon drop is more underhanded than other versions—the found money is not only kept, it must also be laundered to hide it from the IRS. If it were true, the conspiracy would have been highly illegal. Tasha should have been reluctant to report it.

However, it didn't work out that way. Tasha was so indignant at being cheated out of her jewelry that she went straight to the police, who were delighted to receive an excellent description of the other women. The police quickly found the scammers, recovered the money and jewelry, and charged the women, who went to prison for six months.

Con artists who carry out this scam need to be careful their "pigeon" doesn't become a stool pigeon.

THE SPANISH HANDKERCHIEF

Aside from the way it builds trust, the Pigeon Drop scam has two cunning features. First, it makes victims believe they are receiving money when it is actually being taken from them. After the thieves have disappeared, the victim's initial worry is not about getting their own money back, but about returning someone else's.

The scam also makes victims feel that their own money isn't worth much. They may be contributing tens of thousands, but it seems like a trifling amount compared to the huge sums they believe they are holding.

The one element of the scam that is difficult to explain is the "good-faith money." It doesn't really make sense that people who find money should add their own money to it, and it makes even less sense that, having added your money as security for the others, you would get to sit with all the money in your possession. A lot of bamboozling is required to make this sound remotely plausible.

But another con works around these problems.

In the early 1990s, two Swedish tourists, "Lars" and "Erika," were visiting New York. They were experienced travellers and spoke excellent English. As they walked down a city street, a man, "Helmut," approached them.

"Please, to help me?" he asked. "I am new to country. I need find this address. You can help?"

According to the *New York Daily News*, Helmut appeared lost and helpless. The couple spoke much better English than he did and wanted to help him. Lars pulled out his street map, and the couple walked with Helmut, trying to help him find the address he needed. After some minutes of walking, they found the place, but it was an empty lot. Helmut was distressed.

Erika asked where he got the address. "Could there be a mistake?"

"Yes, yes," agreed Helmut. "I will call the man who gave me this. I will go find phone."

But as he was about to leave, Helmut was suddenly filled with doubts. "I am scared to carry all my money with me." Helmut pulled out an impressive wad of cash. "If I am robbed, it is all I have. Please, will you take care of it while I am gone."

Lars and Erika were touched by Helmut's naivety. Lars told him that, in New York, you really shouldn't hand money to strangers. Helmut told them he trusted them completely. Lars was sympathetic. If it made Helmut feel that nervous, he and Erika would be glad to wait behind and look after his money.

Helmut was grateful. "I trust you like my family," he said. He brought out a large and ornate handkerchief and started to wrap it around his money.

"You put your money here, too," he said. "Then, I know you will take care of my money like you take care of your own."

Lars and Erika put their money and valuables into the handkerchief, then Helmut, greatly relieved, wrapped the cloth around the money and carefully tied the corners with half a dozen elaborate knots.

"This is how we do it my country," he said. "It is safer."

Helmut was about to hand it to Lars when he had another idea.

"In my country, when we carry money, we do not place it in the hand. No. We hide in, how do you say? In jacket pocket, like this."

Helmut placed the wrapped package in his jacket pocket, then removed it again. "You do this, too, please? To make safe?"

While Erika tried not to laugh, Lars said he would be happy to do things Helmut's way. He tucked the package firmly under his jacket. Satisfied, Helmut left, promising to return as soon as he had found the address.

Lars and Erika waited in the empty lot. Helmut did not return. They became concerned. Then they became suspicious—the business with the handkerchief was strange. At last, Erika picked open the little knots and opened the handkerchief. It contained a wad of newspaper.

They realized that when Helmut had placed the handkerchief in his jacket, he had substituted it with an identical knotted package. They had lost their money, their passports and their airline tickets.

"The Spanish Handkerchief" is another old scam, and while some of the methods overlap those of the Pigeon Drop, the con artist provides a slightly more plausible reason to handle the victim's money.

In the 1973 film *The Sting*, two Illinois grifters, played by Robert Redford and Robert Earl Jones (father of James), perform the Spanish Handkerchief on a gangster and come away with more money than they can safely handle. The scam probably wasn't that common in 1930s Illinois, but it was an epidemic in 1970s New York.

In another variation of the scam, the con artist may pose as a wealthy philanthropist who wants to give money to a stranger (the victim) so that they can donate it to whatever good cause they want to support. The philanthropist's bean-counting assistant insists that his boss is being too naive: "How do you know this person can be trusted to distribute so much money to the poor? We need to make sure they have money of their own." The boss claims to trust the victim, but goes along with it to teach his employee a lesson, and the victim is encouraged to visit a bank. The cash the victim produces is then placed into a handkerchief "for safety," and the victim walks home guarding a handkerchief full of newspaper.

New York is a huge city, and in most cases, victims of the Spanish Handkerchief will never see the con artist or their money again. But Lars and Erika were lucky. The following day, they were riding the subway and spotted Helmut. One grabbed him while the other found a police officer. Helmut was arrested and ended up going to prison.

CHAPTER 2
PRINCES AND PRISONERS

In the 1980s, Nigeria was a wildly corrupt country. The oil industry was booming, but much of the money was being channelled to corrupt government officials and their cronies. Amid this wealth, chaos and corruption, a scam emerged that fit the times. It was about a corrupt leader or official and his son, who wanted to get his hands on the father's ill-gotten gains.

This was the famous "Nigerian Prince" scam. It first appeared in the form of printed letters (sent using counterfeit postage) and then, as the internet took off, as spam emails.

But, as we'll see, this is just the latest version of a con that has been raking in the cash literally for centuries and looks set to keep working into the future.

THE NIGERIAN REFUND

In 2005, Derek, a self-employed handyman from Wichita, Kansas, received an email from a prince in Nigeria. Most of us are familiar with the type of offer, but it impressed Derek.

The prince was due to get a vast inheritance from his deceased royal father, but he was unable to transfer it to his account in Nigeria. If he did, the government would confiscate the money. His solution was to move the money to the United States first. For that, he needed Derek's help. The prince's lawyers would see to it that Derek was named the beneficiary in the father's will—the authorities wouldn't stop a payment to America. The prince could then leave Nigeria for America, where Derek would hand over the bulk of the cash, keeping a cool $64 million for himself, to compensate him for all his time and trouble.

Derek asked for details and was told that moving the money would require some upfront payments. That didn't sound right to Derek, but the prince explained that moving large sums of money from one country to another was fraught with bureaucracy. It could cost thousands of dollars to move the vast sums involved in this case.

Derek paid the money through Western Union and, as the months rolled by, he made more payments, covering legal fees, processing fees, bribes and so on.

He stayed hooked for three years. He often had doubts, but the prince and his entourage reassured him, urging him not to give up now, not when the money was so close.

By 2008, Derek had handed over $110,000 to the prince. In the process, he had remortgaged his house three times. He still believed the stories—he had sunk so much into the scheme that he couldn't afford not to.

Finally, the big day arrived. The prince was sending him the money in cash. They told Derek to go to the airport and meet the courier: he would be carrying two large trunks.

Derek went and scoured the terminal building looking for an overloaded Nigerian courier. Nobody showed. He finally realized that he'd been cheated.

Millions of "Nigerian Prince" emails were sent during the early 2000s, and many thousands of people lost money to the scam. In Derek's case, he lost most of his assets.

Many victims of these scams never see their money again, but Derek's story was unusual and does have a happy ending. The U.S. Department of Justice was displeased with Western Union's lax business practices when it came to online scams. The company admitted having knowledge that some of its employees had worked with scam artists, and it set aside a large fund for American and Canadian victims—if those victims could prove how much money they had sent.

Derek might have been too trusting, but his record-keeping was second to none. He was a man used to running his own business and he had kept track of every payment and piece of correspondence. He presented all his emails and receipts to the attorney general's office and ended up receiving a refund of the entire $110,000 he had lost.

LETTERS FROM JERUSALEM

The Nigerian Prince was one of the first big email scams, but it's just the latest incarnation of a very old con.

Around 1796, a twenty-year-old French criminal named Eugène-François Vidocq was caught and sent to prison.

He made friends in the prison and soon discovered that it was possible to make a good living behind bars. One method was to write fraudulent letters.

These were known as "Jerusalem Letters," and they were an old scam even then. They would be addressed to wealthy people: French citizens who had survived the French Revolution with their necks intact but were secretly nostalgic for the good old days, when kings were kings and peasants knew their place. Everything in the letter was calculated to appeal to such a person.

The letter would begin with an apology.

> "I am just a lowly servant and I apologize for writing to someone so great and important, and so far above me in status. I would not do so if the need were not desperate."

This set the right tone and explained any spelling or grammatical errors that might follow.

The "servant" claimed he had been a trusted employee of a wealthy marquis.

During the revolution, he said, the noble marquis had to flee for his life, taking his most valuable items with him. The valuables included a chest full of gold and diamonds. He was accompanied only by his most loyal servant, the humble letter-writer.

At one point in their travels, the two men were chased by revolutionary soldiers. The marquis ordered the servant to get rid of the chest—he knew if they were found with it, the soldiers would know he was an aristocrat, and he would be killed.

The servant did as he was told and buried the treasure. Unfortunately, although he and his master escaped, the presence of the soldiers made it impossible for them to retrieve the chest, and they had to continue on without it.

They finally escaped France and reached safety, but it wasn't long before the marquis found himself short of money. He wished he could get that treasure back.

The good servant offered to fetch it. He had made a careful note of the treasure's location when he hid it. He was sure it would still be there. Nobody would be looking for him. He could return to France, retrieve the chest, then come back to do the thing he most loved: serve his dear master. The marquis agreed to the plan.

The servant went back to France, but on his travels he stayed at an inn owned by an enthusiastic revolutionary. One evening, the innkeeper made a toast to the revolution. The servant knew he should show the same enthusiasm, but he couldn't bring himself to lie. The innkeeper noticed the servant's awkwardness and reported him to the authorities. Now, penniless, he was in prison as a suspected criminal.

The servant cared nothing for his own life, but he wanted to deliver the treasure to his lord and master. He needed the help of a good, trustworthy person to locate the treasure for him and return it to the marquis. In return, he was sure the marquis would offer a generous reward.

According to Vidocq, about one in five of these letters received a reply. Some recipients might genuinely want to return the marquis's wealth. Others might see an opportunity to keep the fortune for themselves. Regardless, the servant would offer to send them a map of the location, but would face a series of expenses and bribes which their correspondent had to pay. The scam might end with the tragic death of the marquis, and the servant making a deal to sell the treasure chest for a bargain price.

Some of the exchanges could be very profitable. The con made enough money that the (real) prisoners writing the letters had no trouble bribing the guards, so they could continue their work.

If the scam went on long enough, the victim might finally receive a set of directions giving the location of the treasure. One Parisian cloth-seller was arrested for digging a hole under an arch of the Pont Neuf bridge in Paris. He was convinced it was the hiding place for a chest of gold and jewels.

Vidocq was fascinated by the effectiveness of this con and he wrote about it later in life.

Vidocq quit crime and became a police informant, then a private detective, using his first-hand knowledge of criminals. Eventually, he founded and headed France's first real police force, the Sûreté nationale. Now, that's what we call a con artist.

The letters Vidocq saw were written in the years just after the French Revolution, and the stories that followed were adapted to the events of the time, but the name "Jerusalem Letters" suggests that the scam was about an earlier generation of wealthy people being held prisoner in some far-off land.

This scam has always changed with the times.

CAN YOU HELP ME DIG UP A TREASURE?

Henry Pearce ran an ironworks company in Tavistock, Devon, in the southwest of England. Most of his correspondence was related to his business and came from local customers or suppliers. But in September 1888, he received an unusual letter in the post. It bore a Spanish stamp and was postmarked from Madrid.

When he tore open the envelope, things became even more curious. The writer was one Don Antonio Galvez, and he was currently sitting in a prison in Madrid. He owned a vast fortune and he needed Mr. Pearce's help to get it.

The Spaniard's tale was a sad one. Fourteen years earlier, Galvez had bravely fought against the government of his country in the Republican insurrection. He had served as the right-hand man to General Don Juan Contreras, who promoted Galvez to the rank of colonel and also made him his private secretary. But when their position came under siege by government troops, the general knew their situation was hopeless. He called Galvez and sent him on a secret mission. Galvez was entrusted with a large sum of money belonging to the rebels.

"Go to London," said the general. "Deposit this money in the Bank of England."

Galvez took the money and travelled to England, but when he arrived in London to deposit the money, he received a new message from General Contreras. The general warned him that the Spanish government knew about the money and had sent a message to the British government asking them to watch for Galvez and to arrest him. If he went to the Bank of England, he would certainly be apprehended. His new instructions: hide the money in some safe place.

Galvez wandered around England, trying to avoid arrest. He finally ended up in Tavistock, not far from the home of Henry Pearce. He stayed in the town several days and found a safe place to bury the treasure at night. He made precise measurements of the spot using a military sea compass, then carefully made a map of the location. He placed the map in a hidden compartment of one of his suitcases, then returned to Spain. But he never reunited with the general. Instead, he was arrested for his involvement in the uprising. He had been in prison ever since.

The rebels had disbanded, so there was nobody now to claim the money. In fact, nobody else even knew about it. Galvez alone knew about this fortune in cash, but was unable to access the money. For many years, strict prison rules prevented him from contacting anyone in the outside world. But recently, the rules had been relaxed, and he was permitted to write letters.

Of course, Galvez was still in prison, so now he needed a dependable Tavistock man to retrieve the money for him. His investigations showed that Mr. Henry Pearce, of the firm J&H Pearce, was the kind of honest man he could rely on.

So Galvez had a proposal for Pearce: if the English businessman was willing to dig up the money and return it, he could keep an eighth of the sum for himself. The money was in a metal box and consisted of Spanish banknotes. The box was sealed to keep any moisture out, and the banknotes were still current.

Pearce wasn't sure what to make of this foreign letter, but he was certainly intrigued by the proposition. The fee Galvez offered was half a million Spanish pesetas—somewhere in the region of £20,000. (In modern terms, that was equivalent to around £3 million or close to four million US dollars.) Pretty good wages for a spot of digging.

There was a catch. Galvez didn't remember the precise location, and the case containing the concealed map was still held by the authorities. To get access to it, Galvez would need to pay legal fees, but he had no money. He needed Henry Pearce to send him £240.

Henry Pearce didn't want to send any money without doing some checking. He asked for more proof.

Galvez sent other documents, with official stamps, supporting his story, apologizing for how old and dirty they were. He urged Pearce to pay the legal fees. Then Pearce could bring the money to Madrid "and rescue my liberty, as everything is bought in this unhappy country, and immediately I will leave with you for England for ever." He said he was "awaiting feverishly a reply which may give me hope, and to us happiness and felicity."

As a hard-nosed English businessman, Pearce was happy to take a share of the cash, but was put off by the Spanish man's overfamiliarity. *Exactly what kind of happiness did Galvez have in mind?*

And the documents looked wrong. They were as dirty as the letter-writer said, yet the ink looked strangely fresh. Wary now, Henry Pearce tested his correspondent. He asked for information on precisely how Señor Galvez had arrived in Tavistock—by boat or by train? And what landmarks had he used when taking measurements from his compass? If Galvez had really come here, he should remember those details.

Galvez replied that he had arrived in Tavistock after taking the train from Plymouth. He also gave other descriptions of the local area. They sounded plausible but might also have been taken from a guidebook.

Henry Pearce was cautious, but wondered: was he being too cautious? He didn't want to throw away the chance to make a fortune. He wrote to the British ambassador in Madrid, explaining the situation and asking for advice. The ambassador quickly wrote back, strongly advising Pearce to have nothing to do with "Don Galvez"—the whole thing was certainly a swindle.

The ambassador explained that the fraud had been carried out so often in Spain that nobody fell for it anymore, and Spanish criminals were now writing to people in England—usually names they found in trade journals or newspapers. He congratulated Pearce on not being taken in and advised him to warn others about his experience. Pearce took the correspondence no further. He did as the ambassador asked and went to the newspapers. They were interested in the story and gave it some coverage.

The "Spanish Prisoner" fraud was carried out on an industrial scale by con artists in Madrid, who, as the ambassador had said, found the British public more open to the fraud than the Spanish.

The details varied from case to case, but they usually involved a military man who was now a political prisoner and was secretly in possession of a large fortune. Sometimes, like in the case of "Señor Galvez," the writer had hidden money near the recipient's home. The letter-writer always needed the recipient to send money. If the sucker sent money for legal fees, the prisoner might ask for more to bribe a guard or pay an official fee, and it continued until the victim stopped paying.

The officer often claimed a connection with the letter's British recipient. He might say one of his parents or grandparents was British. He always insisted on secrecy, in case word about the money should get back to his Spanish captors.

It may seem strange that the fictitious prisoner's claim on the fictitious money is dubious. For example, if the facts in the letter "Don Galvez" had written to Henry Pearce were true, the money was entrusted to Galvez and it doesn't seem like it is his to give away. Why not claim to be the legitimate owner of the money—perhaps a wealthy man who invested his own money in a failed rebellion?

There are several reasons why this underhanded aspect of the scam works well.

If the letter's recipient is greedy, they may see an opportunity for a bigger profit: they can dig up the money and keep it all for themself, leaving the thieving officer to rot in prison. While they're thinking about this, they're not thinking about whether the letter is legitimate.

Perhaps it is also psychologically easier for the scammer to rob the victim if they can blame them for making an unethical choice. Getting a victim involved in a conspiracy that is slightly criminal is a feature common to many scams.

The underhanded nature of the deal may help protect the scammer from arrest. When victims realize they have been cheated, they may be reluctant to explain to police that they were trying to get a share of stolen funds.

PLEASE TAKE CARE OF
MY BEAUTIFUL WEALTHY DAUGHTER

One stumbling block in the Galvez-Pearce correspondence was the request that Pearce should come to Spain, release Galvez and bring him back to England.

But the scam had variations which overcame this problem. In one well-played version, the letter-writer is sick and weak. He knows he will soon die in prison, but he has a dear wife or a beautiful daughter aged sixteen or so. He has heard about the honesty and integrity of the recipient and begs the reader to help get his daughter to England and to look after her. The daughter and her chaperone (or governess or priest . . .) will bring a map showing where his secret fortune is buried.

A genteel British man or woman was more likely to play host to an innocent Spanish woman than an imprisoned soldier and revolutionary.

In this version, the travel costs can deliver a final payoff. The British correspondent is instructed to send money for two people to travel in style from Spain to England on a certain date. The host family waits patiently for their fortune-bearing guests to show up, which, of course, they don't. Only then do the hosts realize they have been taken for the supposed travel expenses.

Many victims were taken in by the scam. In 1876, the *Times* (of London) carried an advertisement asking for information on a lady heiress and her travel companion, a priest, who were coming to stay with a family in England. The missing persons were almost certainly fictional characters invented for a Spanish Prisoner scam.

Again, this scam offers different inducements to different types of people. A high-minded recipient may feel genuinely moved to protect a vulnerable woman, while a "cad" may like the idea of having a wealthy and attractive Spanish señorita in his house and under his control.

THE SPANISH-AMERICAN PRISONER

The Spanish Prisoner scam continued to change with the times. During the Spanish-American War in 1898, the United States fought Spain, supporting Cuba's independence.

Spain was kicked out of the Caribbean, but like criminal conquistadores, Spanish letter-writers discovered America.

The new versions were crafted to appeal to American sensibilities. The letter-writer might say he was Cuban, an American ally against the cruel Spanish. Sometimes he claimed to be a distant relative of the recipient. He had been arrested because he fought for freedom. Now he was dying in a Spanish prison, but he had money and a lovely daughter.

A flood of letters reached the United States. As with the "Nigerian Prince" a hundred years later, the plight of the "Spanish Prisoner" became a national joke. Even so, many people continued to be taken in.

In 1908, a New York lawyer (who really should have known better) wrote to William M. Collier, American ambassador to Spain, and asked about an offer he had received from a Spanish prisoner with a beautiful daughter and a fortune contained in a trunk.

According to a New Jersey newspaper, Collier told him it was a swindle. He complained that his legation had received hundreds of letters from American citizens asking about the same fraudulent story.

"Recently," he said, "within one week, one man in Iowa and another in New Hampshire have each sent $500 here to pay the expenses of the reputed daughter to America. Two other men have arrived in Madrid, having journeyed all the way from Montana, for the purpose of taking the same child to their home, and a priest in Columbus, Ohio, has informed me that members of his parish have started to mortgage their farms to raise money to send to the swindlers. In the last few months, victims from nearly every state in the Union have written to this legation."

POLICE RAIDS ON THE SCAMMERS

Many of the Spanish Prisoner scam operators worked out of Madrid. The swindlers used various methods to hide their addresses from the authorities, and local police found it surprisingly hard to identify each gang's headquarters, but sometimes they got a break.

A 1904 newspaper report described how one prolific gang had recently started targeting victims in Germany.

The German consul-general in Madrid received a letter from a German businessman named Max Mathenberg, who wanted to know if the Spanish prisons held a Major Jaquet. He was interested because Jaquet knew the location of a treasure consisting of half a million pesetas, and it would all be Mathenberg's once he had paid 5,000 francs to the prisoner's contacts at a Madrid commercial office.

Mathenberg was obviously very naive and about to be scammed. The German consul-general passed the letter on to the Madrid authorities, and two police inspectors, named Visedo and Puga, decided to contact Mathenberg.

They told the businessman that the person he was looking for did not exist, and the whole thing was a fraud. They intended to arrest the swindlers, they said, and they wanted Mathenberg's help in doing so. If he refused to help, he would be considered an accomplice. Faced with these alternatives, the businessman agreed to help.

The police instructed Mathenberg to write back to the scammers, telling them that he wanted to come to Madrid to hand over the money in person. He would be on a certain train, the South Express, and would be carrying a blue handkerchief. He was also told to provide other details of his appearance and to tell the scammers that he was slightly deaf.

The scammers agreed to the meeting, and on the day of the rendezvous, Inspector Puga, who spoke excellent German, pretended to be Mathenberg. At the station were two police officers disguised as railway porters. As Puga left the carriage and pulled out his blue handkerchief, a well-dressed man approached him and asked him in German if he was Max Mathenberg.

"Yes, I am," said the detective. "Are you the representative of the commercial agency I have been corresponding with?"

The man said he was and led the fake businessman to a waiting car. The two fake porters followed, carrying the traveller's suitcases, and listened carefully to the conversation. If the conversation dipped low, the police inspector feigned deafness—"Could you say that more loudly?"—so his colleagues could hear it.

The stranger suggested they drive to Mathenberg's hotel for their handover. "Mathenberg" thought it was unwise. They would have to talk loudly (again, the deafness), and people might overhear them. He suggested a meeting at the agency. The stranger agreed and drove to an office that, from the outside, appeared to be an ordinary business.

The police raided the office and arrested the entire gang. They found a mass of fake documents and letterheads, which the gang used to convince victims of the writer's credentials. One member was the disinherited son of a wealthy Barcelona family. He spoke several languages and took care of the letters sent to England, America and other countries. The gang kept careful account books of each scam, recorded as "Mining Affairs."

The tone of the newspaper article is sensational, and we wonder if some parts are invented or exaggerated. Certainly, bringing any victim to their real headquarters was a dumb choice by the criminals.

Most successful Spanish Letter gangs went to considerable efforts to keep their headquarters hidden, and scammers used all the technologies of the day to avoid detection by the police.

According to a 1913 report in the *Derby Daily Telegraph*, one successful Madrid gang always requested replies by telegram to be sent to the address of a random house. Sometimes, police would follow up a complaint and investigate the house, but it never led to any arrests.

In fact, even if the police had placed a twenty-four-hour watch on the house, they would have been wasting their time. They would never have seen any deliveries, spotted any criminal activity or discovered any clues to the gang's location. That's because nothing was ever delivered to the house in question.

One of the gang members, a man named Ortega, had once been a messenger in the telegraph office and knew its procedures well. He bribed telegraph delivery boys to collect any telegrams sent to the false address and hand them secretly to him at a prearranged location. The salary of a telegraph boy was very low, so this was an appealing offer.

The police eventually managed to trace the route of an individual telegram. They intercepted one of the delivery boys in a back street at the moment he was delivering a consignment of telegrams to Ortega. The police arrested them both.

Ortega tried to bribe his way out of the situation, but the telegraph boy gave a full confession. With Ortega in their custody, the police were able to discover the gang's real headquarters in Madrid. Their base looked like an ordinary house from the outside, but it had been specially constructed with false doors and a secret room. The head of the gang was assisted by his brother, his father-in-law and a private secretary. They sent hundreds of letters daily from the address.

THE RUSSIAN PRISONER
AND HIS SPANISH FRIEND

In 1915, Russia was in a state of political turmoil. Soldiers were dying in Europe, while conditions were bad at home, with high taxes and food shortages. The Bolsheviks were preparing for a revolution, and the tsar responded with mass arrests.

Spain was still the hub of these mail scams, and once again, the Spanish letter-writers moved with the times.

Many American citizens around this time received a letter from a man who claimed to be a wealthy but corrupt Russian banker who had lost a large sum of his bank's money. He knew he was about to be arrested and had fled Russia, taking a large sum of cash with him.

He had also sent his daughter out of the country in the care of his girlfriend. They carried a large sum in cash. The two women travelled to Madrid.

The banker explained to his American victims how he took a trip to the United States, where he deposited a half-million dollars in a secret account, then wrote a cheque for the full amount. He placed the cheque, payable to "bearer," in a secret section of his suitcase, then returned to Madrid to meet his daughter and his lover.

Unfortunately, while he was busy going back and forth across the Atlantic Ocean, the faithless lover stole most of his cash and fled, while her brother denounced the banker as an embezzler.

The banker caught up with them in Spain. He shot and killed the brother and was arrested for murder.

His poor daughter was sent to an orphanage. The banker was found guilty of murder and now sat in a Spanish prison.

He explained that he still had the half-million-dollar cheque hidden in his suitcase, but it was being held by the court registrar in Madrid. He asked the reader to pay a few fees to the authorities. Once the money was paid, the suitcase could be released to the care of his new American friend and helper, who would be compensated with a one-third share in the fortune.

So, by 1915, the treasure map and chest of diamonds has evolved into something more modern—a cheque payable to bearer and a secret bank account—but the elements remain very similar to those of the scams of a century earlier: a prisoner, a daughter and a suitcase with a hidden compartment.

The recipient claims he is unable to receive mail in prison, so replies should be sent by cable to his trusted friend in Spain. As we've seen, the telegram will likely go to a false address in Madrid and be rerouted by the scammer's confederates in the telegraph office.

SPANISH PRISONER SAYS, "SORRY, SEÑOR"

The criminals usually disappeared when they had extracted all they could from their victims, but in some cases, a con man's conscience seemed to get the better of him.

In 1905, the *New York Times* reported on a British man who had sent money to a Reverend Chaplin in order to help a Spanish prisoner named Antonio Garcia.

In his final letter, the writer thanked the victim and said he was grateful for his kindness.

He added, in his awkward English:

> *I must say you are a perfect gentleman. Now I must confess you are a victim of a deceit. I am not Antonia Garcia nor the Rev. Chaplin. There are neither such a fortune nor a child.*

After advising his correspondent not to bother going to the press or the police, he continued,

> *I am unhappy the fate had brought in such a vile a way, and you will suffer the consequences for. Nothing is true. When this letter reaches you, I will be far from Barcelona. You must have compassion with me. The fate is always the fate. Someday I will write you plainly, and then you will convince yourself that I was merely a secondary implement in this history, and the actors are in your country. God bless you.*

SON OF THE NIGERIAN PRINCE

The Spanish Prisoner scam re-emerged as the Nigerian Prince, and that, too, adapted and evolved into newer and more modern forms.

In 2013, Iraq was at war with the Islamic State, and many US military personnel were posted there. In the same year, a newly designed American $100 bill was issued. These facts led to a new shady but lucrative con targeting American recipients.

In one version of the con, an American sergeant has come into possession of millions of dollars' worth of older American $100 bills, which are scheduled to be destroyed and replaced with the new design.

He needs a reliable associate who can take delivery of the money. In return, he will give his helper a portion of it: a $6-million fee.

The fact that the letter-writer was a military man made the pitch more appealing to many American readers, who respect members of the armed forces, even shady ones. It was an effective new adaptation of the Spanish Prisoner. The sergeant was not exactly a prisoner, but he was unable to return to the United States because of his military duties.

In another version, the plot resembles the movie *Three Kings*: the military man is an officer conducting counterterrorism operations in Afghanistan and during a raid has confiscated millions of dollars from terrorists. As usual, he apparently has no friends of his own and must contact a total stranger by email to help him move the money.

In one audacious scam from 2017, the letter claims to come from a Nigerian government department tasked with stamping out these terrible Nigerian Prince scams: they need your help to recover the countless millions taken by the scammers. Your reward for helping them will be millions of dollars. It will be deposited to your bank account, so if you would be so kind as to provide them with your financial information. . . .

GROUND CONTROL TO MAJOR TUNDE

The Spanish Prisoner/Nigerian Prince scams have lasted hundreds of years and show no signs of slowing. In fact, it seems as if the con artists already have their eyes firmly on the future. A 2019 email must be the wildest version of the scam so far.

The email claims to come from Dr. Bakare Tunde, the cousin of Nigerian astronaut Air Force Major Abacha Tunde, who went on a secret flight to the Soviet Salyut 6 space station in 1979, making him the first Nigerian and first African in space. (Don't bother looking for him—we did say it was a *secret* flight.)

Tunde returned safely from that first flight. The trouble is, ten years later, Major Tunde made a second secret flight to the secret Soviet space station, Salyut 8T, in 1989. Unfortunately, while he was up there, his Russian colleagues needed to take equipment back to Earth, so they put the equipment in his seat, and left him on the space station. But then came the breakup of the Soviet Union. Poor Major Tunde was left up there. Supply flights have sent him all he needs to stay alive, and he's a trooper, but after more than thirty years in space, it's understandable that he wants to return to Earth.

Fortunately, the Nigerian military has not forgotten to pay him, and "he has accumulated flight pay and interest amount to almost $15,000,000 American Dollars . . ."

The astronaut's one hope of coming home is to pay the Russian Space Authorities for a return flight, which will cost $3 million. Obviously, he's good for the money, but the Nigerian bureaucrats aren't allowed to open or use foreign bank accounts, and those Nigerians are sticklers for the rules. The major needs your help to withdraw the money from his account and send it to the Russians.

You will get a 20 percent cut, as soon as you have paid a few fees, which will turn out to be astronomical.

CHAPTER 3
SCAMILY FAMILY

The trouble with schemes like the Spanish Prisoner and the Nigerian Prince is that the con artist has to persuade people to give money to a total stranger. The scammer can play on the mark's sympathy or their greed, but it will always be an uphill climb to make them like and trust the associate.

It would be so much easier for the con artist to convince people if the victim were talking to a member of their own family.

GRANDMA, I'M IN TROUBLE

In 2023, eighty-eight-year-old "Rose" was at her home in Richmond, British Columbia, when she received a call from a young man.

She didn't recognize the voice at first, but he said he was her grandson and he'd been in a car crash. One of the other people in the car was wanted by the police, so the grandson had been arrested, too.

According to *CityNews* Vancouver, he said, "Grandma, I love you so much—you're the first person I thought of."

Rose offered to help in any way she could. A little while later, the phone rang again. It was a different caller. He said he was an RCMP officer. If Rose wanted to help her grandson, she would need to provide $5,000 cash in an envelope.

"One of our officers will collect the money and deliver it to the judge. You'll get your money back after the trial. Once you've got the money together, wait outside your building. Our undercover officer will pick it up. You'll know who he is—he will identify himself using the code word 'blue.'"

Rose took careful note of the instructions and did exactly as she was told.

She went to the bank and withdrew $5,000 in cash. She wasn't used to carrying large sums of cash and she was worried that someone might steal from her on the way. But she made it safely back to her building and waited outside. When the officer showed up and gave the secret word "blue," she handed the money over with relief.

A few days later, the RCMP officer phoned again. There were still some legal problems to sort through and, unfortunately, the money she had sent wasn't enough. Her grandson needed another $5,000.

Rose didn't have another $5,000. She only had $4,000. But she did have a valuable pearl necklace her late husband had given to her on their twenty-fifth anniversary. It was worth $1,500.

The RCMP officer said that $4,000 and a pearl necklace would do just fine.

"You'll get it all back after the trial."

This time, the officer couldn't pick up the money in person. Rose was instructed to send it to a Toronto address by UPS. Rose left her home and travelled from Richmond to Vancouver, about half an hour away, to send the money.

The trial date came and went, but Rose heard nothing more. Then she read a news article about scams that targeted seniors.

At last, she phoned her grandson. It was both good news and bad news to hear that he hadn't been in a car accident and hadn't phoned her for help.

||||||||||||||

Rose had fallen victim to the classic "Grandchild" scam. The scammer calls seniors, claiming to be a grandchild in trouble. It's not always a highly focused operation. Some con artists call numbers randomly until they hear a voice that sounds like an older person. Many grandparents don't see their grandchildren that often, so there's a fair chance they won't question a voice they don't immediately recognize.

The con artist tries not to spend too long in the grandchild's persona—one slip-up could give the game away. After an initial contact, subsequent calls come from strangers associated with the case: police officers and lawyers.

The fake grandchild usually needs money after an accident or because of a legal problem to pay for a lawyer or for bail. The caller will often ask the grandparent not to tell anyone or not to let the grandchild's parents know what happened. This stops the grandparent from checking with other family members and increases their sense of responsibility.

Some scammers do more research before calling. They might discover the name of an actual grandchild by looking on social media. It's not difficult to spoof caller ID information, and there are even reports of scammers using digital technology to imitate the voice of the real grandchild.

In Rose's case, the thief met her in person for the first payment, but didn't want to gamble on a face-to-face meeting for the second payment.

It is risky for the scammer to make contact in person. In the next case, we'll see why.

In 2022, "Laura," a seventy-three-year-old woman from Long Island, New York, received a call from her grandson.

"Grandma? I've been arrested for drunk driving."

According to *WCBS-TV* news, Laura said she would help. Her grandson said someone from the court would call her. She waited for the phone to ring.

The next call came from the boy's lawyer.

"We're going to need $8,000 in cash to cover your grandson's bail."

"Of course, I will pay it," said Laura. "In fact, I have the money right here in my home."

"That's good," said the lawyer. "And I see one of our bail bondsmen happens to be in your neighbourhood. I'll phone him and have him stop by your home to pick up the money."

Laura was instructed to place the cash in an envelope and have it ready to hand to the bondsman.

As promised, the "bail bondsman," a twenty-eight-year-old man, came to Laura's house, and she handed him the stuffed envelope.

As he walked away, a team of police officers rushed in and arrested him.

Laura had scammed the scammers. She knew the call was fake immediately: she didn't have a grandson who could drive. As a former 911 dispatcher, she kept a cool head and played along with the story. As soon as she was off the phone with the scammer she contacted police, and they told her to agree to the cash transfer so they could arrest the criminal.

When she told the scammers she had $8,000 at home, she was afraid she'd gone too far with her story, but they believed it. In creating the cash-filled envelope, she'd used another classic scammer's trick—it was filled with old newspapers.

The scammers were charged with grand larceny.

HI, MOM

In early 2023, "Maura," a sixty-four-year-old woman in Sydney, Australia, received a text message from her adult son, "Finn." He said he had got a new phone and new phone number and asked her to delete the old one.

The style of his texts seemed different from usual. Maura asked if something was wrong.

Finn texted back. Everything was fine, but the change of phone number had caused him some problems. His bank had blocked his online banking for forty-eight hours, and he had some payments he needed to make urgently. He asked for help.

Maura said sure, she could spot him some money. She asked him how much he needed.

He texted back that he needed $8,900. He would repay it once his bank account was accessible in two days.

It was more money than Maura expected. Her credit card would only cover a $5,000 payment. She offered to send him that much.

Finn agreed. The five thousand might be enough.

Although her son's request for money was a little uncharacteristic, Maura knew that Finn had recently moved house. It made sense that he might have some big expenses.

Finn texted instructions for an online payment, and Maura was about to send the money through when "a little voice" in her head asked, *Is that really him?*

She felt a little silly, but decided to check with one last text.

"I know this sounds weird . . ." she began and she told him that, because there were a lot of scams floating around on the internet, she wanted to check he was really her son.

She asked him for the name of his maternal grandfather.

Finn replied that, yes, it did sound weird. He added that the payment was urgent and he needed her to send the money right away.

She asked him to answer the question. He became churlish: "If you don't want to help me out, just say so!"

Maura knew then that this person was not her son. She had just spent an hour offering money and support to a criminal.

She was smart to have double-checked the caller's identity. Many people are taken in by this scam, or others like it, which often involve a child texting from an unfamiliar number, claiming that their phone has been replaced or damaged at a time they face a cash emergency.

The person texting may know the identity of the real child, but some will text blindly and hope for the best. One exchange opened with the following text:

"Hi, mom, it's me."

The mother answered, "Which me is it???"

"Your oldest and cutest child."

The mother replied with laugh emojis, and the scam proceeded smoothly from there.

This scam, which has become very common, is known as the "Hi, Mom" scam and nets the con artists millions each year.

MOMMY NEEDS MONEY

The "Hi, Mom" scam targets parents, but a newer variation scams money from their adult kids.

One message came from a parent who was stuck at a gas station but had brought the wrong card. "Can you send me $150?" she asked. "I'll pay you back when I get home."

Most tech-savvy kids will find it completely plausible that their parents would get confused over cards and accounts, and some send the money before they think to phone and check.

The advantage to this scam is that the con artist doesn't need to worry about names. Senders can refer to themselves as "Mom" or "Dad," and that label will work in many families.

PAY, OR THE COMPUTER GETS IT

In 2023 in Arizona, "Luba" received a frightening call from one of her daughters, who was supposed to be away at a ski resort. Luba heard shouting and sobbing on the phone, then her daughter's voice saying, "Mom, I messed up."

A man came on the line. He said he had kidnapped the daughter. He wanted a million dollars in cash from Luba. If she didn't pay, she would never see her daughter alive again.

Luba was in the middle of picking up one of her other daughters from a dance class. There were a few other parents around. She put her phone on mute and asked them for help. They started calling 9-1-1.

Luba returned to the call. There was no way she could pay a million dollars and told the caller so. She said she could raise $50,000.

The caller agreed. He gave her instructions for handing over the money. It sounded sinister. He said he would drive to Luba's house in a white van, then put a bag over her head so she couldn't see where she was being taken.

But while he was talking, another mother had finished her call with the police. She waved to attract Luba's attention. "It's an AI scam!"

Luba wasn't sure what to believe, so while the "kidnapper" was still talking, she called her daughter on another line. Sure enough, her daughter was enjoying herself at the ski resort and had no idea what all the fuss was about.

The scammers had likely taken a short sample of the daughter's voice from social media. They had then used AI technology to clone a very convincing plea for help. Once Luba was convinced, a real person had come online to conduct the negotiations.

The police had been receiving many reports of cases like Luba's. As of this writing, the law is still catching up to the technology, and the fake kidnapping that terrified Luba is still considered a prank. It seems inevitable that AI voices and images will be more widely used in the future to create a new, very disturbing category of con.

IT'S BEEN A WHILE

If a con artist wants to impersonate a family member today, they can hide their appearance by using a telephone and hide their voice by using text messaging. Those options didn't exist hundreds of years ago, but that was when one French con artist pulled off what might be the ultimate identity theft.

It all started sometime around 1552, when a French soldier named Pansette was recognized and greeted by a group of other soldiers. He didn't know them, but they seemed to know him.

"Hello there, Martin Guerre!"

He told them they had the wrong man, but when they discussed it, they all agreed that the resemblance between Pansette and Martin Guerre was remarkable.

Pansette had a history as a petty criminal, and he started thinking about this incident. It offered interesting opportunities. If his own appearance was so close to that of Martin Guerre's that he could fool Guerre's close friends, perhaps he could fool other people.

Pansette set about learning more about this Martin Guerre. He found his doppelgänger, the real Martin Guerre, and befriended him. He got Martin talking about his background. The more he found out, the more interested Pansette became.

Martin Guerre came from a French village named Artigat, not far from Pansette's own village of Sagias. Guerre was a peasant, but he was a peasant with more money than Pansette.

Guerre had also married well. His wife was named Bertrande de Rols, and her family also had money. To Pansette, things looked better and better.

One more thing intrigued Pansette: Martin Guerre's family and friends hadn't seen him for a long time.

Like many newlyweds in the 1500s, Martin and Bertrande had married very young—she may have been as young as nine, and he was around fourteen. They had stayed together for ten years, but when Martin was twenty-four, he got into legal trouble: he was accused of stealing grain from his father. Martin hurriedly left the village, abandoning his family, his nineteen-year-old wife and his son.

Nobody from his hometown had seen him in eight years.

It all added up to a perfect opportunity for Pansette. He could become Martin Guerre, own his property, take his wife. Although the wife had been abandoned, church rules stated that she couldn't remarry unless her husband was known to be dead.

Pansette learned everything he could about Martin Guerre and memorized every detail. And, in 1556, he began what must be one of the most brazen imposter cons in history.

Pansette marched into the village of Artigat and introduced himself. "I'm back! It's me, Martin Guerre!"

In those days, there were no documents or ID that could confirm a person's identity, but this man certainly looked like Martin Guerre, and he seemed to know everyone. He also remembered a wealth of details that confirmed his identity.

A few people were unconvinced and spread rumours that a different man had returned, but Guerre's family, including his own sisters, said they recognized him. More importantly, so did his wife, Bertrande. Most of the community accepted that he was indeed the real Martin Guerre.

Pansette lived with Bertrande for three years, and the couple had more children. He made extra money by selling some of the property Martin Guerre owned. His con went very well at first.

Both Martin's father and Bertrande's father had died, but when Martin claimed his rightful share of the inheritance, some of the other relatives became resentful, especially Martin's Uncle Pierre.

The uncle had married Bertrande's mother, meaning that both he and Martin could make a claim on the money from Bertrande's wealthy family. Martin's return to the village was more of a problem for Pierre than it was for others. He started thinking about—and encouraging—the rumours that his nephew was an imposter.

A random event provided new doubts. A soldier happened to be travelling through the village. When Martin Guerre was pointed out to him, the traveller said, "That's not him. I knew Martin Guerre in the army. The real Martin Guerre lost one leg in a battle and now has a wooden one."

The rumours didn't go away, and eventually a group of villagers formally accused Martin Guerre of being an imposter.

Facing a court case, Pansette could either make a run for it or hold to his story. He picked the second option, insisting that he was the real Martin Guerre. Fortunately for him, his wife stood by him and assured the court that he was quite definitely the same man she had married. The court was convinced. He was acquitted.

But Uncle Pierre was still busy asking questions and stirring up trouble. He did some detective work and concluded that the man who claimed to be his nephew was actually a rogue from a nearby village. He suspected the man's name was Arnaud du Tilh, who went by the nickname "Pansette."

Uncle Pierre took the case to the courts again to expose the fraud. This time, he didn't want Martin's wife messing things up. To prevent it, he added a little fraud of his own. In his application, he falsely claimed he was acting on behalf of Martin's wife. Uncle Pierre and his own wife then persuaded Bertrande to play along.

With Bertrande now speaking against him, Pansette was found guilty. The court decided he had committed fraud and adultery, and he was sentenced to be beheaded.

But Pansette had come too far to give up without a fight. He doubled down. He appealed to a higher court in Toulouse, claiming that it was his uncle who was the fraud, using the courts to try to kill his own nephew.

"My uncle," said Pansette, "has persuaded my weak-willed wife to go along with his deceit. They have accused me, Martin Guerre, of being an imposter so they can cheat me of my rightful inheritance."

This was a serious charge. Uncle Pierre was arrested and put on trial.

Many other family members still believed Pansette was the real Martin Guerre, remembering (incorrectly, as it happened) Pansette's birthmarks as ones that belonged to Martin. Others said he was a fake and believed in Uncle Pierre. The court officials didn't know what to believe. They'd never seen a case like this.

Pansette put on an excellent show in court. He seemed passionate and sincere, and the judges started to believe him. By the time he had finished, they were persuaded that Uncle Pierre was a greedy man who would stop at nothing to get the family fortune.

Things were looking very bad for Pierre and very good for Pansette. But then something happened that astonished everyone present.

According to one official, its timing was like an act of God. As the court was about to pronounce its judgement, Martin Guerre hobbled in.

Martin Guerre had lost one leg in battle and walked on a wooden leg, just as the travelling soldier said. When people saw Martin and Pansette together, they were struck by the resemblance between the two men, but when the family saw the new arrival, they immediately knew the truth. This one-legged man was the real Martin Guerre, and the man who had lived among them for the past few years was an imposter.

It was all over for Pansette. For his crimes, he was sentenced to death. The church officials wanted to know if he had used witchcraft to fool people. Pansette denied it. He told the whole story, how he had spent years learning everything he could about his subject. He apologized to the family. He was taken in front of the house where he had lived. There he was hanged, then strangled, then burned, which may have been overkill.

As for the real Martin Guerre, he was welcomed back by his family. He accepted the children his wife had given birth to in his absence as his own, but he remained angry at Bertrande for not recognizing the imposter and bringing shame on the family name—which was rich, coming from the man who had abandoned his teenaged wife after stealing his father's wheat.

This bizarre case of identity theft has been the subject of and inspiration for a number of books, series, films, an opera and at least two musicals. Martin Guerre returned twice, and his story keeps on returning.

FAKES AND DRAKES

Martin Guerre's con ended long ago, but another family-based con from the same era kept going well into the twentieth century.

Sir Francis Drake was a famous British sea captain who had impressed Queen Elizabeth I in his battles against the Spanish. His most famous victory was against the Spanish Armada, but his most profitable work was as a "privateer"—basically, a pirate working for the government.

He attacked and raided many Spanish treasure ships on their way back from South America. The ships were loaded with gold and silver plundered from Central and South American civilizations. Drake plundered their plunder and took the treasure to England instead. His work was unbelievably lucrative. In one year, a single mission provided more money to Queen Elizabeth I than all her other income combined.

Drake died on his ship in 1596, and rumours soon spread that his vast fortune in stolen gold would go to his son.

There were two problems with that. First, he didn't have a son. Second, he didn't have a vast fortune in gold. Still, people were convinced that he had died with an enormous fortune that hadn't been distributed, and in the early 1600s, this became the basis for a common scam. Fraudsters contacted people with the surname Drake, trying to persuade them that they could claim their share of the fortune. All the lucky dupe had to do was pay a portion of the legal fees.

The scam may sound familiar. Like the Nigerian Prince scam, it often involves con artists connecting with someone who shares the deceased's surname and telling them they can claim part of a large inheritance. There really is nothing new under the sun.

Over time, the scam evolved. The swindlers found they could do just as well with people whose name wasn't Drake. They might promise to sell the dupe a share in the inheritance.

The scam continued for a few years after Drake's death, bringing big profits to seventeenth-century scammers. What's surprising, though, is that it didn't stop. In fact, the same con was still going strong well into the twentieth century, thousands of miles from England.

In 1915, two con men approached an elderly widow in Iowa. They knew she had $6,000 and they told her she could use it to buy a share in the Drake inheritance. That way, she could parlay her $6,000 into $6 million.

Her son, a man named Oscar Hartzell, learned about the proposition and confronted the scammers. He happened to be a deputy sheriff.

It might seem like the con men had picked the wrong widow to fleece, but surprisingly, Hartzell was not out for revenge and didn't arrest the pair. The way he saw it, the scammers were doing it all wrong, making thousands when they should be making millions. And, as an underpaid deputy sheriff, he wanted to be making millions too. He proposed a partnership in the Drake swindle. The con men said, "Welcome aboard."

Hartzell seemed to be a natural con man. Like the swindlers hundreds of years earlier, he started by contacting people in Iowa who had the surname Drake. He claimed he was a distant relative, and that they were both related to the sea captain.

"Our many-times great-grandfather died a wealthy man," he told them, "and our money has never been paid out."

He claimed he was going to sue the British government so Drake's descendants could get their rightful inheritance. Thanks to the accumulation of interest, Drake's fortune was now worth tens of billions. And it wasn't just from gold—he said the inheritance also included the entire city of Plymouth, England, where Drake had spent much of his life and served as mayor. Hartzell claimed that the seafarer had owned the city.

Once the Drake fortune was paid by the British government, said Hartzell, it would be shared among the investors. For every dollar they put in, they could expect to receive $500.

Hartzell told a good story, and gullible Iowans handed over their money. Hartzell expanded his operation to people named Drake outside of Iowa. More money came rolling in. Like the scammers centuries earlier, he expanded the con to people without the Drake surname and hired agents—some of whom were genuinely convinced of his story—to seek out more investors. Hartzell was making a fortune. He took a trip to England, supposedly to meet an heir of the Drake estate. He stayed there, living a life of luxury.

By the 1920s, Hartzell had accumulated tens of thousands of donors, all anxiously awaiting the big payout. He wrote regular newsletters updating the "descendants" on the progress of the case.

The FBI heard about Hartzell's work and became concerned. They looked into the inheritance, investigating what had actually happened to Sir Francis Drake's money when he died in 1597. It must have been one of their colder "cold cases." They discovered that there was no unpaid money. Most of his plundered gold had gone to the Crown, and the rest of Drake's estate had gone to his wife. Hartzell was a con artist.

But his followers wouldn't believe it—they refused to give up on the dream. Hartzell was still collecting money into the 1930s. Lawmakers tried to act against Hartzell, but the investors protested, saying they were happy about their donations and the government should keep out.

When the British government confirmed that there was no unclaimed fortune, the followers refused to believe it. Hartzell gave his own explanation. The reason there was no unclaimed fortune was that it had been given to the (imaginary) descendant Colonel Drexel Drake, who had assigned the rights to Hartzell.

His claims were nonsense, but Hartzell hadn't broken any British laws. The British police couldn't arrest him, and the American police couldn't reach him. But, at last, the law caught up. Oscar Hartzell was deported back to the United States and put on trial.

Hartzell had his day in court in 1933. His eager followers sent him nearly $70,000 to cover his legal bills, but it didn't save him. He was fined $2,000 and sent to prison for ten years. Even after Hartzell was convicted, some supporters were unable to accept the loss or give up on the fantasy, and they continued sending money.

Around the same time, Dashiell Hammett wrote *The Maltese Falcon*, a fictional story about a group of people obsessively chasing a gold treasure from centuries past. Perhaps it was influenced by the thousands then chasing the Drake fortune.

Hartzell's final years are ironic. While he was confined in Leavenworth Penitentiary, he became insane. He was later transferred to a mental institution. In 1943, he died there, believing that he himself was Sir Francis Drake.

CHAPTER 4
CAN YOU CASH A CHEQUE?

Writing dud cheques has always been one of the con artist's most profitable activities.

Of course, most people are wary of this kind of scam, but the perpetrators are ready with some ingenious and unexpected cons.

MYSTERY SHOPPERS

"Nora" had worked for years at a Nova Scotia convenience store. In this job, one of her duties was to visit other stores in the chain and report back on the customer service, so when she came across an ad for a "mystery shopper," she felt it was a job where she had some experience.

She contacted the company that had posted the ad, and they replied promptly. They were willing to hire her for the job. It all sounded reasonable—a representative said the company worked with major retailers and banks, assessing the quality of their customer service. The representative didn't ask Nora for a social insurance number or her banking information, only her mailing address. The company would send her a cheque and give further instructions.

Sure enough, a cheque for $2,100 arrived in the mail. Nora was told that she could keep $400 for herself. The rest should be used for making purchases. Nora deposited the cheque into her account at the bank.

Her first assignment was to buy $100 of merchandise at Walmart, while assessing staff performance.

Nora felt like a secret agent as she entered the store, but she tried to hide her excitement and act like an ordinary member of the public. She noted the polite greeting as she entered. Full marks for that. She wandered the aisles and selected around $100 worth of random merchandise, then she went to the checkout. Again, she noted that the store's employees did their job well. They were polite and efficient.

Nora left Walmart and went on to her next assignment. This time, she would be reviewing a bank—her local branch of BMO Bank of Montreal. Her instructions were to carry out an ordinary bank transaction: deposit around $1,600 into an account number she had been given. She stood in line, noting the cleanliness of the floors and the efficiency of the staff. They dealt with her politely and moved her money into the account number she gave them.

She left the bank and, following instructions, contacted her employer to let them know her first mystery shopping assignment was complete.

She felt she had done well, moving inconspicuously through the crowd, blending in with the ordinary shoppers.

Her employer obviously agreed, because a few days later, she received sent her a second cheque and new instructions.

Nora went to deposit it, but she had a shock when she checked her account. The balance was negative. Her account was overdrawn. When she asked why, the teller told her that the first cheque was bad. It had been deposited into her account, but when the cheque didn't clear, the bank reversed the payment. They had also charged Nora a fee for depositing a bad cheque.

Nora realized she had been scammed. The Walmart transactions had lulled her into a false sense of security—she had bought $100 of merchandise she didn't need. And when she transferred money at the bank, the scammers had quickly withdrawn it at their end. Essentially, she had taken their worthless cheque for $2,100 and given them $1,600 of real money from her account.

Nora's experience is typical of "the Mystery Shopper" scam. It usually involves the victim receiving a cheque, then sending money using Western Union or some other form of wire-transfer service.

There are legitimate companies that run mystery shopper programs, but they don't issue large cheques upfront. The work is usually low-paid "gig" work—participants might be paid between $5 and $20 for each shopping trip, not the hundreds offered by the scam version.

WORKING AT HOME GETS EXPENSIVE

A Detroit woman, "Lee," was the mother of four young children. She had experience in data entry and posted her resumé on a number of job sites. She heard back from a business that sold medical devices: the company wanted to interview her for a work-at-home position. Lee went online and investigated the company. It seemed the company had been in business for a few years, so she said yes to the interview.

The online interview went well, and Lee got the job. Not only was the pay better than she expected, but she would also receive good benefits.

Lee was told she would need to set up a home office. She already had her own computer, but the people at the medical devices company said she shouldn't use it. She would need to use their software on a computer system that met their specifications. But she shouldn't worry— they would take care of all expenses.

It made sense to Lee. Health records need to be kept secure, after all.

A couple of days later, Lee received a FedEx package. It contained a cheque for $3,800, which was to pay for her work computer and the necessary software. The people at the medical devices company told her to deposit the cheque using the banking app on her phone. She should then wire the payment to their computer supplier.

Lee did as she was told. She withdrew $3,000 from a drive-through window of her bank, then used it to send a MoneyGram from her local Walmart.

A few days later, the cheque bounced. When Lee tried to follow up with her company contacts, she got no reply.

Lee contacted company officials through their web page. It turned out the company was real enough, but they hadn't talked to her or hired her. She had been the victim of a "Work from Home" con. The scammers had used the company's identity to fool a number of victims in the Detroit area.

She had been sent a dud cheque, and the $3,000 she had wired, supposedly to pay for a computer, had actually gone straight to the scammers.

By getting Lee to deposit their cheque using an app, they had reduced the chances that an alert bank teller might spot a scam in progress.

Work-from-Home scams lure victims with the promise of a well-paying job they can do at home. The scammers make money by getting the victim to cash a bad cheque, under the guise of paying bills, buying equipment, doing training, or ordering supplies. It all happens fast—the criminals have to get their money before the bank flags the cheque as bad. Sometimes their haste raises suspicions.

"Gabriela" was a university student in Palm Desert, California. During the pandemic, she was unable to work her regular job and didn't know how she was going to pay her tuition, rent and other bills. Then, an interesting job listing came through her email from her school's job portal. The position was for a personal assistant. The work was well-paid and could be done entirely at home.

Gabriela applied for the job, and to her delight, she was immediately hired. It seemed like her prayers had been answered. Better still, she didn't have to wait long for her first paycheque: her employer, "Renfrew," immediately sent her a cheque for $2,850 and told her to deposit it to her personal bank account. He told her that some of the money was for her salary and the rest was to cover business expenses.

Once the cheque was in her bank account, he told her to transfer some of the money to other accounts.

Something about the deal sounded fishy to Gabriela. Renfrew had been too quick to send her money, and it seemed odd that she had to make payments from her own account. What were these accounts she was sending payments to? It was all moving too fast. Was she really taking care of paying his bills or had she been drawn into a money laundering operation?

She told Renfrew that she wasn't comfortable with this arrangement and didn't want to do the transfers.

That was smart. But her next move was a mistake. She told Renfrew that she didn't want his cheque and would return his money.

She used the mobile payment service Venmo to send the $2,850 back to Renfrew and, feeling relieved, went back to her job search.

A few days later, she received a notification from her bank. Her account was overdrawn. She hadn't realized that banks give their customers credit on deposited cheques before they have completed the clearing process. The cheque from Renfrew was a dud, and she had "returned" money to him that he had never actually sent. Gabriela was out $2,850, plus the bank fees for processing a bounced cheque.

A bank will tell you never to deposit a cheque from someone you don't know. Legitimate companies aren't in the habit of sending money to employees they've only just hired.

Having made the mistake of depositing the cheque, she should have waited a few days before returning it. Gabriela felt like a fool, but she filed a report with the police and she contacted the bank. Neither thought it likely she would recover her hard-earned money. She went to the press with her story as a warning to others, and a GoFundMe account raised enough to cover her losses.

Work-from-Home scams frequently offer generous pay for jobs that sound easy: stuffing envelopes, assembling products, filling out surveys.

Apparently, there are even scam Work-from-Home jobs for people who want to be psychics, but first they have to spend money to buy telephone equipment. Perhaps that one is okay. Maybe it's even a bizarre job interview. After all, if you don't see the scam coming, you probably shouldn't be offering your psychic services to others.

YOU'VE BEEN 'AD

An Oklahoma woman, "Melanie," received a text from a stranger we'll call "Ralph," asking if she was interested in making money by putting advertising on her SUV.

According to a report on *KSWO TV* in 2021, Ralph gave Melanie a very plausible explanation. He told her that "wrap advertising" involved sticking brightly coloured vinyl graphics on a vehicle. The wrap didn't affect the driver's ability to see out, but the advertising would attract the attention of other drivers and people on the street. His company was looking for people willing to promote their soft drink. Participants would be paid to have their car covered for one to three months. The vinyl would be professionally installed and was guaranteed not to damage Melanie's car. The pay was $300 per week. She would receive an upfront payment for the first week. She would not have to pay anything to be part of the program—no "application fees" or anything of that sort. If she was interested, she should write back with her address and phone number.

It all sounded like a pretty good deal to Melanie. She had seen cars and trucks with advertising around town. While the pay sounded good, it didn't seem too good to be true—it didn't sound like a scam. Many of the questions Ralph had asked were the sort you might expect: "How long have you been driving? How many miles do you drive a day?"

She sent her personal details to the company and got a quick reply from Ralph. He thanked her for her interest and welcomed her to the program. He would send a payment to her soon, as promised. She should deposit the cheque when she received it. She would then need to contact the graphic artist they used, providing details of her car's model and year. There was a cost involved in producing the decals, but the soft drink company would cover that, and the money would be included in her first cheque.

A week later, Melanie received the promised cheque, for around $2,300. Ralph checked in to see if she had received it and gave instructions on sending payment to the head of the graphics company, who lived in Florida. The graphics people would arrange for a local artist to print Melanie's customized decal. She did what she was told and wired the payment directly to the graphic artist, together with information about her car.

Melanie waited for an update about getting the advertising decal installed, but she heard nothing. A week later, she checked her bank account and found it was overdrawn. She contacted the police, who said she'd been taken by the "Car-Wrap" scam. It had fooled hundreds of people. The cheque from the soft drink company was a dud, and the money she'd paid to the graphic artist actually went to the scammers. It was all just a complicated way of getting Melanie to cash a bad cheque.

Most people who fall for this scam lose around $2,000 and also end up paying fees to the bank for depositing an NSF cheque.

In 2013, "Anthea" in Wisconsin had a lucky escape after spotting some discrepancies with the car-wrap deal.

Like many victims, she was impressed at first by the offer, which sounded legitimate and above-board. The ad her car would be sporting was for an energy drink. But when she received her first payment, she noticed that the company name on the cheque was that of a local clothing store. She then checked the return address on the envelope—it was for an individual in Maine.

Puzzled, Anthea called the clothing company and asked if they were involved in car-wrap advertising for an energy drink.

The person on the other end didn't seem surprised by the question and asked Anthea to describe the design and colour of the cheque. Was it blue?

"No," said Anthea. "It's kind of green."

"The cheque is a fake," said the person on the phone. "You should call the police."

In the days that followed, Anthea received a number of emails from her soft-drink contact, pressuring her to deposit the cheque and pay the graphic designer. She didn't, and the scammer finally gave up. She wrote about her experience on the website ivetriedthat.com and received more than a thousand replies from others who had been taken in by the scam.

The car-wrap solicitations take many forms: emails, text messages and even flyers in shopping centre parking lots. And don't think you need to own a car to apply—the fake advertisers will also claim they can put ads on motorbikes or even bicycles.

The scammers often use the names of real businesses and may issue cheques appearing to come from them, but it is all fraudulent—the companies have no knowledge of what's going on until they hear from angry victims.

BLANKED CHEQUE

"Kyle" was a Boston resident. In 2023, he sent a birthday card to a friend in Texas, dropping the envelope in a local mailbox. According to *NBC News* in Boston, the card contained a cheque for $50.

Kyle later learned that the birthday gift had not arrived. Had it been stolen? He went to his bank to ask if the cheque had cleared. The teller said it had, then showed him the computer monitor. To his astonishment, the amount on the cheque was nearly $16,000.

It was Kyle's cheque and his signature, but the amount on his cheque had been altered.

In the old days, opportunistic criminals changed cheques by adding words and digits. If there is space on the cheque, it can be easy to change "five" to "five hundred" and just as easy to adjust the digits: $5 to $500. But not every amount is changeable, and careful cheque-writers can foil any attempt to modify the amount by filling extra space with a horizontal line or the word *dollars*.

But today, scammers are more likely to start from scratch, using chemicals like bleach or acetone to wash off the ink, then writing in a completely new amount. It's a whole new definition of money laundering. And that's what had happened to Kyle. The crooks had stolen envelopes from the mailbox and searched them for cheques.

During COVID-19, the U.S. Postal Service cut back on its policing budget, and the number of thefts and cheque-washing cases skyrocketed. Sometimes crooks fish envelopes out of the box using glue on a string, and other times they open the box with a stolen key—a single key opens all the mailboxes in an area, and locks are rarely changed. In a few cases, they've stolen the whole mailbox. Of course, it's just as easy for thieves to lift cheques from mailboxes by the doors of homes.

Check-washing has become so widespread that security experts now advise people not to use cheques at all if they can avoid it, and if they must send them by mail, to stay clear of street mailboxes and double-check their bank account after writing a cheque.

Unfortunately, this didn't help Kyle. He complained to his bank that the cheque had been altered. The bank initially denied it, saying there was no sign of alteration, even though traces of previous ink were still visible on the cheque. This kind of blame-the-customer foot-dragging seems to be a common strategy for some banks. The bank eventually refunded Kyle's money, but it was a slow process.

Some of these scammers have chutzpah. The AARP (formerly the American Association of Retired Persons) reported a case where a fifty-nine-year-old man, Gerry, sent a $445 cheque to his insurance company. The cheque was stolen in the mail and washed, leaving no trace of the original writing. It then became a cheque for $2,949, supposedly to cover electrical services. In the "Memo" box, the thief praised the quality of the work with the words "Great job!"

In Gerry's case, the cheque-washer was apparently so pleased with his work that he tried depositing the cheque in person. The bank spotted a discrepancy and refused to accept it. The scammer panicked and ran from the bank, leaving the cheque behind. Hubris strikes again.

THE CHEQUE YOU CAN'T DEPOSIT

These days, the internet abounds with pornography and sex-related products, but in decades past, it was less common to see such material, and more shocking when you did. People seeking out these products tended to be discreet about it.

Some people wanting to avoid the embarrassment of buying in person might instead order merchandise by mail.

This laid the groundwork for an ingenious scam.

During the 1960s and '70s, con artists ran advertisements in smutty magazines offering a range of raunchy products for sale. When they received an order, they sent back a letter of apology: "We're sorry to say that your item is no longer in stock. We enclose a refund for your payment."

A cheque was enclosed for the full amount the customer had paid, but prominently emblazoned across the top of the cheque was the name of the company, which was something like, "Inflatable Sex Toys and Rubber Fetish Supplies, Inc."

In those days, depositing a cheque meant going into the bank and handing it to the teller. A person nervous enough to order by mail probably wouldn't want to hand that kind of cheque to a bank teller, so most of the cheques went undeposited.

Anyway, that's the story. We don't know if it's true or an amusing urban legend. If it happened, it's definitely something victims kept under wraps.

FAKING IT IN HOLLYWOOD

"Stefan" lived in Los Angeles and was trying to make ends meet as an actor, so he was excited when, in early 2023, he received a notice from a well-known casting director, "Vaughan."

The acting gig was a commercial for Bitcoin. Vaughan messaged Stefan asking for an audition video. That's a commonplace request for actors these days, and Stefan had provided audition videos to the director in the past, but this audition was slightly different. Vaughan needed footage of Stefan going to his ATM, withdrawing money and then depositing it into a Bitcoin account.

According to a *KABC-TV News* report, the casting director told Stefan that the client wanted the transaction done through an ATM, not a teller, because they wanted to test the efficiency of the machines. That struck Stefan as a little strange—producers of commercials aren't usually worried about the day-to-day operations of a business—but he agreed to do it.

Vaughan also wanted Stefan to do the transaction with real money, so the actor could give a testimonial. He sent Stefan an envelope by priority mail. It contained a cheque for nearly $5,000. He was told to use this money for the Bitcoin purchase.

With all this money flying around, it seemed to Stefan as if the producers must be pretty serious about using him for the commercial. After depositing the cheque, he turned on his phone camera and made a video of himself withdrawing money from the ATM, then depositing the cash into a Bitcoin account.

Now he only had to wait to see if his audition was successful.

Unfortunately, he had been conned. The Vaughan who had contacted him was an imposter. When Stefan checked his account later, he found that the cheque had bounced, and he had sent the money to an untraceable Bitcoin account. As a struggling actor, he had had very little in his account to start with, so he was now overdrawn by nearly $5,000.

The "audition" was a cheque-cashing scam that had been given a unique Hollywood slant. "All that glitters isn't gold," as they say.

LET'S TRY THAT AGAIN

When people have been scammed, they're often confused, upset and not thinking clearly. In other words, they're in a perfect situation to be scammed again. This technique is known as the "double shot."

"Ruby" had been scammed in a Pigeon Drop. Two strangers she'd met at a mall had found a bag of money and a note that said something about a guns shipment. Against her better judgement, instead of reporting the find, she had agreed to share the money with the strangers, then gone to the bank to add money of her own. She had fallen for their plan hook, line and sinker.

She felt ashamed and embarrassed at how she'd been taken. How could she go to the police now? They would laugh at her. Then again, perhaps admitting her mistake would help prevent other people from being scammed in future.

As she agonized over what to do, the decision seemed to be made for her. She got a phone call from an FBI officer who told her he had spent some time following the activities of the team that had scammed her. The officer was kind and understanding.

"You're not in trouble. They fooled you, but don't feel too bad—they fool a lot of people."

"That's such a relief."

"But I need to warn you, Ruby, the way this team operates is always the same. After you've taken money out of the bank, they go back to the same account and empty it. We need to prevent that from happening."

The officer advised Ruby to withdraw the rest of her money from the account. He would send a special agent to pick it up from her house, and it would be held for "safekeeping."

The scam had already cost Ruby thousands, and she certainly didn't want to lose the rest of her money, so she went to the bank, made a huge cash withdrawal, and handed it over to the nice plain-clothes officer who came to her door—who was, of course, a con artist working with the original team. Fool me twice . . .

HELP OUR INVESTIGATION

The "Double Shot" scam works all too well, but con artists soon discovered that they didn't need to bother with the initial scam. The second one worked just as well on its own.

A Massachusetts woman, "Joan," received a shocking phone call one day in the summer of 2022. The man at the other end was an official at the Drug Enforcement Administration (DEA). He warned Joan not to hang up or they would have to send police officers to her door.

This ridiculous claim is a line often used by scammers, and, of course, Joan was talking to scammers.

According to the *Daily Hampshire Gazette*, the fake official, who called himself Oscar White, told Joan that drug dealers had compromised her bank account and were using it to launder money. Joan was horrified when he said that she was at risk of being prosecuted herself for her involvement in the scam. But he reassured her that she could protect herself by helping the DEA with their investigation.

Joan wanted to cooperate—anything to help the police.

Oscar told her that the first step was to empty her bank account so it could no longer be used by the criminals. Joan's account contained around $300,000. Oscar advised her to withdraw the money, then convert it to gold bars. These should then be handed over to the DEA for safekeeping. It was important not to make the criminals suspicious, so everything must be done discreetly. She was told to leave the gold bars in an unlocked car at a certain parking lot. A court officer would then collect the gold.

Joan did as she was asked: she went to her bank and withdrew all her money, then went to a local jeweler to buy the gold.

Oscar had told her to place the gold in two buckets and drive to a restaurant parking lot, then walk away from the car, leaving it unlocked, so the "court officer" could pick up the gold.

The scammer discreetly followed Joan's vehicle in his black BMW. She pulled in at the restaurant and left the car as instructed. When she was out of sight, he drove up next to her car, entered it, transferred the gold to his own vehicle and drove away.

Fortunately, Joan had not been entirely duped. She had initially believed "Oscar White," but after emptying her bank account and buying the gold, she started to have doubts.

She contacted the local police. They quickly coordinated with the FBI and other local police departments and laid a trap to scam the scammer. The car the scammer had followed was not Joan's, but an undercover car driven by an undercover officer. While he watched the woman he thought was Joan, the police were watching him.

Once he had taken the gold and started to drive away, the police moved in, blocking his exit. Oscar White tried to reverse and make an escape with the gold, but he found himself surrounded by police. He surrendered.

Two men were arrested, and one went to prison for a year less a day after pleading guilty to conspiracy to commit wire fraud.

As for Joan, once she contacted the police, her money was no longer at risk. The gold in the car was fake, and the jeweler took back the gold bars and returned Joan's money.

Many criminals get away with this kind of scam, but sometimes their own greed can snatch defeat from the jaws of victory.

"Doris" was a woman in her mid-seventies from Long Island, New York. In May 2023, she received a call that her computer had been hacked. The man on the other end said she needed to take immediate steps to keep her finances safe.

Doris was shocked and afraid, but the scammer reassured her. According to the *Nassau Daily Voice*, he told her to withdraw all her money from her compromised bank accounts and use it to buy gold bars.

Doris was ready to take whatever lifeline was thrown to her, and she did exactly as she was instructed. She withdrew more than $190,000 and purchased the gold. A "federal employee" came to her door to pick up the gold for safekeeping.

If the scammers had quit at this point, they would probably have made a clean getaway. Instead, they tried to squeeze more cash from poor Doris. A week after their first request, they contacted Doris again, advising her to withdraw more money. Doris took out another $190,000 in cash and purchased more gold. This time, the scammers instructed her to leave the gold under a tree in her yard, where "federal agents" were supposed to pick it up.

It was an odd way for federal agents to behave, and Doris became suspicious. She contacted the police and told them her story. When the pickup came, they were watching. Two men were arrested and charged with attempted grand larceny, 2nd degree.

As of this writing, it's not known if Doris got back any of the money she lost in the first scam, but she avoided getting robbed a second time.

CALL THE POLICE

Here's a fun con you can try at home.

On a regular land line, putting the telephone handset down doesn't necessarily end the call immediately if the person who made the call is still on the line—there's often a delay. This quirk in the system means the person receiving the call can hang up in one room and pick up the phone in another, so long as the caller hasn't hung up.

Here's how you use this as a hoax or a magic trick. You arrange for an assistant, who is at another location, to call your land-line phone. You answer and then hang up. The line should stay connected for a while. (If it doesn't work, you could also answer with a second extension and leave the other phone off the hook.)

Now you just need to choose a victim for the trick.

Standing in front of your land-line phone, you ask your subject to pick a name out of the blue.

She makes up a name: "Emerson Blenkinsop."

Next, you ask her to think of a random phone number. She should make it up, but it has to be a phone number that would actually work, with a real area code and the right number of digits.

The subject reels off some random digits and, as she says them, you lift the receiver on the land line and dial the number.

"It's ringing," you say. (It isn't. Your assistant is waiting silently at the other end of the line.)

You say to the subject, "When they pick up, I will give you the phone. I want you to ask who it is. It will be Emerson Blenkinsop." (As you say this, your assistant, at the end of the line, hears the name.)

You listen to the phone, then react as if someone has just answered. "Hello? I have someone here who has a question for you."

You pass the phone to your friend, who asks, "Who is this, please?"

"My name is Blenkinsop. Emerson Blenkinsop. What's this about?"

It's an entertaining trick and will probably get a laugh at a party. But this harmless hoax has also been used as the basis of a multimillion-dollar con.

In 2019, "Gerald," a Vancouver senior, received an unexpected call from a jewelry store.

"Did you make a credit card purchase for $6,000 worth of jewelry?"

Gerald certainly had not made a purchase like that, and he said so.

"That's what I was afraid, of," said the jewelry store manager. "It looks like your credit card has been used fraudulently to make several large purchases.

She told him that, before doing anything else, he should immediately contact the police to report the theft and gave him information about the purchases.

"The most important thing is to contact the police. As soon as you're off the phone with me, call 9-1-1."

Grateful for the advice, Gerald hung up his land line, then picked it up and dialed 9-1-1.

Unknown to him, the con artists were still waiting on the line. They had patched in a recording of a dial tone. When Gerald dialed 9-1-1, he thought he was making a new call, but the button presses had no effect.

The scammers created a convincing 9-1-1 call. Gerald heard a recording of a phone ringing. Then he talked to a fake emergency operator who transferred him to a fake police officer specializing in fraud.

Gerald was convinced that he was talking to the police—after all, he had phoned them—so he was ready to do what he was told.

The "fraud officer" advised him that they had to take quick action to deal with the theft of Gerald's money (which was true, in a way). Over a series of calls, the officer guided Gerald through the process of transferring his money from his own "compromised" bank account into what he was told were safe "police accounts."

Gerald moved more than $3 million this way, sending it all into overseas accounts controlled by the criminals.

The scam is a variation of the "bank investigator" fraud, but the telephone trick makes it much more convincing.

Fortunately, after his discussion with the fraudulent fraud officer, Gerald also phoned the real police. They moved into action fast. They couldn't retrieve all his money, but they did recover the bulk of it. However, it was impossible to trace the criminals, and the same team has almost certainly continued the scam with fresh victims.

CHAPTER 5
IT'S JUST A GAME

When you're playing a game, the usual rules of life are put on hold. Players suspend their disbelief to take part in the fun—and that's the perfect atmosphere for frauds of all sorts. It doesn't matter if it's poker, dice, lotteries or carnival concessions, almost every type of game has its own specialized scam.

So, step right up and try your luck. Here are just a few game-related cons.

THE LOST LADY

In 2022, a Georgia woman, "Samantha," was going into the mall when another woman, "Chelsea," approached her and asked her help.

"I'm heading to a card game," said Chelsea, "but I'm afraid I'm going to get cheated. Can you just stand nearby and be a witness, so I don't get ripped off? I'll give you $200 if you can help me. It won't take long."

That sounded like easy money to Samantha. According to *WXIA-TV News* in Atlanta, she followed Chelsea to a table, where she found a group of players participating in a game she'd never come across before. The dealer had three cards: two black tens and a red queen. He threw the cards face-down on the table and shuffled them around a little.

"Find the lady, my friends," he said. "Find the lady."

Chelsea and the other players placed their bets on which card they thought was the queen. Samantha saw these players put down big money on the outcome—thousands of dollars at each turn. She saw Chelsea win a game, then lose it all on the next game, then win again.

But what amazed Samantha was the way the players struggled to follow the movements of the queen. For Samantha, it seemed so easy. She played along silently in her head. She watched deal after deal and saw the players biting their lips, trying to decide, but Samantha was able to pick the right card every single time! Why weren't they able to see what she could see? Perhaps she was just naturally good at the game—a savant.

Samantha knew she was only meant to be here as a witness and she was doing her best to keep quiet and just watch, but it was incredible to see the money these people were making—or more often, losing—on a game where she had natural ability.

A new deal, and Samantha was sure the queen was the centre card, but Chelsea put $10,000 on the rightmost card. When the cards were turned over, Chelsea's card was a ten. The winning card was in the centre.

Samantha couldn't help speaking. "I knew it!" she said.

The dealer turned to her. "Don't be standing there making comments. Do you want in? If you want to play, you can play. The pot is up to thirty thousand."

Samantha considered it. Maybe she should give it a go. It was a lot of money, but she knew she could do this. These guys were going to be in for a shock.

"You'll have to put in some good-faith money," said the dealer. "Ten thousand."

Samantha considered it. She had that much in her savings.

"Okay. I have to go to my bank, though."

"We'll wait. But don't be long."

Samantha ran to her car and paid a quick trip to her bank. She was soon back with an envelope stuffed with cash. She placed the money in front of the dealer.

He held up the queen, then threw down the cards. He moved them around a couple of times, but Samantha's mind moved faster than his hands. She had no difficulty tracking the queen. It was on the right.

"This one!" She pointed to the card and prepared to be $30,000 richer.

The dealer flipped the card. It was a black ten. "Sorry."

He grabbed the cards and her envelope of money and walked away.

Samantha had been taken by one of the oldest card scams around—"Three-Card Monte," also called "Find the Lady" and "Three-Card Trick." Some games, like poker or blackjack, can be played either fraudulently or honestly, but there is no legitimate version of Three-Card Monte. It is a card adaptation of an age-old deception using three cups and a ball. It is only ever a scam—a card trick disguised as a game.

The con almost always involves a team of con artists—a dealer and a group of shills pretending to be players—who bet excitedly on the game and occasionally appear to win. And that's the persuasive genius of Three-Card Monte—the other players who make the game seem legitimate. The mark enjoys watching the action and starts to feel that they are more perceptive and intelligent than the players. When the mark sees that other people are betting large sums on a game they've never seen before, it makes it feel more normal to join in.

The card-dealing side of the scam involves a simple sleight of hand where the dealer makes the mark think the card is in one position when it's actually in another.

A magician can do this trick in many ways—for example, by hiding and palming extra cards—but the street version is much simpler. The dealer really does use exactly three cards, and the trick depends on a simple move. Before each throw, the dealer holds one of the tens in one hand and the queen and the second ten in the other. The dealer raises a hand to show the queen, then appears to throw it to the table, but depending on how the two cards are held, the dealer can release either the queen or the ten above it. It is impossible for an onlooker to tell if a dropped queen is actually a ten.

The dealer shows the cards, throws them casually onto the table, then shuffles them around a little. The moves are slow and easy to follow, so it appears obvious which one is the queen. The mark should guess correctly every time—unlike the dimwitted shills—but when the mark actually bets their money, the dealer puts down a ten instead of a queen, and the mark will follow the wrong card.

Sometimes, the fake players will cheat. While the dealer is pretending to pay attention to something else a player will check the cards, then fold the corner on the queen. The dealer returns to the game, not noticing the fold, moves the cards around as usual, then asks players to place their final bets for the day. Following the card with the folded corner is easy, so the mark puts down a large sum to make money on the final round, but when the cards are turned over, the folded card turns out to be the ten. The player who folded the queen pretends to be as astonished as the mark.

Again, this trick is done with sleight of hand—the dealer bends a different card and unbends the queen—but what makes it convincing is the support of the fake players. They accept their defeat, so the mark does the same, not even realizing they've been scammed.

Sometimes, a mark will correctly identify the location of a card. Here, too, the shills can help. When the player puts down money on the correct card, a shill puts down even more money on the same card. The dealer declares that only the highest bid on each card counts. The shill appears to win money, but it's all part of the group's pot.

Sometimes the group may rope in two or three passers by. If one is interested and the other is wary, the team will push forward, feigning enthusiasm to place a bet, but putting their bodies between the person who looks like their pigeon and the other who might advise caution.

FACE-UP POKER

Some cons take the form of simple proposition bets, usually something where the suckers think they can't lose.

On a break from a private poker game, "Larry" struck up a conversation with a friendly player, "Sal." Larry had lost a few dollars to Sal in the last game and now he complained about the terrible cards he was dealt. "Just bad luck, I guess."

"It's not luck," laughed Sal, who had consumed a few too many drinks. "It's skill, man. It's skill. I can't lose, because I've got the skill. Even if you could pick the cards you want, right out of this pack, you can't beat me. Because I've got the skill."

"That doesn't make any sense," replied Larry. "Obviously, if I could choose which cards I get . . ."

"I never lose!" shouted Sal loudly. "I'll bet you on it. In front of all these people."

Sal took another shot of bourbon and grinned. He spread out the cards face-up on the table.

"Go ahead. You choose any cards you want. Any cards. Then I'll do the same. Then we change cards if you want. Just a regular poker game, but you can see all the cards. I bet you can't beat my hand. C'mon, buddy. A hundred bucks. Whaddya say?"

The other players listened in amusement.

Larry considered for a moment. This was a good opportunity to make a quick hundred from this cheerful loudmouth—and recoup some of his earlier losses.

"Okay. Sure."

Sal gestured to the cards. Larry picked out the ten, jack, queen, king and ace of spades. A royal flush. It was the highest hand in poker, and was unbeatable.

Sal made his own choice. The same cards, but in clubs.

"Want to change any cards?" asked Sal, slurring his words.

"No, I don't think so," laughed Larry. "I already chose all the cards I wanted. Why would I want to make my hand worse?"

Sal thought about it and nodded. "Yeah . . . yeah. Me neither, buddy."

"Well, that was predictable," said Larry. "We've both got the best possible hand, so I guess neither of us wins."

"Whoa! Hang on," said Sal. "I didn't bet I'd win. I bet you couldn't beat me. And you didn't beat me."

"Yes, but . . ."

The other players agreed—that was what Sal bet, all right.

Larry was down a hundred bucks. And he wasn't happy about it.

"All right, all right," said Sal. "No need to sulk, buddy. Tell ya what, I'll give you a chance to win your money back. Double or nothing. Same bet, but this time I have to beat you. And I'll go first."

That sounded like a good opportunity to Larry. It was an idiotic bet—clearly, both players would choose a royal flush again and they would tie. Since it was impossible for Sal to beat Larry's hand, Larry would win his money back.

Larry put down another hundred and fanned out the deck of cards face-up for Sal to choose.

Sal picked four tens and a two. Larry saw what his drunken opponent was thinking. Sal had taken all the tens, preventing Larry from choosing a royal flush. What Sal seemed to have forgotten was that four tens was an easy hand to beat. Larry might not be able to form a royal flush, but he could choose a straight flush, which would beat even four aces.

Larry picked out the five, six, seven, eight and nine of diamonds—the highest poker hand it was possible to form without using tens.

"I guess I win," said Larry.

"Not so fast, not so fast," said Sal. "I'm gonna change some cards."

Larry had forgotten about that part of the game. Sal discarded the two and three of the tens, keeping only the ten of spades. Sal then pulled the jack, queen, king and ace of spades from the face-up deck. Now he had a royal flush.

Larry prepared to do the same, but he realized he couldn't. He needed a ten to match Sal's royal flush, but Sal had the only ten—all the others were in the discard pile, unavailable to Larry. The best hand Larry could make was the hand he already had—a straight flush, which was beaten by Sal's royal flush.

As Larry left the game, he suspected that Sal wasn't quite as drunk as he'd seemed.

CARNIVAL CONS

By law, games at fairs and carnivals must be winnable. But even when they adhere to the law, that doesn't mean the games are fair. Most carnival games have some sort of trick, and many use a misleading demonstration.

SHOOT THE STAR

Players are shown a paper target with a red star in its centre. Using an air BB gun and a hundred BBs, the challenge is to shoot the target so no trace of the red star remains. This is quite difficult in the first place, but it's harder when the gun's air pressure is set too low, the ammo is smaller-than-normal shot and the sights are misaligned. Winning is just possible if you try to shoot a circle around the star, but almost impossible if you aim for the red marks.

TUBS OF FUN

Throw a softball into a hard plastic tub to win a prize. The tubs give a lot of bounce to any ball that falls in, meaning it's likely to bounce out again. The carny will demonstrate by dropping a ball in, then offer you a free practice turn. On the practice, a ball that goes in will likely stay in, because the carny's ball is already at the bottom of the tub, stopping a second ball from bouncing out. But when you try it for real, the tub is empty and extra-bouncy. In 2013, a New Hampshire man lost $2,600 trying to win this game. Determination makes the best marks, it turns out.

MILK BOTTLES

This looks easy. Three bottles are stacked in a pyramid. Players have to throw a ball and knock down all three bottles. It seems as if aiming between the two lower bottles should do the trick. The "gaff" is that one bottle is weighted. If that bottle is placed on top, the game is easy to win—that's the way the game is demonstrated. If the heavy bottle is on the bottom, the game becomes much harder. Adding to the difficulty is the special lightweight softball the players are given to throw.

RING TOSS

Throw a ring so it lands over the neck of a bottle to win a prize. There are plenty of bottles to choose from, and the ring will fit over the bottle top—just. The ring goes on easily when the carny drops it down (it helps that the carny's ring may be slightly larger and made of a softer material), but when thrown horizontally, it will almost always bounce off.

BASKETBALL

Just throw the ball through a hoop to get a prize. The hoops look round, but are actually oval. And they're higher than normal. And the balls are overinflated. Only a very precise or very lucky throw will go through.

BALLOON DARTS

Throw a dart at a balloon to pop it. This should be easy if you are any good at darts—that is, unless the darts have dull points and the balloons are only partially inflated, which happens to be the case here.

DUCK POND

A game for toddlers, where they use a fishing rod to catch a duck. It sounds like an unlikely method of hunting, but not as unlikely as winning a good prize. The kids will always win something, but almost all the ducks have "junk" prizes. Welcome, children, to a world full of cons.

RAZZLE DAZZLE

Jerome, a guy in his early twenties, was wandering through a mall parking lot in Arizona in 2014 when he spotted the game. A few other people around his own age were gathered around the operator, Max, who talked fast and put on a good show.

The rules were simple enough. Max rolled eight balls onto a board with holes, each hole marked with numbers from one to six. Then he checked the total against a chart with all the combinations. Some totals give the player nothing, some earn points and some add new prizes to the pool. Reach one hundred points and you get to take home the accumulated prizes. Some combinations could give you one hundred points on a single roll.

There were some pretty good prizes on display, and it was only a dollar a turn. *You only live once, right?* Jerome decided to try his luck.

"What prize do you want to start with, sir?" asked Max.

Jerome's eyes were on a game system on the high shelf—the latest PlayStation. That was more than $500 in stores.

"Can I choose anything?"

"Anything, no. Anything on these racks, yes. I'm a genius, not a genie."

Everyone laughed. This guy was fun.

"The game system, please."

"You got it. Game system it is. Good choice. Gaming for a game. Let's roll them balls, see how they falls ..."

The balls tumbled into the numbered holes, and Max rapidly counted the total as he plucked them out. "That's a three ... niner ... makes fourteen ... and nineteen ... twenty-five ... thirty-one ... thirty-seven ... for a total of forty-two." Jerome checked the chart: that total was worth twenty points.

Jerome played a second round, and this time the total was thirty-one—no points for that. But the next roll totalled seventeen, which was worth another five points, and the next roll added a second prize to the pot—a nice pair of headphones.

He had to get to one hundred points to claim the prizes and, after spending four bucks, he was already at twenty-five points—a quarter of the way there!

Jerome spent another $5 and earned another twenty points, as well as another prize in the pot: a mobile phone. He didn't need a phone, but he could give it to his sister. The kids around him were impressed at his progress.

After a few more rounds, Jerome had a bad roll. Max groaned. The total was a twenty-nine. "You don't want to get those." That doubled the price of a play—instead of $1, the price now went up to $2. But Jerome figured it was still worth it. He kept playing.

He kept earning points, and his total kept climbing. Twenty minutes later, he was at eighty points—just twenty points from a win, and the prize pool now included $5,000 worth of merchandise. But it was now costing Jerome $8 a play, and he was out of funds.

Max was understanding and wanted to help. If Jerome needed to get more money, he would pause the game. When Jerome returned, he could pick up where he left off.

Jerome wasn't sure. He'd already spent more than he intended.

"Tell you what I'll do," said Max. "I'll add a special prize to the pool: if you win, you get back all the money you've played."

This sounded pretty good to Jerome. He was so close to winning, after all. He went to the cash machine and took out more money. He picked up where he left off, but somehow, he couldn't seem to get those last few points. He carefully watched where the balls fell and double-checked the totals, but the key numbers remained elusive.

After two more trips to the cash machine, Jerome admitted defeat. He didn't have much money in his bank account, and now he'd taken it all out—more than $600. As Jerome left, Max commiserated and gave him a stuffed toy. Jerome felt like he'd been scammed, but he couldn't see how.

The game, known as Razzle Dazzle, can turn up at carnivals, at night-clubs, in parking lots and on the street. It is a particularly clever and insidious scam.

You might expect that the balls or the board are rigged somehow, but no, the balls roll fairly. What works against the player is the law of probabilities. Only high and low totals earn points, and it is extremely unlikely that the player will ever get a winning combination.

The chances of rolling an "instant win" are less than one in a billion, but the odds of earning any points at all are remote. Mathematicians who have studied the game say that a player will have to play an average 5,239 times to win.

What makes it worse is the fact that the cost per play doubles each time the player rolls twenty-nine. That number is a common total, which happens on average every ten or eleven rolls. It is theoretically possible to win the game, but because of the constant doubling, the average cost of doing so would require far more money than exists on Earth.

So, why did Jerome get as far as he did? That's where the con comes in. Most crooked games are rigged to make players lose, but the Razzle Dazzle scam is just the opposite. The operator helps the player at first, miscounting the totals, so the player wins on rolls he actually lost. Players don't usually check a successful result, and if they do notice an error that worked in their favour, they are likely to keep quiet about it. Players feel like winning is pretty easy and grossly misjudge their chances.

It's only later in the game, as the points are getting closer to the big payout, that the game is played honestly. At this point, a typical player will be spending much more and watching the results like a hawk. They can double-check all they like, because everything is above board. Victims pour more and more money into the game—sometimes thousands of dollars—but they are extremely unlikely to reach that one-hundred-point target.

Razzle Dazzle is illegal in the United States, but it often sneaks under the legal radar by taking other forms. In the Auto Races version, players must advance their car one hundred miles. In Play Football, the goal is to move a football one hundred yards down the field. They're all the same game. Some versions use dice. Most offer impressive prizes—they can afford to, because nobody will win them.

THE JACKPOT THAT'S NOT

Many people fantasize about a big lottery win. One day you're just one of the crowd, the next you're a multi-millionaire, and any money cares you once had have evaporated. "Winning the lottery" has become a synonym for your dreams coming true.

So it's hardly surprising that lotteries are fertile territory for con artists.

A ninety-three-year-old Tennessee woman we'll call "Livia" received a call one day. As reported by *WATE-TV News*, the caller told Livia she had won the jackpot on the Mega Millions lottery. That was wonderful news, but even more amazing was how much she had won: $187 million.

What made it more remarkable was that she had never bought a ticket for a Mega Millions lottery. But she did remember filling out a card inviting her to participate in some kind of international lottery. She had signed her name and sent it off, along with a $50 registration fee, and now, not long after, she had won the big prize.

After congratulating Livia, the caller said he would send her the money. It wouldn't happen immediately. First there was the matter of insurance. And then a few fees. But once those were taken care of, Livia would be rolling in dough.

Livia sent off the insurance money and paid the fees. But then new payments were required. The requests kept coming. Every few weeks, the lottery people needed more money from her. Some of it had to be sent in the form of prepaid gift cards.

The calls kept coming, month after month, until one day the caller asked for another payment and Livia said she had no money left. Over the course of a few years, she had sent around $190,000 to the scammers.

Livia was so embarrassed that she kept quiet about the whole experience, then she changed her mind, deciding that it was better to be open about it so other people could be warned.

This kind of scam is an example of an "advance fee" fraud, where the con artist says they will send you money, but first you must pay the advance fee.

It goes without saying that the scam has no association with any real Mega Millions lottery. Victims pay the advance fee but will not usually see any money—unless it's a small amount to encourage them to pay the next big advance fee. Livia's loss was a large one, but others have been even larger.

In 2022, *CTV News* reported on an elderly Ontario couple who were told they had won a large American lottery. They sent $1.2 million to the scammers. The police didn't reveal the details, but it's likely the couple were told they had won a huge sum, many millions, then told they had to pay the US taxes before the money could be released. The only real million-dollar jackpot was the one the con artists received from the couple.

In Canada—as in most places—it is illegal to charge fees, taxes or service charges to lottery winners.

Common characteristics of this scam are that the winner often hadn't purchased a ticket and the lottery is held in another country. Callers often insist that the winner must keep their win secret or they won't be able to claim their prize, which helps isolate the victim from people who might see that it's all a scam.

And the one thing all these scams have in common is that the "winner" must pay money to get money. If the lottery were real and the lottery authorities needed an administration fee, it should be possible to say, "No problem, just deduct it from my winnings."

OH, NO! I WON THE LOTTERY!

"Elena" was a seventy-six-year-old woman living in Los Angeles. Around 2019, she came across a younger woman, "Sofia," sitting on the ground, weeping. Elena asked her what was wrong.

Sofia showed Elena a lottery ticket. "I won the lottery."

Elena didn't understand. Sofia's tears were not tears of joy. "But . . . why are you so upset?"

Sofia shook her head. "I can't collect it. I'm not here legally."

It turned out that Sofia was an illegal immigrant from Colombia.

Elena's heart went out to Sofia. Elena was a US citizen, but she was Hispanic, too, and she knew other people who were worried about their status in the United States. She comforted the young woman and offered to help. First, the lottery ticket. Elena checked the numbers on the ticket against the numbers in the newspaper. It was a match.

Sofia had a winning ticket, all right. And it was probably true that she would have a hard time claiming it. If she showed up to claim the cheque, she would have to present ID, and when they realized she wasn't a citizen, she would be deported.

Another woman, "Camila," came up to find out what was going on. Camila was also Hispanic. As they talked about the situation, Camila had a good idea. She knew someone who was a lottery official. They could call him. He was also Hispanic, and he might be sympathetic. Perhaps there was a way to work this out.

The tearful Sofia was very grateful. If there was some way, she would happily share her winnings with Camila and her new friend Elena.

Camila phoned her friend who worked at the lotteries. He said he could help them, but they would need to pay a deposit in advance.

Sofia didn't have any money, but Camila said that was fine—she could pay her share later. As for Camila's contribution, it wasn't a problem. Camila immediately pulled out cash. Now, what about Elena?

Elena had wanted to help the tearful Sofia, and now she saw that, if she contributed to the fund, she would be part of the group and would be rewarded with a share of the big lottery win.

If you remember how the Pigeon Drop works—the scam where someone finds a bag of money—this series of events may sound familiar. It is a variation of the same scam. Sofia and Camila were pretending to be strangers, but were actually working together, along with two others who posed as lottery officials on the phone, confirming that the payout would occur if the deposit was paid.

The whole con had been designed to get Elena's money. And it was successful. They drove Elena to her bank and then her home, where she handed over $14,000 in cash and $10,000 in jewelry.

The group that scammed Elena was later arrested. All were from Colombia, and they had been approaching four women a day. Over the course of two and a half years, they had conned at least sixteen women, taking in close to $200,000.

The fraud earned them prison sentences ranging from six to thirty-three months. They were also required to repay the money they had taken from their victims, so Elena might eventually get her money back.

Some versions of the lottery scam involve a bag switch, just like the Pigeon Drop. Typically, the lottery ticket and the victim's valuables are placed in a pencil case, which is then substituted for an identical case stuffed with newspaper.

The most interesting difference between this scam and the Pigeon Drop is the use of a winning lottery ticket. It's a real ticket, and the numbers do match the winning numbers for the last big win. The trick is that the ticket isn't for the past lottery—it was bought more recently, for the next lottery, using the numbers that won on the previous one. People might scrutinize the lottery numbers to make sure they are legitimate, but it is actually the date that has been carefully changed.

CHAPTER 6
WINNING THE LOTTERY

Con artists have used fake winning lottery tickets as part of various scams. But what if you could find a sure fire way to con the lottery system itself?

Many con artists have tried—and some have succeeded.

6-6-6: THE NUMBER OF THE CHEATS

Nick Perry was a well-known TV presenter in Pittsburgh, working on the ABC affiliate *WTAE-TV*. Like many staff presenters on local stations, he had multiple roles: he was a news presenter and a weather reporter, and he hosted *Bowling for Dollars*. One of the shows that had fallen in his lap was the nightly broadcast of The Daily Number, a Pennsylvania lottery draw held in the station's own studio.

The lottery numbers were drawn from three machines, each containing ten numbered Ping-Pong balls. Jets of air blew the balls around until one random ball exited through the selection tube at the top of the machine. Each draw produced three numbers, one from each machine. A ticket holder had a one-in-a-thousand chance of choosing the right combination, and the winnings were shared among all the ticket holders who had chosen the correct numbers.

As Perry stood behind the machines, watching the balls bounce around to make someone else wealthy, he came up with an idea. If the Ping-Pong balls could somehow be substituted for heavier ones, leaving just one or two of the original, lighter balls, only the lighter numbers would be selected. It wouldn't be that hard to do. Perry knew the security around the machines was lax. He had two partners in a vending machine business, brothers named Peter and Jack, and he talked to them about the possible con. As a celebrity host, he couldn't be seen buying winning tickets, but perhaps they would like to lend a hand. Peter and Jack were excited by the prospect and willing to invest in it.

Perry couldn't do it alone, so he brought in a few confederates: a graphic designer helped create balls with the right appearance, and a lottery official made sure he had access to the machines so he could carry out the switch. In total, eight people were in on the plan.

The weighting of the balls had to be subtle—the balls should bounce around, but not quite high enough to reach the tube. The designer tried injecting powder into the gaffed Ping-Pong balls, but that didn't work. Then he tried injecting the balls with latex paint—an ingenious and much more successful method. The paint evenly coated the inside of the balls so they were only slightly heavier than the original ones.

According to Pennsylvania newspaper the *Morning Call,* reporting on the case in 1980, the team needed to be certain their method would work, so they arranged for one of the lottery machines to be left in an accessible area for "repairs." They loaded the machine with a set of heavier balls and one or more lighter ones. The test worked perfectly. When the machine was turned on, the heavier balls appeared to be blown around normally, but only the lighter balls could reach the top tube. The team carried out many tests, and in every test the results were the same: the heavier balls never reached the top, so only the lighter balls were selected.

Once they had tested the system, the group planned to make the same changes to all three machines. They would replace the Ping-Pong balls with weighted balls just before the draw, then restore the original lighter balls immediately afterwards in case the machines were inspected. They decided to choose the same two numbers for each machine: four and six. That meant the winning number would be some combination of those digits, such as 4-4-6 or 4-6-4. There were only eight possible combinations—much better than the one-in-a-thousand odds the other citizens of Pennsylvania would face. They might have used a single unweighted ball in each machine, which would let the criminals choose the number precisely, but it would also run the risk of a long, suspicious delay if the chosen ball took a while to find the tube.

The vending machine brothers, Peter and Jack, went around town buying multiple lottery tickets with all the six-four combinations. On the big night, Perry's associates smoothly switched the regular balls for the weighted ones. Nick Perry presided over the draw, as usual, and tried to look calm as the numbers came up. It worked as planned, although the combination was an unusual one: 6-6-6. Was the Devil trying to tell him something?

As soon as the draw was over, team members removed the machines and replaced the gaffed balls with the genuine ones. The rigged balls were removed and destroyed. A few minutes after the draw, all the incriminating evidence was gone.

The payout from the draw was the largest in the lottery's history: $3.5 million. Some went to legitimate players, but more than a million dollars went to Peter and Jack, who shared it among their eight partners. It seemed like the con had gone without a hitch. They had rigged a lottery in front of millions of viewers, and having done it once, they could easily repeat it, using different numbers.

Unfortunately, Peter and Jack had been careless in buying tickets. People around town noticed when they put down large wads of cash on different combinations of the same two numbers. The brothers had also shared the upcoming winning numbers with friends and family. Worst of all, they had also placed some large private bets with underworld bookmakers. The bookies noted the unusual bets and tipped off the police.

An investigation showed phone calls between Nick Perry and the brothers, and everyone in town was soon talking about the "Triple-Six

Fix." After a police grilling, the brothers confessed their involvement and snitched on the rest of the gang. As a result, they avoided jail time, but the rest of the group were convicted. The lottery official received a two-year sentence. Most of the others pleaded guilty and received light sentences. As for presenter Nick Perry, he received a seven-year sentence. He came out after two years, but never managed to return to TV.

It was a mistake to play with the lottery Ping-Pong balls for millions. He should have stuck to *Bowling for Dollars*.

EASY PICKINGS

The so-called "Triple-Six Fix" cost taxpayers millions, but that's nothing compared to a lottery con in Milan. Lottos are hugely popular in Italy, and the proceeds are used to pay for art projects and to support museums.

Most North American lotteries use machines with bouncing balls to randomize the results. The system used in Milan is simpler: the balls are placed in a round cage similar to the ones used in bingo games. The cage is rotated, then a blindfolded child reaches into the cage and selects a ball.

In the late 1990s, some people seemed to be racking up a surprising number of wins. An official said there was fraud going on; he claimed that the lotto results had been manipulated more than a hundred times between 1995 and 1997. When police looked closer, they realized that many of the children chosen to pick the balls from the cage were relatives of the officials who were paid to safeguard the lottery.

But if it was fraud, how was it being done? What method could be used to enable blindfolded children to select the balls the crooks had chosen?

The answer seems to be: every method you can think of. Some kids were taught how to peer through the blindfold, as many blindfolds leave a gap at the bottom, a feature that stage magicians exploit. Other kids worked by touch. They chose balls that had been previously frozen, or balls that had been previously heated, or balls sprayed with a glossy coating. The children were not only good at their job, they were also cheap to bribe: those who weren't related to the corrupt officials were kids from orphanages. For their role in the scam, they got toys.

Eventually, the people behind the scam were arrested, but the amount they earned from their con was enormous. Over several years, they may have sucked more than $174 million from the system.

VOLTAIRE'S LOTTERY CON-DIDE

It's never been easy to make a steady living as a writer. The French writer Voltaire topped up his modest writer's income through a very profitable lottery scam. Or *was* it a scam? You decide.

In 1728, the French government sold bonds to raise money, but after an unpopular rate cut, people didn't want to buy them anymore. As writer Andy Williamson describes on the website TodayIFoundOut. com, the French government decided to sweeten the deal and added an incentive to make the bonds more appealing. Anyone who bought one of the bonds could also buy a lottery ticket. The ticket would give you a chance to win a prize of 500,000 francs—a huge fortune.

The government had thought it all through. The bonds came in many denominations, allowing people of all ranks to buy them, and to make things fair, the cost of each lottery ticket was adjusted to be more affordable to the smaller buyers. Each ticket cost one thousandth of the price of the bond. All tickets were created equal and had the same chance of winning. Égalité, fraternité . . . lotteré?

Perhaps you have already identified a flaw in this plan. If the lottery ticket you bought with a cheap bond has just as much chance of winning as the one you bought with an expensive bond that cost twenty times more, you would be much better off buying twenty cheap bonds than a single expensive one—multiple cheap bonds would give you more lottery tickets.

A French mathematician named La Condamine spotted this problem

89

and did some number crunching. He calculated that, if investors were to buy up all the cheap bonds and the lottery tickets that went with them, they would have an excellent chance of winning the jackpot. They might not win on the first attempt, but it should just be a matter of time before a win became inevitable.

The mathematician shared the information with his close friend Voltaire, and the two men decided to give the plan a try. Voltaire used his social connections to pull in partners and form a syndicate. He sweet-talked one of the officials in order to buy large numbers of cheap bonds as soon as they came out, then buy lottery tickets without arousing too much attention.

Their system worked like a charm. The syndicate won the lottery—not just once, but many times. They were making money hand over fist.

Eventually, when the authorities realized that the same people were always winning, they took the syndicate to court. But the prosecution didn't have much of a case. The way the court saw it, what Voltaire and La Condamine had done wasn't illegal—they had just played the odds well.

The government cancelled the lottery, and Voltaire went back to his other work, writing classics like *Candide*. He established his reputation working with words, but only after making a fortune working with numbers.

ONE WINNING TICKET, PLEASE

Voltaire may have got away with exploiting a lottery flaw in eighteenth-century France, but it didn't work so well for a man in modern-day China.

Zhao Liqun was a lottery seller in the city of Anshan. He owned three stalls, which were wired to the network that recorded lottery purchases.

Around 2007, he noticed an oddity with the system. It was supposed to stop purchases of tickets once the lottery numbers had been drawn, but the block was slow to take effect. In fact, you could still buy tickets a full five minutes after the winning numbers had been announced.

In theory, this would mean that you could see the winning tickets on television, then buy them on the machine. But surely that wouldn't work in practice.

Liqun put it to the test. It worked perfectly. He was able to see the winning numbers, then order a winning ticket. It was like having a time machine, without the inconvenience of ending up lost in dinosaur days.

Unfortunately, Liqun was not subtle in the way he used his new-found powers. He repeatedly bought winning tickets, then he asked friends and neighbours to claim the winnings and bring him the cash. His tickets earned the equivalent of more than $3.6 million. The unusual surge in big wins attracted official attention, and when police looked at the claimants and saw they were all related to the same ticket seller, it wasn't hard to figure out who the mastermind was.

Liqun was arrested and tried. He was found guilty of fraud, and the sentence was harsh. He lost all his property and was sent to jail for life.

IT'S OKAY, I GOT A SYSTEM

A man named Victor Gjonaj (pronounced *JOAN-eye*) ran a real estate company, but he was fascinated by lotteries, particularly a lottery in Michigan where players try to match just four single-digit numbers. In 2022, *The Atlantic* magazine described how this obsession led to an unusual con.

Like many lottery numbers, the digits on the Daily Four are drawn using a machine. Four compartments hold bouncing Ping-Pong balls numbered from zero to nine. In each compartment, one ball is sucked through a tube into a tray that holds the selected numbers. It's a simple method, but as long as nobody has rigged the machine or weighted the balls, the results should be quite random.

But what if the results are not as random as they seem? What if the numbers generated earlier in the week could help predict numbers that have not yet been generated?

If you talk to a statistician or a physicist, they will tell you this is impossible. The bouncing balls don't know or care what numbers turned up yesterday. A string of losses doesn't mean the world owes you a win—that's the classic "gambler's fallacy."

But Gjonaj could "feel" patterns in the chaos. He was good at mathematics and knew how to program, so he turned his intuitions into algorithms. He wrote an app that applied his principles, predicting upcoming numbers based on subtle patterns. His rules were complex— even arcane—but he started getting wins.

He refined the system, incorporating more subtle patterns. On one day, he purchased five hundred tickets, all with the same number combinations. He won. The system had worked. He walked into the lottery claim office and presented his winning tickets. He walked out with $2.5 million.

He used the same system again. In an upcoming draw, he calculated the numbers that were likely to appear, although he didn't know the order. But the lottery rules allowed for such a bet. Again, he bought big: 800 tickets at $24 a ticket. And again, he won the lottery, collecting $4 million. He reinvested his money in more tickets, buying them in larger and larger quantities.

Over the months that followed, Gjonaj became a regular visitor to the claims centre. He was cashing in tickets for millions of dollars. Alarmed lottery officials tried to slow him down, limiting how many tickets he could buy at any one location. He spread his spending over multiple sellers and kept turning up to collect his winnings.

The lottery's security division started investigating Gjonaj. It shouldn't be possible to play a lottery like a business—the odds didn't work that way. But if Gjonaj was running a scam, they couldn't see how it was working. He couldn't control the draw—it was random. His tickets appeared authentic and had been issued before the draw took place. He paid the correct amount for each ticket. But something was screwy. When he came in to collect his money, he seemed so unsurprised, so sure of himself. What was the secret to his success? He couldn't see into the future. *Was there a con going on here?*

The truth was that Gjonaj was in the middle of a huge fraud, but he wasn't conning the lottery. The staff at the lottery claims office only saw him when he won a jackpot, but they weren't seeing his losses. He was buying colossal numbers of tickets—so many that some wins were inevitable. In the big picture, however, he was losing a fortune. His "mathematical" system was statistically worthless, but like many gambling addicts, he believed in it and constantly chased the next win using any money he could lay his hands on.

The money to buy the tickets came from his real estate clients. They thought they were investing in property deals, but the funds went into lottery tickets. When Gjonaj got a win, he would pay some money out to his investors as part of their return, but most of their money was gone, eaten up by a lottery Ponzi scheme. Even his occasional big wins were not enough to save him. Gjonaj was millions of dollars in debt. He borrowed and lied. He sold the same property to more than one investor.

It was just a matter of time before all his creditors came asking for money. He couldn't pay. When investigators took a closer look at his books, the scale of the fraud became clear. In court, people were astonished to learn that a trusted investor had blown millions on lottery tickets.

In September 2021, he was sentenced to fifty-three months in prison. He was released early, in June 2023. Keep a weather eye on those mega millions.

CHAPTER 7
GOLD AND JEWELS

It would be nice to have piles of cash, but somehow those stacks of green paper pale before the primal appeal of gold, silver and precious gems. Those feel like real wealth.

Sometimes, a hoard of jewelry is the tempting target of a con artist's efforts. At other times, the promise and allure of such wealth has been used to attract victims to other scams.

THE DIAMOND NECKLACE

A plan to steal a piece of jewelry earned the scammers very little, but it may take the prize for being one of the most disastrous cons in history.

The scam was carried out by a French woman named Jeanne de la Motte. She came from a poor background. Her family had distant connections to French royalty, but her mother was a servant, and her father was a drunk. De la Motte schemed to improve her social standing. She married a cavalryman and claimed he was a count, which made her a countess. She looked for opportunities to meet the queen, Marie Antoinette, and use her charm to get herself a fat royal pension. Unfortunately, the queen had heard what kind of woman de la Motte was, and de la Motte couldn't get close to her.

In the meantime, de la Motte wasn't happy in her marriage, so she fooled around. One of her lovers, a man named Rétaux, was a gigolo who had a sideline in blackmail and forgery. She moved on from him, and did better with her next lover, Cardinal de Rohan—not only a cardinal, but also a prince. He gave her gifts and money, and even got her husband a more lucrative job in the military.

As de la Motte got to know the cardinal, she found he had the same problem that she did: Marie Antoinette didn't like him. He had a sleazy lifestyle that didn't look good for a church official. He'd also made some blunders: before Marie Antoinette was married to the French king, he had spread nasty rumours about her mother. If only there were a way to win her over, he would be more powerful and more wealthy.

De la Motte told the cardinal that she could help build up his relationship with the queen. She claimed she had a very close relationship with Marie Antoinette.

"But I thought she hated you!"

"That's just what she wants people to think. It allows me to hear what people really think of her. I am one of her most trusted companions. I'll talk to her about you."

The cardinal believed de la Motte and was delighted to have an insider working for him. And when de la Motte told him to write to the queen, he did. She said she would deliver the letter personally.

The cardinal wrote a letter to Marie Antoinette, and de la Motte brought back a reply that was friendlier than he expected. He continued the correspondence, and the letters from the queen became more and more affectionate.

"Could it be that Marie Antoinette is in love with me?" asked the cardinal.

"Yes, I think she is," said de la Motte.

"I must see her!" he said. "Arrange a secret meeting at night."

De la Motte arranged the meeting for her lover. The cardinal met the queen in the gardens of Versailles. The first meeting was brief. He gave her a rose. She gave him a letter saying that she forgave him everything. The cardinal was ecstatic.

Sadly for the cardinal, it was all a fraud. De la Motte didn't have any influence with Marie Antoinette. When the cardinal had written a letter, de la Motte took it to her forger ex-boyfriend, Rétaux, who wrote a convincing reply from the queen. And the woman the cardinal had met at night was not Marie Antoinette, but a high-class prostitute hired by de la Motte. The woman bore a passing resemblance to Marie Antoinette, and with the right dress, on a dark night, she fooled the cardinal completely.

Now that the cardinal thought he was in with the queen, it was easy for de la Motte to tap him for more cash. She told him the queen needed to borrow money for charity work, and he handed it over. With a steady supply of funds from her gullible lover, de la Motte could buy the finest clothes and mix with the rich and powerful. Foolishly, she raised her status further by telling other people about her close connection to the queen. Word got around that she was someone with influence.

Things all went horribly wrong when two men heard her boasts and figured she was exactly the person they needed to meet.

The men were Paul Bassenge and Charles Auguste Boehmer. They were jewelers to the royal court, which should have been a good thing, but in their case the position had driven them to the edge of bankruptcy. A few years earlier, they had crafted a lavish diamond necklace for the king of France to give to his mistress. They borrowed money to buy the finest matched diamonds, because His Majesty wanted a piece of jewelry that would outshine all others. Unfortunately, in the time it took to create the necklace, the king who had commissioned the necklace died, and now there was a new ruler.

They had tried selling the necklace to the current monarch, Louis XVI. "Perhaps your queen, Marie Antoinette, would like it?"

But the necklace was tainted. Marie Antoinette wasn't enthusiastic about a gift intended for her father-in-law's mistress, even if she had liked the woman, which she hadn't.

The jewelers found themselves stuck with a massive debt, a necklace priced for a royal budget, and nobody who wanted to buy it. They were desperate, and when they heard about de la Motte's influence over

Marie Antoinette, they thought she might be able to solve their problems. They asked if she could have a word with the queen. If she could persuade Marie Antoinette to buy the jewelry, they would pay de la Motte a healthy commission.

De la Motte saw an opportunity for a dangerous but extremely lucrative con. She agreed to help the jewelers, then went to her lover, the cardinal. Through conversations and more fake letters, she persuaded him that the queen was desperate to have the necklace. Unfortunately, with a bad economy and French citizens starving in the streets, Marie Antoinette couldn't make the purchase openly. De la Motte said the queen wanted the cardinal to buy the necklace on her behalf.

The cardinal placed the order, and the jewelers gave him the necklace, which he passed to de la Motte so that she could discreetly deliver it to the queen.

As soon as she had her hands on the necklace, de la Motte pried out the huge diamonds, and she and her husband sold them on the black market in Paris and London. In modern terms, the gems were worth tens of millions of dollars. All they had to do was cash it in and make a discreet exit before the cardinal realized he'd been royally scammed.

Unfortunately, things came to a head sooner than de la Motte expected, because the necklace was too expensive even for a cardinal-prince to afford. When the cardinal's notes of credit weren't enough, the jewelers complained directly to Marie Antoinette. "We realize you wanted to be discreet, but we made you a necklace and we still haven't been paid for it."

Now the whole con exploded. "Necklace? What necklace?" Who had been buying a fortune in jewelry under her name?

Arrests quickly followed. The queen figured the sleazy cardinal was behind it, so he was arrested and thrown in jail. De la Motte was arrested, and so was her lover, the forger, as well as the prostitute who had pretended to be the queen. De la Motte's husband made a getaway to London.

The king and queen could have hushed up the whole business, but instead decided to defend their reputation by putting everyone on trial

The witless cardinal, who was mostly a victim, was eventually acquitted, but still ended up losing all his offices and was exiled. De la Motte was sentenced to be flogged, branded and imprisoned for life.

For the king and queen, it was a public relations disaster. The treatment of the cardinal seemed harsh and arbitrary. And many regular folk were amused by the audacity of de la Motte's scam. As for Marie Antoinette, she might not have been involved, but the public already hated her spending habits, and buying a diamond necklace seemed like the sort of thing she would do. Some people thought she had engineered the whole story to ruin the cardinal.

De la Motte didn't stay in prison, but she might have done better if she had. She broke out, disguised as a boy, then fled to England. A few years later, in London, she was trying to hide from debt collectors and fell to her death from a hotel window.

The "affair of the diamond necklace" increased the anger of the French public toward their rulers, and many historians say the scandal contributed to the French Revolution. It was a high-stakes con that played a major role in the guillotine deaths of the king and queen, ending a thousand years of French monarchy.

THE LOST RING AND FRIENDS

In his book *Gambling Scams*, Darwin Ortiz describes a con called "The Lost Ring."

A woman pulls into a gas station. She is well-dressed and drives an expensive car. After filling her car, she asks if she can use the washroom. When she comes out, she is about to leave, but then becomes distraught.

The staff ask her what's wrong.

"My ring!" she says. "It must have fallen off somewhere. I know I had it when I came in here."

The gas station staff help her search, scouring the counter, the washroom, the area around the car. As they search, she can't stop talking about the ring—how valuable it is, and its sentimental value to her.

The staff do everything they can to try to comfort and reassure the poor woman, but there's no sign of her lost ring, and she is already running late for an appointment.

She despairs. There's nothing else for it—she will have to leave without the ring.

"I'm sorry ma'am. Maybe it will turn up later."

"Oh, I hope so. If it does, please call me."

She writes out her name and the phone number of an expensive hotel where she will be checking in tonight. She will give a reward if they can find her ring: a thousand dollars!

Sad and anxious, the woman drives off down the highway.

A short time later, a tramp walks down the road and cuts across the gas station. As the staff watch him, he spots something on the ground and picks it up, looking pleased at his find.

Of course, the gas station staff run out to stop him.

"What did you pick up there?"

"Nothing."

"It was a ring, wasn't it!"

"None of your business. It's mine now."

The people at the gas station try to claim the ring, but the tramp won't hand it over. He's a big fellow, so they're not going to fight him. They offer him money for it. "Fifty bucks!"

"Nah, it's worth more than that."

They negotiate with the tramp and eventually end up paying perhaps $500 for the ring, figuring that they can still turn a profit when they collect the reward. The tramp pockets the cash and leaves.

The employees try to call the woman's hotel, but she hasn't arrived yet. They keep checking, but she's not there that evening, or the next day. In fact, she doesn't show up at all. They have no way to get in touch with her.

But that's okay—more than okay—because they still have the valuable ring. Eventually, they try to sell it to a jeweler. They then discover that the ring is just cheap costume jewelry. They have paid $500 for a $30 ring. The gas station employees are probably too embarrassed to report the scam to police.

Of course, the hobo and the lady are working together on this scam—and are often a husband-and-wife team. She never had a ring—he just kept one in his palm and pretended to pick it up. Once he's left the gas station, he will walk down the road to her waiting car, and they will drive on to the next gas station.

A number of other scams follow a similar pattern to The Lost Ring. In one version, a shabby violinist forgets his violin at a restaurant. A second scammer, posing as a violin expert, finds the forgotten instrument and offers the restaurant owner a fortune for this rare violin. When the player returns, looking for his violin, the restaurant owner tries to buy it and may pay thousands for an ordinary violin.

In the 1800s, the same technique was used in a horse-trading scam, where a man leaves his horse to be boarded at a farm, and a passing stranger offers the farmer a huge sum for it. The farmer is then induced to buy an ordinary horse from its owner for an inflated price.

THE PEARL

In 1935, the Australian newspaper *The Age* reported on a con that had been practised in the United States a few years earlier, until the Depression hit.

A man we'll call "Taylor" enters a jewelry store, "Finchley's," one of the most exclusive in the city. From his clothes and his manner, it's clear he's a wealthy man. He boasts that he owns a huge ranch in Oklahoma. He says he wants to buy a birthday present for his wife. A real nice pearl.

The salesman shows him some of the fine pearls they have on display. Taylor is disappointed. He was hoping to find something really special. He had heard about Mr. Finchley's establishment and came all the way into the city to shop here, but the pearls they're showing him just seem like ordinary pearls. "Don't waste my time with these little blobs, son. Show me something really good and I'll buy it."

The salesman excuses himself for a few minutes and consults with the owner, Mr. Finchley himself. Mr. Finchley emerges from his office and deals with the customer personally. He escorts Taylor into a little room where the company keeps its most precious treasures.

Finchley opens a drawer to reveal a number of much larger pearls.

"This is more like it!" says Taylor, as he reviews the pearls on offer. He settles on the largest pearl in the store. The price is $20,000. That's not a problem for Taylor. He confides to the jeweler that they recently struck oil on the ranch. He pulls out a bankroll of cash (thousand-dollar bills) and asks the jeweler to have the gem sent to his hotel, which is the best in the city. Of course, the jeweler checks the money before sending the gem. The money is real. He has the pearl delivered to the hotel.

Mr. Finchley and his salesman are pleased with their day's business—a very profitable sale.

A few days later, Taylor returns. This time, Finchley comes out immediately to attend to him.

Taylor has been thinking about that pearl, and he's not happy. No, sir. It doesn't seem enough for a fine lady like his dear wife. He would like a second pearl, just like the first, so they can be made into a pair of earrings. His wife just loves earrings.

Finchley is anxious to please but explains that the pearl was an unusual item. It may be difficult to find an exact match at short notice.

Taylor doesn't believe what he's hearing. Why, his wife was talking to her friend "Miss Wilberforce" just the other night, and she had a pearl of identical size.

Finchley is skeptical. Indignant, Taylor insists that it is true. Finchley can go look her up if he won't believe it. He angrily writes down the woman's name and address, and throws it onto the counter. Finchley calms down the Oklahoma millionaire, assuring him he'll do everything he can to find a second pearl.

"Price is no object," says Taylor. "I'll give you $40,000 if you can find it. I'll be at my hotel for the next week."

When Taylor has left, Finchley worries about how he is going to be able to find a pearl to match the first one. Such treasures don't come on the market every day. He glances at the crumpled paper on the counter. Is it possible this Miss Wilberforce that Taylor mentioned really has a matching pearl? It was worth investigating.

Finchley sends his representative to pay a call on Miss Wilberforce. She shows him her pearl, and sure enough, it is as large as the one they sold to Mr. Taylor—a perfect match, in fact. The representative asks if she is willing to sell the pearl. She is not interested. The representative says he can give a very good price. He keeps raising his offer, and she keeps saying no, but when he gets to $35,000, she finally succumbs.

The representative takes the pearl back to Finchley. It was a high price, but it will still give the company a tidy $5,000 profit. Finchley phones the hotel in triumph to give Taylor the good news. But the reception desk tells him that Taylor has checked out. "No, he did not leave a forwarding address."

Finchley then takes a closer look at the pearl and realizes it is a better match than he realized. He has just paid $35,000 for the same pearl he recently sold to Taylor for $20,000.

Finchley calls the police. They interview Miss Wilberforce, who denies knowing any Taylor and refuses to say how she got the pearl. Why should she? Was the pearl stolen?

At this point, the police can do no more.

The money that changed hands was all legitimate. Finchley chose to approach the woman and made the offer on the pearl. If he paid too much, that was his business.

MINE, ALL MINE

In 1870, financier George D. Roberts was working late in his San Francisco office when he heard a knock at the door. He opened it to see two men in shabby, weather-beaten clothes. Outdoor types, clearly.

The men said they had a leather bag of valuables they wanted to deposit at the Bank of California. However, they had arrived late, and the bank was closed. They asked Roberts if he had a safe where they could store their bag.

The men weren't local—both had Kentucky accents. Roberts guessed they were prospectors. He assumed the bag contained gold. He asked them about it.

They looked awkward. They didn't want to talk about what was in the bag. They just needed a place to store it for the night.

Roberts pressed for information. Finally, they confided in him. As Roberts suspected, they were prospectors. They were also cousins. Their names were Philip Arnold and John Slack. And they had made an extraordinary find. Not gold, but diamonds.

They showed Roberts the contents of the bag. It contained a large number of rough diamonds. Roberts was amazed. He asked where they had found so many gems. The cousins refused to say. The location had to stay secret, and so did the fact that they had found the diamonds at all. They insisted that he must tell nobody about their find. Roberts placed the diamonds in his safe and swore that he would not tell another soul.

It wasn't a promise he took too seriously. The prospectors, after all, were just simple folk from Kentucky, and this find needed to be handled by people with some business sense. He contacted two friends. One was William C. Ralston, who had founded the Bank of California and made a fortune investing in silver. Another man, Asbury Harpending, was a former privateer (a licensed pirate), who also knew a thing or two about mining. They were amazed to hear about the find.

America had been through the California gold rush in 1848, followed by a silver rush in Nevada. People had made vast fortunes from being in the right place at the right time. It seemed inevitable that other mineral fortunes were out there, waiting to be found. This discovery could be the start of the next big thing. But the businessman had to get rid of the two dirty prospectors at the first opportunity.

While Roberts was busy putting his deals together, bringing in other investors, Arnold and Slack returned with more gems from their diamond field. They claimed they had sixty pounds of gems and not just diamonds, but also other valuable stones, including rubies, sapphires and emeralds. Roberts and his associates knew that if they didn't lock up the rights fast, other investors would soon move in.

Roberts, Ralston and his associates offered to buy out Arnold and Slack. What did they want to sign over the rights? The cousins didn't want to sell; they had found the diamond field and they intended to keep earning money from it. But Roberts kept up the pressure. If they were to sell now, for a lump sum, how much would they ask?

Arnold still wasn't budging, but Slack considered the question. He liked the idea of cash in hand. Yes, he figured that he might sell his share for, say, $100,000, which is about $2.3 million in modern money. The price was not only acceptable—it was a bargain. The buyers, however, didn't want to seem too eager. It was eventually agreed that Slack would get $50,000 up front and another $50,000 after he had made another visit to the diamond field. Slack got his money, and the prospectors went back to the wilderness. They brought back an impressive haul of gems, which they poured out onto a billiard table for the investors to admire. A second sack just like it had been lost during a river crossing.

The banker Ralston took a representative sample of the gems and sent them to the jeweler Charles Tiffany in New York. Tiffany and one of his experts inspected the rough stones and was impressed at their size and quality. Based on his assessment, the most recent sack of stones the prospectors had delivered was worth $1.5 million.

The syndicate recruited new members—high-ranking military men and politicians. Their names would help bring in more investors, and their influence with the government would help if it turned out that the diamond field was located on federal land.

By the following year, 1872, Arnold had agreed to a deal for his half, which gave him a mix of cash and stocks in the new venture, and the investors formed the San Francisco and New York Mining and Commercial Company. They sent a mining engineer, Henry Janin, along with several other investors, to inspect the site. Still keeping the location secret, Arnold led the group on a convoluted route to his diamond field. When they arrived, he suggested sites where they could dig. The area was rich in gems, and they found one after another. Janin, a mining expert, let the investors know that this was the real deal.

The site was now revealed: it was on the border of Colorado and Wyoming. Janin staked out a claim to thousands of acres around the diamond field. Finally, Arnold and Slack were both paid off. Their cut was around $650,000. It was a lot of money, to be sure, but their entire take from the vast underground wealth was much less than Tiffany's assessment of the single bag they'd brought back earlier. It seemed like the cousins had been duped, but the rich investors didn't see a problem with that. They sat back and prepared to get a lot richer.

But a chance encounter on a California train sent things in a different direction. Henry Janin met a government geologist who had been surveying the same region of the American West. Without revealing too much about the location, Janin talked about the cousins' find, which was on a mesa to the north of a cone-shaped mountain. The geologist was shocked that his survey hadn't identified the diamond field. But some details of this find were odd. Diamonds are formed from carbon. Rubies and sapphires are a compound of aluminum. Emeralds are a compound made from beryllium. The gems form from different materials under different conditions. It was strange to find a mix of gems in the same location.

Back at the office, the government geologist shared news of the encounter with his superior, a geologist named Clarence King. He, too, was skeptical, but he was also concerned that his official survey might have missed something important. The geologists used the descriptions Janin had provided and did some detective work. They found the cone-shaped mountain (today named Diamond Peak), deduced the location of the diamond field and went on a difficult journey by train and mule to investigate the site.

They found an unusual assortment of precious and semi-precious stones. They also discovered strange holes poked into ants' nests in the area. When they dug into each of the ants' nests marked with a hole, they found a gem buried underneath.

The government scientists concluded that the gems from this site were a geologic impossibility. It was clear to them that the area had been deliberately "salted" with gems. The investors, jewelers and mining engineer had been ingeniously conned.

The Kentucky cousins had planned it all to perfection. They both had real experience as prospectors, but before their first meeting with businessman George Roberts, Philip Arnold had worked as a book-keeper for a San Francisco drill manufacturer. The company bought industrial diamonds for use in drill bits, and it seems likely that Arnold had borrowed some of these inexpensive diamonds to offer as his first find.

When Slack was paid the first half of his buyout fee, he and Arnold didn't go to any diamond field. Instead, they took a ship to Europe and purchased rough gems from dealers there.

The con artists had an unexpected stroke of luck when the investors gave the purchased stones to Charles Tiffany: he and his associate were used to dealing with cut stones and had very little experience with rough ones. By his estimate, the bag of stones presented by the swindlers should have been worth $1.5 million. In fact, Arnold and Slack had purchased the stones from dealers for just $20,000. Tiffany's overvaluation was a gift to the cousins, and made it much easier for them to get the price they wanted.

Philip Arnold and John Slack were indicted for fraud in California, but by that time they had both gone back to Kentucky, and the case never came to trial. Arnold was sued by the defrauded investors and settled out of court. He remained wealthy and set himself up as a banker. That business proved just as dangerous as mining; he was later shot by a rival banker.

John Slack lived longer. Perhaps he had become more aware of the fragility of life. He became an undertaker.

Of course, the investors lost a fortune from the con, and they also looked like fools to the public. They gave up trying to bring the fraudsters to justice. It was better to walk away and let their bruised reputations recover.

In the end, the person who benefited most from the con was the government geologist Clarence King. When the newspapers announced the fraud, they sang the praises of the geologists and their dogged investigation. King's careful, expert work in uncovering "The Diamond hoax of 1872" made him famous on both sides of the Atlantic.

The words *superstar* and *geologist* don't usually go together, but that is what King became, and his accomplishment made him famous for the rest of his life.

PARKING LOT DIAMONDS

In 2014, a fifty-eight-year-old Texas woman, "Rhonda," was walking through the parking lot of a local mall when she was approached by another woman, "Candy."

Candy asked if Rhonda wanted to buy some diamonds. "Because if you do, I can sell you some for half price." She showed Rhonda the stones. They were small and sparkly, as you would expect diamonds to be. "I'll sell you these. You can sell them to a jeweler and double your money."

Rhonda wasn't quite sure, but another woman had approached them. She seemed to know a thing or two about diamonds, and when she saw the ones on offer, she immediately wanted in. She bought a diamond from Candy on the spot, paying $10,000 in cash.

Rhonda was impressed by the other woman's decisive purchase. You only live once, and she could see that this was an unusual opportunity. It's not every day that you meet a woman in a parking lot selling tens of thousands of dollars of half-price diamonds. Were they stolen? Perhaps it was better not to ask too many questions.

Rhonda had some money saved in her bank account. A spot of diamond trading could allow her to quickly multiply her funds. She thought of the things she could do with that money. Her son needed a new vehicle, and with the money she could make here, she could buy it for him.

She decided to go for it. But she told Candy she didn't have enough money on her to buy the gems. Unlike Candy's previous customer, she wasn't in the habit of carrying thousands of dollars in cash.

Candy couldn't have been nicer about it. If Rhonda wanted to stop by her bank, that was just fine. She would even come with her. Rhonda hurried to her bank and withdrew a large sum of money. Cash in hand, Rhonda purchased four of the precious gems. We don't know how much she paid, but given the going rate, it was many thousands.

Later, when Rhonda was back home, she called her daughter to tell her about the bargain deal. The daughter was less supportive than Rhonda had hoped.

"You bought WHAT? For HOW much?"

"Other people were buying them, too. I saw a woman pay $10,000."

"Mom, you've been scammed."

The daughter took the diamonds to a jeweler. He confirmed her fears.

The stones were not diamonds. They were cubic zirconia. They are nice gems, in their way. They look like diamonds. They are very hard, very sparkly—and very cheap to produce. Factories have been turning them out since the 1970s. Rhonda had spent thousands on a few dollars' worth of stones.

Rhonda reported the con to the police. They told her that the other woman, who had been quick to buy one of the diamonds, was certainly one of the scammers. Using a shill, in this case, a fake customer who appears knowledgeable and enthusiastically buys into the con, is a powerful technique for persuading the mark that they're getting a good deal. It can also create a sense of urgency: if you don't buy it now, someone else will.

But even when shills are working to make the deal look legit, a mall parking lot is a sketchy place to buy expensive jewelry. Don't look at the diamond—look at the setting.

THE FAMILY JEWELS

Cons tend to rise and fall in popularity, and they also move around. When a scam has been overplayed in an area, people become wary of it, but in another area, the same scam will still seem fresh, and the local population will be naive to it.

One common scam worldwide begins with a person who needs to sell their jewels to pay for urgent expenses. Around 2020, this scam became popular in British Columbia.

In one case in 2020, "Roger," a sixty-one-year-old man from Victoria, was flagged down by two men parked beside a road. They offered to sell him gold rings and chains. When he told them he wasn't carrying any money, the men drove him to an ATM so he could withdraw it. Then Roger spent nearly $500 on what turned out to be worthless jewelry.

Roger was perhaps more trusting than most. In some places, getting into a car with two unknown men could cost you more than a few hundred dollars. But other British Columbia residents have been scammed by con artists who seemed more wholesome.

In April 2023, two residents of Langford, "Sam" and "Chris," were approached by a couple who needed help. The husband's wallet had been stolen, and they urgently needed money to buy gasoline. The couple were well dressed, and they had kids waiting in the minivan.

The couple weren't looking for a handout. The wife offered to sell her gold jewelry in exchange for cash.

The price she asked for the jewelry seemed well below its true value. Here was an opportunity to help some strangers in need and make a healthy profit. To Sam and Chris, it seemed like a win-win. They took the gold and handed over a few hundred dollars in exchange.

When they checked the jewelry later, they found it was fake, worth only a few dollars.

According to Victoria's *Times Colonist* newspaper, the "Family in Trouble" scam is growing in popularity. The con artists claim they need money for gasoline or ferry tickets to deal with a family emergency. They then offer to sell jewelry at a price they say is far below its true value.

Another victim, in Kelowna, was cheated out of $800. The con artists were travelling as a family. "They were dressed nice, had kids in the vehicle."

The jewelry was stamped as 18 karat gold, and the scammers accompanied the victim to the bank machine.

CBC News reported on another group operating in British Columbia, using a different strategy to sell cheap fake-gold necklaces and rings. They claimed it was from a hoard smuggled out of Iraq that formerly belonged to Osama bin Laden. One fifty-year-old man paid more than $700 for several necklaces and rings. The prospect of a quick profit overrides the mark's skepticism.

Like some other teams, this one operated in mall parking lots. In one case, they tried to sell a man a worthless gold chain and helped him put it on. The man said no to the deal, but when the men had gone, he realized they had stolen his own gold chain, which was worth $500.

ARCHIMEDES

Fake gold has a very long history. Archimedes's famous "Eureka moment" was related to a scam involving gold. According to one account, a Greek king had ordered goldsmiths to make a crown using gold he had provided to them. The crown probably resembled a wreath of laurel leaves. It wasn't for the king himself, but to use in the temple as an offering to the gods.

The king received the finished crown, which was well-made and weighed as much as the gold he'd provided, but he was uneasy. The word on the street was that these goldsmiths had taken some of the gold for themselves and mixed the remaining gold with silver. He turned to Archimedes and asked how the crown's gold content might be tested. The young inventor went away to think about the problem.

According to legend, Archimedes was taking his bath when he realized that if the gold in the crown had been mixed with silver (which is much lighter than gold), the crown must have a larger volume than it would have if it were made only of gold. If the crown was placed in a bath, the water it displaced would show the volume of the crown, which should exactly match the volume of the gold. If it didn't match—if the crown needed more "stuff" to make up the same weight—it meant the king had been cheated.

Archimedes is said to have been so excited about his discovery that he shouted "Eureka!" ("I have it!"), then jumped from the bath and went running naked down the street, later shouting whatever the Greek is for "I can explain everything, officer."

Although Archimedes's method works in theory, it is difficult to prove in practice. A crown of gold leaves doesn't take up a lot of volume, and any useful comparisons would require very precise measurements of the displaced water.

Some scientists have suggested Archimedes may have used a different and more accurate water-based approach, one he described in his other writings.

Lighter metals are more buoyant than heavy ones. The crown could be balanced on a scale against the same mass of pure gold. Once the balance is perfect, the scale is immersed in water. If the gold in the crown is pure, the scale will go back to being balanced, but if the crown's gold has been mixed with lighter metals, the crown will be slightly more buoyant than the pure gold on the opposite side, and the scale will no longer balance.

Whichever method was used, Archimedes is said to have carried out his test and discovered that the crown had indeed been mixed with other metals. It's not known what happened to the goldsmith con men, but it probably wasn't pretty. There's a story or two in Greek mythology about cheating the gods, and it doesn't usually go well.

It's an early example of a long battle between scientists and con artists.

ALL THAT GLITTERS

In 2008, Ethiopia's national bank exported a batch of gold bars to South Africa. The gold bars looked normal, but the South Africans only had to pick up one of them to realize that something was wrong. The gold bars used by banks are not very large—about nine inches long and perhaps three inches wide—but they are very heavy. A single bar might weigh more than thirty pounds. But the bars they had received from Ethiopia were less than half that weight. They were clearly made of a lighter metal.

The South Africans complained to Ethiopia. "These bars are not gold. They are gold-plated steel. We're not taking them." The rejected bars were sent back to the seller.

The event led to panic in Ethiopia, where officials realized that someone—or, more likely, a large group of someones—had carried out a multimillion-dollar swindle against the country's national bank. Dozens of arrests quickly followed: the person who originally supplied the gold, his associates, the bank officials, and the chemists who worked for the bank and were supposed to test gold.

The Ethiopian case was a clumsy scam—the bars would only pass a visual inspection— but it still took some time before it was caught. If the scammers had used a heavier metal for the fake bars, the switch might have been harder to detect.

In 2012, a Manhattan jeweler, "Sam," bought four ten-ounce gold bars from a dealer. The bars had the correct stamps and came with valid certificates, but Sam had heard that some jewelers bought counterfeits, so he drilled into the bars to check they were pure gold. They weren't. Sam's heart sank when he looked under the gold exterior. The block contained a drab, grey material—tungsten.

Tungsten is a strange metal—it doesn't look or act like gold. Gold is soft, while tungsten is extremely hard; gold is easily melted, while tungsten can be heated to very high temperatures without melting. Tungsten's physical properties make it extremely useful in manufacturing: tungsten wire is used as a filament in incandescent light bulbs, and tungsten coatings produce super-tough drill bits.

But if you're a con artist, it's the weight of tungsten that you'll really love. A cubic centimetre of gold weighs 19.3 grams. The equivalent volume of tungsten weighs 19.25 grams. That's a difference of only a quarter of a percent—close enough that it will pass most weighing tests. And while tungsten is expensive compared to metals like iron, it costs only about a fifth as much as gold. Four hundred percent profits, anyone?

You can take a block of tungsten and wrap some gold around it, and it will look and feel like a real gold bar or a gold wafer or a gold coin. The buyers probably won't find out the truth until they try to melt down the metal. The gold on the surface will melt away, revealing the dark, non-meltable tungsten monolith inside.

Other fakes have emerged in other countries. The criminals may take real bars, with valid documentation, and drill out much of the gold from inside, replacing it with tungsten. Or they may manufacture high-quality fakes from scratch. The true extent of this scam is unknown, and some people don't want to know. Detecting a tungsten interior is impossible without high-tech equipment, and for those who already own gold bars and would like to resell them, it may be easier not to look.

CHAPTER 8
TROJAN HORSE SCAMS

The Trojan Horse story (if it's true) was a military con.

The Greeks left the horse outside the walls of Troy, then departed. The Trojans let their guard down and pulled the horse inside their gates, not realizing it contained a hidden force of Greek soldiers.

The same idea is the basis for many different kinds of cons. A small lapse in security can be exploited for bigger losses.

WORLD'S MOST EXPENSIVE PIZZA

In April 2023, "Anita" was near her vehicle in a supermarket parking lot in Brampton, Ontario, when a distressed teenaged girl approached her.

According to *CBC News*, the teen said that she and her friends had ordered a pizza, but the delivery driver wouldn't accept cash. She asked Anita if she would take $20 in cash and use her debit card to pay for their pizza.

Anita was sympathetic and agreed to help. The driver had a point-of-sale machine. She offered him a credit card, but he said he couldn't accept it—only a debit card would do. Anita found her debit card and, since the machine didn't allow tapping, inserted it and entered her PIN.

The next day, she logged into her bank account. To her shock, she found that the account, which should have contained more than $4,000, was completely empty.

The teenager and the delivery driver were con artists. The machine was a fake and recorded her keypresses. When she looked at her debit card, she realized it wasn't hers: at some point, the scammers had palmed her card and switched it for one that looked similar. It was then an easy matter for them to use the same card to withdraw money from her account using the PIN they had recorded.

She filed a complaint with the police, but as of this writing, she has been unable to get her money back, and the con artists are still on the loose.

USB STICKUP

In 2015, "Josie" had just left her car and was walking through the university parking lot when she spotted a key ring on the ground. It had two keys and a USB flash drive, but no other identification. She considered handing it in to security, but decided instead to take it with her to her office.

She plugged the flash drive into her computer, hoping to find some clue about the owner. It contained HTML files—web pages. She clicked on one to open it.

She had been conned.

The moment she opened it, her computer downloaded a file from the internet. People watching at a distant location instantly knew that the drive had been picked up and inserted into a networked computer at the university. They were ready to carry out their next step.

Fortunately for Josie, the con artists monitoring her activities were computer security researchers at the University of Illinois, and their next step was to present her with an anonymous survey on why, as a computer-savvy woman, she had plugged a strange USB drive into her computer.

Hackers often drop USB sticks in public places in order to place malware on computers. The researchers wanted to measure how effective that technique really is. The answer is: very effective. They dropped nearly three hundred flash drives around the university campus. More than 45 percent were quickly picked up and plugged into a computer.

Some people did it because they were curious to see what was on the USB stick. (On a university campus, marking a stick "Exam answers" can add another incentive.) Other people were helpfully trying to find clues to the user's identity so they could return the key ring.

Whatever the motivation, plugging in a random USB stick is a very risky activity. Depending on how a computer is configured, it may automatically run software on the drive. Malicious software can track the user's keyboard input and take periodic snapshots of the screen, allowing hackers to figure out a person's banking information.

Another sneaky con is to configure the USB stick so the computer thinks it's a keyboard. When the user plugs in the stick to see the contents, the drive starts typing instructions that have been put there by a hacker.

Even computers that have been designed for higher-security environments can be vulnerable to USB sticks, because a computer communicates with a USB device as soon as it is plugged in. It has to, so that the computer can tell what kind of device has been attached: a drive, a keyboard, a mouse or any of thousands of possible devices. For hackers who know their stuff, that brief burst of communication can be used for evil purposes.

In 2008, an employee of the US military working at a Middle Eastern base found a USB drive and plugged it into their work laptop to see what was on it. What was on it was a computer "worm" named agent.btz. The malicious code spread through military computer systems, allowing Russian hackers to gain access to US intelligence information. It took fourteen months to remove the infection, and one Pentagon official said it was the worst breach of US military computers in history. The incident led to the creation of a new command within the military just to deal with digital attacks—the United States Cyber Command. We hope they began with a policy to never plug unknown USBs into military computers.

But the United States has also used this style of attack for its own purposes. In the early 2000s, the United States and Israel developed software designed to interfere with Iran's nuclear program. Iran was using giant centrifuges to separate different weights of nuclear material. The hackers wrote a program that would infiltrate the computer systems and discreetly change the speed of the huge devices, making them alternate between faster and slower speeds until they were damaged or destroyed. The sabotage was a success, destroying a fifth of the country's centrifuges.

But getting the software into the tightly guarded nuclear facility had been a challenge. The method they finally, and successfully, used was the same con: USB flash drives dropped in a parking lot.

QR CODE SCAM

A dropped USB stick is one way to spread malicious software to passers-by, but there are even cheaper methods.

"Enid" was a sixty-year-old woman in Singapore. According to the *Straits Times*, she was in a bubble-tea shop and noticed a sticker on the door, inviting customers to fill out an online survey to get a free drink. She scanned the QR code with her Android phone and downloaded an app, which allowed her to complete the survey.

That night, the app went into action. The next morning, $20,000 had been removed from her bank account.

QR codes are the successors to the bar codes used on food labels. Bar codes work like the old Morse code, with numbers represented by combinations of thick and thin lines. A QR code uses a grid of black-and-white squares. Where a bar code usually stores a short run of numbers, a QR code can hold a brief text message or a web address.

Scanning the code on its own can't harm a phone, but if it makes the phone open a web page, it might not be obvious what page you've been sent to. In Enid's case, the sticker on the door was a fake, and the website it linked to did not belong to the bubble-tea store—it was a site set up by hackers.

Downloading the app was a mistake. When it ran, it asked for permission to access certain features of her phone—the microphone and camera, as well as Android's Accessibility Service, which is designed for users who need help operating a phone. Enid clicked the buttons to allow this, as many people would, not knowing what it meant or what it would be used for.

Once these permissions were granted, the app had access to her phone's screen and it started monitoring her activity. When Enid went onto a banking site, it captured the information and recorded her login details, sending it back to its masters. It was then easy for them to log into her account and move the money to their own.

QR codes are often placed strategically by criminals. Common locations include phone poles and restaurant menus. There are reports of QR codes stuck to the backs of parking meters. Drivers assume the codes allow them to pay for parking, and when they scan the code, a site opens asking them to enter their credit card information.

WHAT'S IN THE BOX?

Of course, in past centuries, criminals couldn't steal money by typing a few keystrokes. Accessing a person's wealth involved getting past walls, heavy chains and locks. But amazingly, criminals of the past used techniques that are now common in cybercrime.

Around 1780, an innkeeper in Liechtenstein had an unusual female visitor. She was travelling alone, a tall, strong redhead, carrying a large box on her back. Her name was Barbara Erni. She put down her money and asked the innkeeper if he could give her a room for the night.

The innkeeper took Barbara to a room, and she was satisfied with it. She then asked the innkeeper if had a place where she could store the box she had been carrying.

"Can't you keep it in your room?" asked the innkeeper.

"No, no," said Barbara. "It wouldn't be safe. This box contains a fortune in valuables. I want it locked up in your safest and most secure location."

The innkeeper was surprised, but pleased by his guest's trust. He told Barbara that he had a room that would serve the purpose. He kept his own valuables there, as well as some precious items belonging to another guest.

Barbara was satisfied and said she would sleep easy knowing that her treasure was well protected.

The innkeeper dragged the heavy box to his safe room, where it was protected by two locked doors.

Barbara left the next day. The innkeeper fetched her treasure chest, and she hoisted it over her shoulders, then went off, striding down the road.

Much later, the innkeeper discovered that his room wasn't quite as safe as he had imagined. His own money was missing, and so were the valuables he was holding for his other patron. He hoped the thieves hadn't also stolen Barbara's treasure.

In fact, Barbara had stolen the money using an unusual con. The box she carried held a small man, her accomplice. She travelled from one country inn to another, and at each location, she made sure the box was stored with the most valuable possessions. At night, the accomplice slipped out of the chest and stole whatever valuables he found around him. When Barbara left in the morning, she carried her accomplice and the stolen property.

She and her partner made a good living from this scam, but

Liechtenstein is a tiny country, and it was only a matter of time before word got around. Barbara's luck finally ran out when she tried the scam in the city of Eschen. In 1784, she was put on trial and admitted to seventeen thefts using the "tiny man in a box" trick. The court sentenced her to death by beheading. The execution was carried out in front of a thousand spectators.

It seems a harsh sentence for the crime. The people of Liechtenstein may have felt so, too. Although the death penalty remained on the country's books for another two hundred years, it was never used again.

CHAPTER 9
CON ARTIST ARTISTS

Fine art has been the subject of many cons, ranging from insurance frauds to forgeries. Some people even claim that modern art itself is a big con.

But art cons take many forms, and not all of them are modern.

A SIGNED ORIGINAL

A story about both Salvador Dali and Pablo Picasso is that they used to pay their restaurant bills with cheques.

In Dali's case, he would sketch a little drawing on the cheque, then sign it. The recipient now faced a dilemma. An artwork by Dali could be worth big money. Should they keep this cheque with its signed doodle or deposit it in the bank and lose the art? If they kept it, it meant that Dali got his purchase for free.

Pablo Picasso is said to have done something similar. In his case, merely the presence of his signature was enough for the restaurant owner to keep the cheque rather than deposit it.

Are these the actions of an artist or a con artist? You decide.

LAUGHING ALL THE WAY TO THE BANKSY

In 2018, the artist Banksy put a copy of one of his paintings up for auction. The painting, titled *Girl with Balloon*, went for $1.4 million, a record price for the artist, but after the auctioneer's hammer had fallen, a shredder hidden inside the ornate gold frame started pulling the painting down, turning it into strips. Banksy had pranked the auctioneers.

The shredder seems to have malfunctioned partway through the process, so instead of shredding the entire painting, it left the top of the painting untouched, while the ruined lower half hung like a paper tassel below the frame.

The stunt received enormous attention in the media, and three years later, the same half-destroyed painting (now renamed *Love Is in the Bin*) was put up for auction again. This time it sold for $25.4 million.

If the original price was correct, that breaks down as $1.4 million for the painting and $24 million for the con.

HOW CUPID DO YOU THINK I AM?

Raffaelo Riario came from a poor family in Italy, but he had a stroke of luck when his mother's uncle was made pope and doled out favours to family members. Riario was given the post of cardinal—a big promotion, considering that he was only sixteen years old and wasn't even a priest. Suddenly, he had a life of luxury—a large income and not much work to do. That might sound like a scam, but it's not the one we're looking at here.

In those days, Italians were rediscovering Greek and Roman culture—that's what the Renaissance was all about. This new-found enthusiasm for the ancient world meant that anything from Ancient Greece or Ancient Rome could fetch big money on the art market. Carvings,

statues, busts, urns—wealthy buyers would snap them up, then display them in their homes to show how cultured they were. So once Riario had settled into his life as a rich cardinal, he started taking an active interest in the arts and spent big money on quality pieces, especially sculptures. A dealer came to the cardinal and offered him a beautiful Roman sculpture. It depicted a sleeping Cupid, the Roman god of love. Riario was interested. It was expertly carved. He was impressed by the work and paid a large sum for it.

But on closer inspection, it became clear that the work was not a Roman antiquity. It was a high-quality fake—a modern carving that had been treated with acid to make the stone appear old. When the cardinal realized he'd been had, he was furious and demanded a refund from the dealer. Even so, he had acquired a genuine appreciation for the arts and had to admit that the sculpture was a beautiful piece of carving. He asked to meet its creator. The artist was brought to Rome. He was a twenty-one-year-old man named Michelangelo. The lad might have been a forger, but they both came from poor backgrounds. The cardinal liked the lad and commissioned new works from him, and soon he was getting favourable reviews from the rich and famous of Italy. The attention Michelangelo received from his forged sculpture launched his career as an artist.

Michelangelo's *Sleeping Cupid* sculpture became more valuable as a fake than it would have been if it were marketed as an original. It was later purchased by another cardinal, Cesare Borgia, and exhibited next to a similar Roman sculpture. Perhaps it was a challenge: "Can you spot the fake?"

Sadly, we can't look at Michelangelo's breakout work today. Nobody is certain what happened to it. According to one theory, it was purchased by King Charles I and moved to England. If that's true, the *Sleeping Cupid* was probably destroyed in a fire at the Palace of Whitehall in London. However, other works by Michelangelo survive, and he is still considered one of the greatest sculptors and painters of all time—a con artist who became a real artist.

FORGER HAN VAN MEEGEREN

A Dutch artist named Han van Meegeren loved the work of Vermeer and other paintings by the Old Masters. He tried to paint in a similar style. Unfortunately, in the early twentieth century, critics and buyers were more interested in abstract art than realism. When van Meegeren presented his works, hoping for praise, the critics were not impressed. Sure, he had technical ability, but his work wasn't original. He was mediocre.

The artist was upset and angry at the way his work had been rejected. But he would teach the critics a lesson. He would con them all and show the world what fools the art experts really were and what a genius he was.

He vowed to take a very profitable revenge on the art world by painting and selling a forgery. The artist he chose to copy was Vermeer, a painter from the 1600s whose paintings had soared in value during the twentieth century.

Many of Vermeer's paintings had originally been sold at modest prices and were difficult to track down. This meant that quite a few were tucked away in strange places. Over the years, an unrecognized Vermeer painting would sometimes be found in an attic or turn up for a bargain price at an estate sale. Vermeer made only a few dozen paintings in his life, so whenever a "new" one appeared, it was an exciting event in the art world. Such paintings were worth a fortune.

Van Meegeren had to plan his fake Vermeer carefully. The painting had to be original but look like the sort of subject Vermeer might have painted. He carefully refined his methods, capturing the same facial expressions and the same high-contrast lighting.

For his subject, van Meegeren chose a religious theme—Jesus having supper at Emmaus, an event mentioned in the Gospel of Luke. The artist Caravaggio had painted this scene, and Vermeer was thought to have studied it, so it seemed a plausible subject for him, too.

The painting would have to pass scientific tests. Van Meegeren chose authentic paints and canvas material, but soon realized there was a serious problem. Oil paints take up to fifty years to fully harden. And old paint develops tiny cracks, which are not found in new paint.

Van Meegeren made his paints look older by using some modern technology: he mixed his pigments with Bakelite, a plastic that had been invented about thirty years earlier, then cooked the paintings in an oven. In a matter of hours, the paint was rock hard. Rolling the canvas over a cylindrical tube created fine cracks, and he could make the cracks more prominent by adding fake dirt—a wash of India ink created a convincing look.

It took van Meegeren six years to get his forging techniques just right. At last, he completed his version of the painting *Supper at Emmaus*. Now he was ready to fool the critics, and he decided to aim for the top.

The foremost expert in Vermeer was art historian Abraham Bredius. He had spent his life studying him and was considered such an illustrious expert that nobody would dare to contradict him. Because his word was final, the art community had given him the nickname "the Pope."

Van Meegeren needed to fool Bredius for his scam to succeed. But if Bredius spotted the fakery, six years of work would be wasted.

Van Meegeren arranged for a lawyer friend to present the piece to Bredius. The painting's backstory sounded convincing. The lawyer was trustee for the estate of a certain Dutch family who preferred to remain anonymous. They didn't know what to make of this large painting. Perhaps Bredius could take a look.

Bredius looked and was astonished: "Why, this is a Vermeer!" Of course it was very old, but aside from the tiny cracks in the paint, it was in perfect condition. Many old paintings had been damaged and restored over the years, but this one was pristine—it showed no sign of restoration. Magnificent! Bredius declared that this newly discovered painting was not merely the work of Vermeer, it was one of his finest works.

Critics and artists lined up to admire the new discovery. The Pope had spoken, and the art world said "Amen."

The painting was subjected to a battery of scientific tests: it was X-rayed and chemically tested. Today, the Bakelite might have set off alarm bells, but the tests of the day seemed to support Bredius's expert opinion: this appeared to be an authentic Vermeer.

The painting was a sensation. The Rembrandt Society spent a fortune to buy it—the equivalent of around five million US dollars today. The money went to the lawyer, who funnelled it back to the discreet Dutch family—actually van Meegeren himself.

At this point, van Meegeren might have revealed his scam and declared victory. After all, the experts had said that his work showed great skill and originality and had set a high value on it. He had proved that the critics were fools and that he was an artistic genius. He had won.

Instead, he lay low and enjoyed the money. He also enjoyed the fuss surrounding his masterpiece, which was now the focus of a big exhibition. In the meantime, he used his fortune to buy a big house and purchase some genuine Dutch artworks. He also set to work creating new forgeries, which he could sell through a group of well-paid agents.

But van Meegeren hadn't got the one thing he really wanted—recognition as an artist. He had shifted from disgruntled artist to wealthy criminal. He continued raking in the cash, forging works by various Dutch artists and selling them to collectors. Even when the Nazis invaded the Netherlands in 1940, he lived well. He bought more properties and more art and enjoyed a lavish lifestyle, but it had bad effects on his health. He smoked and drank heavily and became addicted to morphine.

Eventually, the law catches up with many forgers, and it caught up with van Meegeren, but perhaps not in the way he expected. In the closing months of the war, after the Netherlands had been liberated from the Germans, van Meegeren was arrested.

The Allies had found the looted art collection of Nazi Reichsmarschall Hermann Göring. Included among the artworks was a Vermeer purchased from van Meegeren.

The charges against him were serious. In selling a Vermeer to

German officers, he was considered to have collaborated with the Nazis as they pillaged Dutch art treasures. The penalty was death.

Van Meegeren's defense caught the authorities by surprise. He said that the Vermeer he had sold Göring was not real—he had painted it himself. What's more, he had traded it for 137 paintings looted by the Nazis, rescuing genuine Dutch art treasures from German hands.

He confessed that he had been forging paintings for years and identified the fakes. The court didn't know what to make of it. They demanded that he prove his claims by painting a new fake Vermeer, a work titled *Jesus among the Doctors*. And so, in a strange twist, art forger Han van Meegeren painted to save his life, trying to prove to the court not that he was innocent of forgery, but that he was guilty.

The resulting painting wasn't his best work, but some people said stress might explain that. It was still a good enough fake, and careful chemical analysis of the other paintings that he admitted to creating seemed to back up van Meegeren's story.

The Dutch public considered van Meegeren a hero for cheating the Nazis and saving Dutch artworks, but the buyers he had cheated disagreed. The artist escaped the death penalty, but was charged with fraud and forgery and sentenced to a year in prison. But before the sentence could begin, his life of booze and drugs caught up with him. He suffered a massive heart attack and died.

Van Meegeren's assets were sold to compensate the buyers he had defrauded, although much of his money remained with his wife, who he had strategically divorced during the war and who claimed to know nothing about his activities as a forger.

CHAPTER 10
FALSE ADVERTISING

Only a fool would believe all the promises made in advertisements. Most consumers view ads with a wary eye, but no amount of skepticism can match the creativity of a rapacious con artist copy writer.

THE OL' BALLOON SCAM

In 1889, an advertising expert named M. de la Houchette made an unusual sales pitch to some of the business owners of Paris. He said he had invented many successful advertising methods, including the sandwich boards that were now common around the city. In recent years, he'd become interested in ballooning.

France was famous as a pioneer of ballooning—after all, the country had made the first successful manned flights back in 1783—and de la Houchette was continuing the tradition of innovation. He said he had invented balloons decorated with advertisements or business logos.

These ventures were very expensive for the participating businesses, but now he was working on an even more exciting opportunity: if the business owners provided him with their literature, he would fly over Paris at regular intervals and drop the papers on the excited crowds below.

A few businesses were interested in his high-tech plan and subscribed to the service. They handed over their money and provided boxes of printed material decorated with woodcut illustrations, neatly folded and placed in envelopes.

On the day of the first flight, the sponsors assembled to watch the balloon rise. A couple had telescopes, so they could see every detail. The pilot placed the precious cargo of promotional advertising into the basket, then climbed in himself.

The ropes tethering the balloon to the ground were released, and the balloon ascended gracefully skyward. The businessmen smiled with satisfaction—this was commerce at its most modern, exploiting the high tech of the nineteenth century. The balloon drifted over the streets of Paris.

An initial flutter of envelopes came down. Most landed on rooftops.

"It's fine. He's just getting started."

More stationery fluttered down. A few papers hit pedestrians. They looked up in confusion to see where the airmail had come from.

Suddenly, M. de la Houchette became very busy in the basket of his balloon. He emptied an entire box of papers, all at once. Then he did the same with another box. What was going on?

The pilot adjusted the bags on the side of his balloon. A mass of sand poured down.

"I do believe he's releasing all his ballast. But why? His aeronautical advertising flight has hardly begun."

As the confused business owners looked on, the balloon quickly rose high into the sky and floated away to the north. They realized with horror that he was not coming back. They had been swindled!

Hours later, de la Houchette landed his balloon in the north of France. The ropes of the balloon were snagged on the branches of a tree, but he managed to scramble to the ground and made a getaway with the money. He wasn't too worried about losing the balloon: he had previously scammed it from its legitimate owner.

THE PONZI USB DRIVE

In this compound con, false advertising, a deceitful USB drive and a Ponzi scheme work together to cheat the victim. In a Ponzi scheme, which we'll hear a lot more about later, the con artist keeps taking in new money and claims to invest it, but actually just pays out a little to investors and spends the rest.

In 2022, some online retailers sold a hard drive that worked in the same way.

The drive was sold as an SSD—a solid state drive, which has no moving parts and is entirely electronic. These drives are usually priced at a premium over older disk drives, but this one offered thirty terabytes of data—roughly thirty trillion bytes—for less than $20. At current prices, this much storage should cost thousands, so it was an absurdly low price.

One cybersecurity expert, "Joel," was curious as to what kind of scam this was and bought one. The drive wasn't very fast, but when he plugged it into a computer, it did seem to offer an enormous amount of storage for the money.

It didn't look so good when Joel pried open the unit. Inside the drive was a circuit board with two small memory cards hot-glued to it. The memory held a total of one gigabyte. The device's firmware was programmed to lie to the computer and say that its capacity was thirty terabytes when, in fact, it only held one thirty-thousandth of that data. It was like buying an aircraft hangar and getting a bedroom closet.

Actually, it was worse than that, because not only was the hard drive designed to misreport the amount of storage it had, it was programmed to think it was capable of storing huge amounts of data. It cheerfully allowed files to be transferred to it. Optimistic owners used it to move data from their computer hard drive, and the file directory showed that the data had been successfully moved to the new drive.

Unfortunately, as soon as the small memory chips were full, the drive started overwriting old files with new ones. If a user looked at their directory listing, the files seemed to be there—like the investments in a Ponzi scheme, the reports showed that what you'd put in was all present. The problems came when you wanted to get it back—the data couldn't be opened or retrieved. It was gone forever.

IT'S NOT JUST FOR OILING SNAKES

"Snake oil" has become a synonym for a fake remedy, and "snake oil salesman" is used to describe someone who fraudulently promotes a worthless product or solution.

Snake oil was a common medicine in the past. Various brands of snake oil were once sold as a cure-all. In Europe, "viper oil" had been used for generations, as it had in China and the Middle East. People used to believe that venomous snakes were immune to their own poison, so an extract from the snake would be effective in fighting poisons in general, including those they believed were causing diseases.

It's unlikely that snake flesh or snake oil offers much medicinal value to a sick patient—it contains some omega-3, but you can easily get that from a fish. However, the dramatic idea of drinking a liquid brewed from a poisonous snake might have had a strong placebo effect.

An ancient Arabic medical text offered a recipe for snake oil, which could be used to cure leprosy and similar skin conditions. "Take three to ten parts sesame oil and pour into a ceramic pot. Throw in five to ten black vipers, depending on their size . . ." Once the snakes were boiled, and the liquid was strained off, it could be applied to the skin. The author includes the wise advice, "If you see that it causes harm, stop using it."

There are considerable risks associated with catching and cooking venomous snakes, especially when some recipes recommended that the snakes should be added to the pot while alive. That's probably why later snake oil producers, particularly those in nineteenth-century America, changed the recipe slightly. They kept the name and they kept the oil, but they didn't bother with the snake part.

William Avery Rockefeller was one of those nineteenth-century snake oil salesmen. When he wasn't selling snake oil, he was pushing other fake elixirs and offering loans to cash-strapped farmers so he could seize their land when they couldn't repay him. The graft continued when he came home. He cheated on his wife—he was a bigamist. He also hustled his kids and once bragged, "I cheat my boys every chance I get. I want to make 'em sharp." He made them sharp, all right—they stuck with oil, but dropped the snakes and the scams. They eventually founded Standard Oil, and John D. Rockefeller became one of the wealthiest people in history.

One of the most famous snake oils was Clark Stanley's Snake Oil Liniment—a well-known brand sold by a Texan cowboy doctor. Clark Stanley said he had learned the secret recipe while studying under a Hopi medicine man in Arizona. His product was popular and widely sold in the United States. The label showed two angry rattlesnakes around an illustration of Stanley and declared the oil to be "the strongest and best liniment known for pain and lameness." It was supposed to provide immediate relief and treat rheumatism, sciatica, toothaches, sprains, bruises, animal bites and more.

Stanley wasn't offering temporary relief either. His snake oil would cure the aches and pains permanently. He pulled no punches in recommending the medicine and insisted that pharmacists stock it. In one advertisement, he says, "Tell your druggist you want a bottle of Snake Oil Liniment; if he says he hasn't got it in stock, you tell him he can get it for you off any jobber in New England. It is the duty of every druggist to sell Snake Oil Liniment because it cures. Everyone knows things that are sold that don't cure."

In those days, manufacturers were using a range of chemical tricks to turn a profit. They could remove the telltale smell of rotten eggs or make rancid butter appear fresh. Honey could be topped up with much cheaper glucose syrup. Some of the frauds, like "embalmed beef," posed a serious health threat. By 1906, the American public had had enough of the trickery, and new laws stopped trade in misbranded or adulterated food and drugs.

Government chemists analyzed Stanley's snake oil and found it contained no snakes at all. It was mostly mineral oil, with some beef fat, turpentine and capsaicin, the chemical in chili peppers that creates a burning sensation. There was nothing in it that could permanently remove pain.

Stanley was a con artist, and his snake oil was a fraud. He was prosecuted and pleaded "no contest." The penalty was not severe—a $20 fine. But after that, "snake oil" no longer meant a medicine—it meant a con.

WHITE-VAN SPEAKER SCAM

One of the oldest and most effective forms of false advertising is carried out face to face, making exaggerated claims about the value of the goods you have to sell.

In 2018, "Colin" was stopped in his vehicle on a street in Orem, Utah, when an SUV pulled up next to him. Two men sat in the front and asked Colin if he was interested in buying a set of surround-sound speakers.

The men looked clean-cut and legitimate, and they wore ID tags, so Colin talked to them. They said they were audio installers, and the distributor had sent too many speakers. If Colin was interested, he could have a set. The speakers were worth more than $2,000, but they would let him have them for $300.

It was a good deal, but Colin hadn't really intended to buy speakers, and $300 was more than he wanted to pay. He was about to leave, but the men called him back. How about $200, for the $2,000 speakers?

"If you don't want them yourself, you can just sell them on the internet and make a profit."

As the conversation continued, Colin was conflicted. He was increasingly suspicious of the two men. Even so, getting speakers at a

90 percent discount seemed too good an opportunity to miss. Finally, Colin paid his money and got a boxed set of speakers. He also made a note of the car's licence plate.

When he looked at the speakers later, he discovered they were very cheap ones. Even at $200, he had paid far more than the speakers were worth. He went to the police, but there was not much they could do. The speakers were junk, but he shouldn't have been surprised. The car's licence plate was also phony.

This con is called the "White-Van Speaker Scam." It was most popular during the 1980s, when more people craved a high-quality stereo system. Then and now, the con artists usually operate out of a rental truck or van (they are typically painted white) with a magnetic corporate logo attached, sitting in a parking lot.

The stories vary—"We meant to order ten speakers, but we ordered ten pairs of speakers by mistake . . ."—but the result is that a customer pays several hundred dollars for speakers they believe are worth thousands but are actually worth $20 or $30. The speakers work . . . if you don't play them too loudly.

The original scam still fools people, but it has also taken new forms over the years. What used to be "stereo speakers" have now become "surround-sound" speakers for a TV. Or it may not be speakers at all—the con artists sell other home entertainment electronics, such as high-definition TVs and amplifiers. They may display websites that show the "regular" price of the devices.

It's not the most creative scam out there, but it's one you might come across.

COMIC BOOK ADS

From the 1950s to the 1980s, kids' comic books had ads for astonishing products, usually at bargain prices. The products weren't exactly cons, but the descriptions certainly stretched the truth and almost seemed calculated to disappoint children as much as possible. It's a style of hyped-up advertising that laid the groundwork for the real cons.

X-RAY SPEX

X-Ray Spex were a pair of glasses that promised X-ray vision. The accompanying drawing showed a man leering at a woman. She wears a dress, but he can see her body in silhouette.

In fact, the glasses had no X-ray powers. The "lenses" were flat pieces of cardboard, each punched with a small hole. A feather placed in the hole distorted light, so if you looked at your fingers through the holes they appeared blurred around the edges and solid in the centre, as if you were seeing the bones. The product was first patented in 1909.

If used as a prank, the joker could offer another person a view of their hand through the glasses, then put them on himself and pretend to see through walls and clothing.

TOY SOLDIERS

Another long-running ad offered one hundred toy soldiers for $1.98, along with tanks, jeeps, battleships cruisers, bombers, jets, cannons and more, delivered in a "footlocker."

This is a case where sellers seem to have gone out of their way to make the product disappointing. These soldiers were not only small, but also flat, as if they had been crushed by a tank. Presumably it allowed the whole set to be squeezed into a small box and cheaply mailed.

YOUR OWN GIANT MONSTER

"Monster-size monsters" were another regular comic book ad for many years.

Beside an image of Frankenstein's monster, the copy read: "A giant 7 feet tall, his eyes glow eerily as his hand reaches out—as awful and sinister as the wildest nightmare . . ."

If Frankenstein's monster wasn't your thing, you could order "Boney the Skeleton," who was similarly proportioned: "A 7-foot monster out of the grave—his bones white, his eyes staring—even glowing in the dark."

The ad promised an item "so lifelike you'll probably find yourself talking to him. Won't you be surprised if he answers?"

Of course, he won't answer, but that's the least of the issues with this sorry offering.

If you sent your dollar (plus 25 cents for shipping), the monster you received would indeed be seven feet tall and between two and three feet wide. The problem was that both monsters were deficient in depth. Frankenstein's creature and the skeleton were basically low-quality posters printed on a sheet of cheap bin-bag plastic. Any moving they did was almost certainly the result of a light breeze.

YOUR OWN NUCLEAR SUBMARINE

What kid wouldn't love a Polaris nuclear sub—"over 7 feet long" for just $6.98?

According to the ad copy, the submarine seated two kids, had working controls,, rockets and torpedoes that fired, a real periscope and an electrically lit instrument panel. "Thrill as you hunt sunken treasures in pirate waters and explore the strange and mysterious ocean floor."

It was constructed of "200-lb. test fiberboard." Shipping was another 75 cents, bringing the total to $7.73.

The submarine was made entirely of cardboard, which you assembled into a vaguely submarine-shaped box. The torpedoes were fired with a rubber band, and it was ruined if it got wet, or even damp, so the ocean floor remained a mystery, except in your imagination.

For a couple of dollars less, you could get a Jet Rocket Space Ship— "the most sensational toy in America." It was slightly smaller than the nuclear submarine but had a similar construction, and it wouldn't get you any closer to space than to the ocean floor.

YOUR OWN CABIN

For a dollar (plus 25 cents for shipping), a kid could get a Frontier Cabin "big enough for 2–3 kids!" The illustration shows a boy in a Davey Crockett hat crouching by a child-sized log cabin. The ad promised that the "huge, western-style cabin is a child's dream come true."

You might expect another cardboard box, printed with a log pattern, but such luxuries were not available in this price range. The cabin was in fact a sheet of plastic, printed with a cabin design. If you draped it over a table like a tablecloth, you could pretend the table was a cabin.

A girls' edition had brick walls, French windows and shrubs.

A REMOTE-CONTROLLED GHOST

According to the ads, a "U-control" ghost was "life sized" at seven feet in height. It cost 95 cents.

The advertisement promised that the ghost could soar up to forty feet into the air, while the operator guided it in secret with a pocket device. "It rises, falls, floats, dances. Spooky effects." The package included a white shroud and a secret control.

The product was a white balloon, printed with a face resembling Casper the Friendly Ghost. The white shroud was a white bin bag. The "secret control" was a reel of fishing line.

YOUR OWN SECRET RADIO

Spy Pen Radio—a real working radio hidden in a pen case! Having your own radio was an exciting proposition for a kid in the 1960s.

What the advertisement didn't make clear was that the pen case had long wires attached: one for the antenna, one to connect to a ground and one for the hard plastic earpiece. The radio was a form of "crystal set" and would pick up a signal if a nearby radio station was powerful enough, but it wasn't the neat James Bond–like gadget most kids expected.

SURPRISE ME!

The densely packed page of comic book ads often included a "surprise package," supposedly worth much more than the $1 asking price. One buyer received a pack of onion gum. Another got a rubber centipede.

SEA MONKEYS

Sea Monkeys were another comic book regular. Today, Sea Monkeys are sold in stores, but in those days, they were mostly bought through comic books, and the comic book ads were all customers had to go on. They were often sold on a page of their own. The graphic showed a family of friendly undersea aliens whose heads were topped with three-pronged crowns. They resembled a middle-class American family gazing in amazement at their tank—a father sea monkey, a mother, an older boy and a younger girl. Although they were unclothed, the father's curved tail modestly covered his nether regions, while his leggy, yellow-haired wife stared seductively at the reader.

The advertisement suggested highly intelligent creatures: "Always clowning around, these frolicsome pets swim, stunt, and play games with each other." The ad said they were "full of tricks . . . eat very little . . ." and "require only minimum care, although they LOVE attention."

The real creatures are brine shrimp, a kind of crustacean that has adapted to drought conditions, meaning its dried eggs can be shipped in a sealed packet and will hatch when water is added. They are fairly easy pets to keep, and watching their growth is interesting, but the name "Sea Monkeys" is a wild stretch. They look nothing like monkeys—they are tiny shrimp that resemble swimming centipedes.

DARLING PET MONKEY

How about a pet squirrel monkey—only $18.95? This "Darling pet monkey" was said to make "an adorable pet and companion . . . almost human with its warm eyes . . . Eats the same food as you, even likes lollipops." It came with a free cage, leather collar, toy and book of instructions.

At nearly $20, this was one of the most expensive items offered in comic book ads. But you knew there had to be a catch. If a "Sea Monkey" was a brine shrimp, what was a squirrel monkey? A grasshopper? A spider? Or was it actually just a squirrel? Or a monkey-shaped balloon?

Surprisingly—and unfortunately for the animal—this item was

precisely what the advertisement claimed. It was a live squirrel monkey. The creatures were captured from the jungles of South America. That meant the customer would be shipped a wild animal. The monkeys were intelligent, very noisy, destructive and had needle-sharp teeth capable of inflicting impressive injuries on the unwary. The ad claimed it was "simple to care for and train," but primate experts say this species is a difficult one to keep—a terrible pet for anyone, much less for children.

According to *CBC News*, more than 170,000 live squirrel monkeys were imported to North America in the late '60s and early '70s. Those who received a monkey in the mail often described the scenes of chaos that followed. Sadly, most of these monkeys did not live long.

IT'S ALL IN THE SWING

Some exaggerated advertisements can lead to disappointment, but others can be deadly—and the deadly ones aren't always the ones you'd expect.

In the 1990s, golfing magazines carried ads for a new product targeted at golfers who needed to find a lost ball. The "Gopher" was a golf-ball locator. Its swinging detector rod changed direction as the golfer moved past the lost ball. It cost $20.

The device was invented by Wade L. Quattlebaum, a former car dealer who was also a commercial diver and treasure hunter.

His device was a cheaply made plastic handle attached by a simple hinge to metal antenna, the type you'd find on any cheap radio. Depending on how you held it, the antenna might swing to the left or right, pulled only by gravity. It was a mass-produced dowsing rod.

Dowsing (or divining, or witching) has an ancient history. Its practitioners use an assortment of tools—a Y-shaped wooden stick or two L-shaped pieces of coat hanger or a pendulum—and walk back and forth over piece of land. The movements of the dowsing rod lead them to areas where there is water, although some people use it to search for gold or oil.

Scientists explain dowsing as the result of an "ideomotor phenomenon." In plain English, that means the dowser unconsciously senses the presence of water and makes tiny physical movements in response. Those minuscule physical reactions are turned into the visible movements of the dowsing rod.

The ideomotor phenomenon really works. You can try this with a needle on a length of cotton. If you let the needle hang and you merely think about the needle moving clockwise as you watch it, you will likely find it does exactly that without any intentional movement on your part. It doesn't work for everyone, but it works for many people. The method uses suggestion and imagination, and the phenomenon is reliable enough that magicians use it in stage shows. An object is hidden, and the magician, blindfolded, has a person guide them around the room. By detecting slight resistance in the volunteer's movements, the magician can home in on the object. The volunteer has no idea they're sending physical signals to the magician.

The ideomotor phenomenon provides a mechanism by which dowsing might work, but *does* it work? Is the dowser unconsciously detecting underground water? When professional dowsers were put to the test by scientists, their performance wasn't too good. In one test, various pipes under the floor were filled with water. When the dowsers were asked to identify which parts of the floor had water underneath, they performed as well as you'd expect by chance.

It's true that farmers often pay dowsers for their services, and many are happy with the results. Then again, you could probably point to any area of a field and say, "There's water here" and, if you dig a hole deep enough, you will be right. That's why people dig wells, and why every mine owner spends a fortune pumping out water.

And if a person spends a good portion of their time looking for areas of land with a lot of water underneath, they may detect other clues, consciously or unconsciously—a different smell in the soil or a change in the vegetation or signs of animal activity. Whether or not there is a scientific basis for dowsing, many dowsers believe that what they're doing is legitimate. And in the sense that the rod is moving in response to their intuition, it works. They're not trying to scam their customers.

Quattlebaum's Gopher was just a dowsing rod for golf balls. An instructional video for the device explained how it was supposed to function:

> The locator uses an advanced technology and is programmed to detect all the elements used in all golf balls. Just like a magnetic compass needle which swings of its own accord to the north pole, the direction-finding antenna will swing of its own accord in the direction of a golf ball as soon as your shoulders line up with the ball. The locator does not generate or transmit any harmful signals and is environmentally safe.

That last part was true: the device certainly didn't generate or transmit any harmful signals. That's because it didn't transmit any signals at all—it was an empty plastic box. The rest was outright lying. The Gopher used no advanced technology and wasn't "programmed" in any way. There was nothing in the device that allowed it to distinguish between the elements of a golf ball and, say, the elements of a nearby tree. It didn't use magnetism. It was just another variation on the L-shaped metal rods used by some dowsers, pumped up by outlandish advertising.

In one video demonstration for the product, a middle-aged golfer, who seemed to be genuinely skeptical and sincere, was guided in the use of the Gopher. The subject already knew where the golf ball was as he tested the device and, as he walked past the ball, the antenna swung to point toward it. The golfer appeared to be quite convinced by the demonstration, but it's a classic example of the ideomotor effect. The device works because the user believes in it and unconsciously makes small movements to tilt the rod.

The device was sold for years. It was unquestionably a scam, but at

$20 a pop, it didn't seem like there was any great harm in it. It might even be argued that, for a golfer who unconsciously knew where his golf ball was likely to be, it might work better than a random search.

The Gopher was sold as a golf-ball detector, but it would work just as well (or badly) on other objects. Its antenna could point unerringly at toys, electronics, jewelry—as long as the person using it believed in its powers and already knew the approximate whereabouts of the object in question.

The makers of the Gopher eventually asked themselves, "Why sell a golf-ball detector when we could sell a drug detector? Or an explosives detector?"

So, they rebranded the product. Instead of the Gopher, "The Amazing Golf Ball Finder," they sold the "Quadro Tracker Positive Molecular Locator." It was the same device, but now it came shipped in a foam-lined briefcase like a piece of high-tech spy gear. The detector slid into a sturdy holster.

A coiled wire connected the handle to a belt clip with a "card reader"—a new addition. If you placed a card into the slot, it was supposed to tune the device. One card would make the device respond to bombs, another would make it sensitive to drugs. There were cards to detect weapons, gold, wild animals, alcohol and even escaped prisoners.

The starting price of the Quadro Tracker was $400—a big markup over the $20 golf-ball tracker. The most expensive version of the Quadro Tracker cost $8,000. For that, you could provide a Polaroid photograph of any person or thing, put it in an "electromagnetic frequency transfer unit" (which looked suspiciously like an ordinary Canon photocopier), then make a custom card for your card reader. The device would show the direction of your desired target up to a range of five hundred miles.

New technobabble explained how the Quadro Tracker cards worked. The photocopier "extracted the molecular structure and its subsequent frequency emission from the photo."

On the inside, the Quadro Tracker was still just an empty plastic box. The cable connecting the box to the belt clip was not wired to anything—it might as well have been a length of wool. One investigator took one of the cards apart and found that it only contained a blob of epoxy glue with some dead ants.

Some people tried to point out the brazen scam, but buyers weren't listening. If potential scam victims weren't familiar with the ideomotor phenomenon, the company's salesman could still put on a good demonstration. School boards and police departments purchased significant numbers of Quadro Trackers until a US court injunction finally banned the device and the FBI declared it to be a fraud.

Three of Quadro Corporation's executives, including Wade L. Quattlebaum, were charged with mail fraud, but were acquitted. According to their lawyers, it came down to the fact that, although the defendants couldn't prove that the devices worked, the prosecutors couldn't prove that they didn't. The case didn't get a lot of news coverage, as most newspapers were waiting on the verdict for the O.J. Simpson trial.

Some aspects of the con are amusing, especially the idea of police departments paying thousands for a non-functional golf-ball detector and grimly sweeping it over cars and lockers.

But the scam had victims other than the taxpayer and police dignity. The device had already been used in schools to scan lockers, which were then cut open. It may have led to false charges. And things were about to get much worse.

The failure to convict the creators of the Quadro Tracker encouraged other brazen imitators. A UK company named Global Technical sold the MOLE programmable detection system, which was almost identical to the Quadro Tracker. (It's hard not to wonder if the name MOLE might have been inspired by the original Gopher.) Other similar-looking devices included Global Technical's GT200, Homeland Safety International's "Sniffex" and the "Alpha 6." Controversies and court cases have swirled around these devices.

The most notorious copy was sold by a UK company, Advanced Tactical Security and Communications Ltd (ATSC), which produced a device it called the ADE-651. Like the original "Amazing Golf Ball Finder," it was an antenna on a hinge, with no power and no electronics. The company claimed it was powered by static electricity. (Operators would shuffle their feet on the ground in the belief that they were charging it up.) And, like the Quadro Tracker, it used "programmed" detection cards. The company claimed it could detect guns, bodies, contraband ivory, banknotes and explosives, among other things. The devices sold for up to $60,000, with many sold in Iraq and Afghanistan. According to military experts, a number of deaths from bomb attacks could be blamed on the use of the fake detectors, which had failed to detect real bombs.

The British government eventually banned the sale of the device. The company founder was convicted of fraud and given a ten-year prison sentence.

CHAPTER 11
A MISCELLANY OF MISCREANTS

The range of scams and cons that have been carried out is mind-boggling, as is the range of motives behind them. Some con artists are greedy, some are incompetent, some are narcissistic and some are just delusional.

Enjoy the following smattering of swindling. Or should we just call it a "con-glomeration"?

THE TREASURE FINDER

We've already seen how dowsing didn't deliver on the promise of finding drugs and explosives. Another dowsing inventor promoted his ability to detect buried gold.

The gold in question was at the bottom of a Canadian waterway. In 1650, the Jesuits brought seven large boxes to what was then New France. The boxes were transported by canoe and raft, but one was lost in the river. It was believed to contain the pay for the troops who accompanied the missionaries. The box also held church ornaments, including a solid gold candelabra.

That corner of New France later became Penetanguishene, Ontario, and the waterway is now named the Wye River. Over the years, many people have tried to find the lost treasure, but without success.

In 1922, an experienced Canadian diver, Captain Bob Carson, turned his mind to the problem. He was fascinated by the stories of treasure, but he knew that finding it in the river would be like looking for a needle in a haystack. However, Carson had heard about a new invention that might improve the odds.

An inventor named Edward Jeffrey had been working on a new detector for gold. He showed his device to Carson: it looked like a small cannon made of canvas, cane and rubber. It contained two steel bars in its barrel. Jeffrey explained to Carson that it had been used successfully to find mineral deposits and that it would be ideal for locating the lost Jesuit treasure. Sure, some doubters had scoffed at the device, but Jeffrey had tested it, precisely locating a gold watch in a farmer's field. On another occasion, the device had led him unerringly to a bag of gold. It worked.

Jeffrey's invention was nothing more than a fancy divining rod. It's not clear whether the inventor was a con artist or he actually believed in his device. What seems certain is that Carson was convinced that it worked.

The two men teamed up to scan the waterway, rowing up and down the Wye and taking measurements with the device. In one location, Jeffrey claimed he was getting a powerful signal: it was gold, he said, and in large quantities. Jeffrey also believed that the size of the object matched that of the lost treasure chest.

Carson knew retrieving the chest would be difficult. The bed of the river was covered with a twenty-foot layer of silt. After centuries, the box would be buried deep. They would need to remove the silt before they could examine the source of the signal.

But Carson was determined. He hired a dredge, the Baltic, and set to work removing mud from the bottom of the Wye river. Again and again he dropped the huge clamshell scoop into the water. It closed its metal mouth on a new load of mud, then hauled it to the surface. Even with the aid of the steam-powered scoop, the work took days, and Carson moved many tons of silt.

At last, the work had created a significant crater in the river bed. In the middle of June 1922, Carson put on his brass helmet and diving suit and descended to look for the treasure. He found a dark object, about six feet long, jutting out from the edge of the hole. It was unquestionably the Jesuit chest. It only remained to lift the heavy box to the surface.

The men announced to the press that, after centuries, the lost chest had been found.

The press were electrified by the discovery of such a huge treasure. The Ontario government said it was important to have a "proper disposition" of the valuables. The local mayor agreed. And Father Bouvrette, a priest at the Jesuit Order, also said that proper disposition was vital. Unfortunately, nobody could agree what the proper disposition should be. Representatives from each group gathered at the river, each ready to rush the treasure away for safekeeping.

The crew constructed a derrick to pull the box from the silt, but the equipment strained to move it. They weren't surprised—gold is heavy.

As the world looked on, Captain Bob Carson put on his diving gear and descended to see what was going on. He came to the surface a few minutes later, apparently in a state of excitement. He removed his helmet and announced, in salty language, that their quest was at an end. He'd been duped by Edward Jeffrey's invention. The chest of Jesuit gold was just a big, flat rock.

WE'VE GOT TROUBLE, MY FRIENDS . . .

One of the great fictional con men is "Professor" Harold Hill, from the musical *The Music Man*. Robert Preston's character is a con man and salesman. He pretends to be a great band leader and promises to train the local boys to play in a marching band, then skips town after citizens have placed their orders for instruments and uniforms.

To create demand and endear himself to the locals, the "spellbinder" whips up the support of the townsfolk by preaching on the moral failings brought to their town by joke books, cigarettes and, worst of all, a pool hall.

Although the Music Man was fictional, this kind of travelling con man was a common visitor to American towns, and whipping up moral indignation was an effective way of winning confidence and making a good impression on locals.

Before the telephone, communication between towns was poor, and a moralizing huckster could run a scam in one town until people started to become suspicious, then "take the money and run" to the next town, where the scam started all over again.

In summer 1817, a man named Jonathan Parks was travelling west from Hartford, Connecticut, and made a stop in Hagerstown, Maryland. Parks was appalled and disgusted by the wickedness he saw around him.

Some of the townspeople agreed with his point of view and they gathered around to listen. Parks spoke out loudly against the evils of the age—evils like drunkenness, breaking the sabbath and profane swearing.

Seeing that he was surrounded by good people, the right kind of people, he invited his new friends to an "optical show" he had ready—a series of colourful painted glass slides projected from an oil-fuelled "Magic Lantern."

The audience was impressed by the slide show and paid large sums to support Parks and the "good works" he claimed to be doing. Parks pocketed the cash and left town to improve the wider world.

Months later, the citizens of Hagerstown started to suspect he had been a swindler. We don't know what caused their change of heart—perhaps they had heard from people in other towns who had also given money to Parks but had never seen any good works come from their donations.

The outraged folk of Hagerstown published newspaper advertisements demanding that Jonathan Parks come forward and provide more information about himself.

If Parks saw the advertisements, he didn't bother replying, so the people of Hagerstown published a newspaper article accusing Parks of being a swindler and asking other newspapers to reprint it, which many did.

We don't know if Parks was eventually caught—more likely, he continued the same sanctimonious business under a different alias—but he was not a unique case or even a particularly gifted con man. There were countless others like him criss-crossing America, whipping up a moral panic for their own profit.

THE SAVAGE LANDOR

In the late 1800s and early 1900s, before aircraft made the world smaller, everyone loved an explorer. These brave souls—usually men from wealthy backgrounds—climbed mountains, found the source of long rivers and raced to be the first to reach the poles.

One of these world travellers was Arnold Henry Savage Landor. In 1897, he went to Nepal and Tibet, intending to explore the area and climb a few mountains. The Royal Geographical Society lent him surveying equipment for the adventure.

When he returned, he wrote books about his adventures. He claimed he had ascended one of the region's tallest mountains, reaching the greatest height yet climbed by a human. He included photographs of the expedition, showing him casually sitting astride a boulder partway up the mountain.

He refused to copy the style of the Alpine mountaineers with their heavy clothes and spiked boots. Instead he reached the peak wearing his regular London street shoes, a straw hat and summer clothes. He carried a regular British walking stick. He made it easily to the top, fending off many attacks by bandits and brigands. He attributed his success to constant consumption of nutritious food.

Members of the Alpine Club, an organization for mountaineers, thought his story was nonsense. So did the Royal Geographical Society—it had helped him with his expedition, but made a point of not inviting him to give a lecture about it.

We can't confirm whether it was all a hoax or not, but the mountains he claimed to have ascended—one was more than twenty thousand feet—would normally require a well-equipped mountaineering expedition using oxygen, rather than casual streetwear and a cheerful attitude. It sounds ridiculous, but the newspapers were impressed by his tale, and they reprinted details from his book without question. As a result, his book sold well.

One story about Arthur Henry Savage Landor shows how unreliable newspapers were in those days. When the adventurer was returning from Tibet, he made a stop in St. Petersburg, Russia. Far away in Australia, the *Melbourne Times* received a short note describing the event.

"A. Savage Landor arrived in St. Petersburg today from Tibet after suffering greatly at the hands of the natives."

The Australian editor misunderstood the story and embellished a little to make sense of it, turning the explorer into something like a yeti:

A savage landor got into St. Petersburg yesterday, and the people of the city were terrified. After considerable difficulty the beast, which comes from Tibet, was captured, taken to a remote place and there dispatched. It is said that this is the first animal of the sort ever seen in Russia. How he reached the city after his fights with the natives of Tibet, which is a comparatively unknown country, is a mystery.

THE BEST GRADES MONEY CAN BUY

How do you turn a bad student into a good one? Hard work may be one solution, but creating a false record is quicker. After all, getting children into a good university can mean a high-paid career for them down the road, so it's a grift that keeps on giving. Many frauds and cons have focused on university admissions boards.

In 2019, a huge college admissions fraud was uncovered in the United States. The case, which is probably just the tip of the iceberg, revealed an organized network of corrupt examiners, school officials and sports coaches that allowed wealthy clients to pay their kids' way into elite schools.

One businessman paid $100,000 per test for someone to write each of his two sons' SATs. That included the cost of making up copies of a driver's licence with the son's name and the test-taker's face. The test-taker was advised not to do too well or the results might not be believed.

Many American universities offer special scholarships to students who have demonstrated athletic prowess, and that can be a gateway for students whose grades wouldn't win any prizes. One couple paid $250,000 to have their daughter acknowledged as the star soccer player she wasn't.

A wealthy family wanted their son to be a water polo player. They paid $250,000 and bought water polo gear, then created a Photoshopped image of their son in action. It's not clear where the son was during this process, but he wasn't training in a pool.

Another family wanted pictures of their daughter playing water polo. One inexpensive solution might have been to encourage their daughter to play water polo. They found a quicker option—using a picture of a different girl. "You can't tell it's not her," said the high-paid expert who advised them in their scam. The girl might not have been a sports star, but she had the academic ability. At least, she did after her parents paid tens of thousands to bribe markers to change her exam answers.

Learning disabilities might be thought of as a disadvantage, but some parents use fake disabilities to their advantage. By bribing a corrupt psychologist, parents could have their children identified as having a learning disability. They were then able to have exams and tests given at certain sites where they knew administrators who were open to bribes.

The mastermind behind this scam was accepted into an excellent prison for three and a half years.

GRADING AND ABETTING

The competition to get into elite North American universities may be intense, but it is nothing compared to India. Delhi University is considered one of the best in the country, and students hoping for admission need to score 99 percent or higher in their final high-school exams, so even a brilliant student will need a lot of luck to make the grade. Access to government jobs, which are highly sought after, is also determined by an applicant's performance in a specialized exam. In India, success in exams can mean the difference between a good job and no job—so it's a fertile ground for scams.

According to a 2022 article in *The Economist*, there are many people offering fraudulent shortcuts for Indian students, and cheating is rampant. A 2015 video showed parents scaling the walls of a building trying to smuggle help to their kids as they took their exams in a fifth-floor room.

Of course, some people try the obvious approaches, like smuggling notes into the exam room, or peeking at the answer sheet, but the authorities are wise to that: students are frisked on their way into the exam, and answer sheets are locked up at the police station. But in such a competitive environment, even these aren't effective solutions. As one former schoolteacher commented, "You think the policemen do not have children?"

Like students everywhere, the test-takers might try to look at the answers of the person next to them. There are different ways to cope with that problem, but one Indian school board may have gone too far when it put cardboard boxes over the heads of students so they could only see what was in front of them.

But much of the cheating is very sophisticated, and education authorities are engaged in a constant arms race against it.

Organized cheats may find a way to break into lockers and get access to exam papers or answer sheets. These are circulated on the internet. However, officials monitor sites as closely as the anxious parents: if an exam is widely circulated, officials can make last-minute changes.

Professional "solvers" offer a personalized but expensive approach. The solver may take an exam in place of the student, or, if that isn't possible, they take it at the same time as the student, sitting nearby, and exchanging answer sheets before the exam is over. The exchange is risky, and Indian newspaper headlines frequently announce the arrest of exam solvers.

Some students manage to smuggle in phones or other internet-connected devices. One student had a tiny phone sewn into the lining of his pants. A connected Bluetooth device had been surgically implanted into his ear.

Cheating on exams occurs in many fields of study. In 2022, twenty-eight men were arrested for cheating on army exams.

Teachers know that shoes can make an excellent hiding place for notes or devices. Prospective teachers know it, too. At one exam for selecting trainee teachers, a number of the applicants were caught wearing modified flip-flops. The shoes had phones built into the soles, connected by Bluetooth to a hidden earpiece. These flip-flops cost nearly $8,000 a pair. The discovery led to a ban on shoes and socks at subsequent exams.

Officials also fight back with technology of their own, using internet jammers to block Wi-Fi signals.

But the most challenging method of cheating that Indian officials must counteract is old-fashioned bribery. One huge operation known as the Vyapam scam ran from the 1990s to 2013 in central India and involved organized criminals, examination officials, professional test-takers and other bureaucrats. It affected a wide range of exams, including those for medical students, police officers, government employees and food inspectors. Those who could afford to pay the bribes would be given illegal help using a wide range of methods. For example, corrupt officials could be bribed to overlook the substitution of a subpar test-taker with a smarter substitute, or test-takers could submit a blank answer sheet, which would then be filled in with the correct answers by a bribed marker.

Exposing fraud can be dangerous, too—literally, a matter of life and death. When the Vyapam scam was eventually uncovered, more than a hundred people were arrested, but some informants and journalists investigating the case died under mysterious circumstances, leading to rumours that the corruption went to high levels of government.

CHAPTER 12
AND YOU TELL TWO FRIENDS . . .

I f everyone in the world gave you a dollar, you'd be very rich, but how do you reach billions of people? One approach is the pyramid scheme, where each participant pays you money and brings in more participants.

Today, pyramids seem like a classic con, but it didn't start that way. They've undergone a strange transformation.

A SNOWBALL'S CHANCE

In the late 1880s, a woman named Mrs. Campbell was involved with a new London charity, the "Home for Destitute Women," which had been founded by the Bishop of Bedford.

The home needed to raise money, and Mrs. Campbell had what she thought was had a good idea. She decided to solicit contributions through a charity "snowball" collection.

A snowball was a system where letters were written to two potential donors. Each recipient then wrote a letter to two more, and the numbers grew larger, or "snowballed," exponentially.

In addition to writing new letters, each recipient was supposed to make a small donation to the charity, just three pennies, in the form of unused postage stamps, sent to Mrs. Campbell at her home, Brook Villa, in Bedford.

A number at the top of Mrs. Campbell's letter showed how many times the letter had been copied. Her original letter was marked with the number one, and each letter-writer was told to increase the number on their copies by one. When the number of letter-generations reached fourteen, the letter writing should stop. At that point, the letter would have reached a total of more than thirty-two thousand people (the final generation on its own would reach more than sixteen thousand) and would have earned about £400 in donations.

The snowball seemed to be a huge success at first. People took the letter seriously, donated stamps flooded in, and the home for women soon had the £400 it was hoping for. But Mrs. Campbell was surprised when the donated postage stamps kept coming.

It seemed that not every letter-writer had copied the text carefully— or perhaps they were so moved by the cause they wanted to increase the letters' reach. One changed the target number of generations from fourteen to 140. Now, instead of reaching a maximum of 32,000 people, it would reach a number in the tredecillions – that's a ten with forty-two zeros, and obviously far more people than were alive in the world or even that had ever lived.

The original version of the letter came to a stop at the fourteenth round, but this mutated version with its damaged telomeres kept circulating.

At first, Mrs. Campbell was happy with the results. She was preparing a move to Scotland, and she must have felt as if she were going out on a high, having secured the future of the women's home.

The number in the letter changed again. It went from 140 to 1,400, then increased again to fourteen thousand. It hardly mattered, because the targets were already insane. But new mistakes crept in, as people misread the handwriting of others. Mrs. Campbell's home address, Brook Villa, became Rook Villa, Rock Villa and Bronte Villa. The town of Bedford was changed to Bradford or Brighton. And Mrs. Campbell didn't even live there anymore. She had made her move to Scotland.

The letters followed her, redirected by the post office at the rate of thousands a week.

Some people tried to correct what they thought were errors in the letter. A different bishop, the Bishop of Bangor, happened to have the surname Campbell. Some readers assumed the letters were from his wife and changed "Bishop of Bedford" to "Bishop of Bangor," redirecting the money and causing more confusion.

With thousands of letters circulating, many people noticed discrepancies with the letters. They sent inquiries to the various bishops involved, asking if this collection was real or if someone was carrying out a fraud.

The income was now more than £1,000, but the Bishop of Bedford and Mrs. Campbell were embarrassed by the accusations and the unasked contributions and tried to stop the letter. They paid for newspaper advertisements, begging people to stop circulating the letters "as very grave mistakes have been made in names, figures, and wording, so that the appeal in its present form is most erroneous."

But it had been much easier to start the process than it was to stop it. The snowball kept rolling, and poor Mrs. Campbell wrung her hands with anxiety every time the postman brought a new sack of mail and unused stamps to her door.

It was not the only case where a snowball became an avalanche. A snowball letter for a London hospital led to similar results. The newspapers had a field day with the stories, criticizing charities that used the method, even if their intentions were good. It would be easy, they said, for an "evil-disposed person" to use the same methods for personal profit.

As we'll see, they were right.

CHAIN OF FOOLS

In the early 1900s, the "snowball letter" was renamed the "chain letter." It still worked the same way. The person who received the letter was supposed to send copies of the letter to two more people, but all recipients sent money to the same address, which was that of the charity listed at the top of the letter. Some were real charities, while others were fraudulent.

There were many ways to scam people. In 1902, one American company started a chain letter that offered to sell a pen for $2.50 and pay the lucky readers $6.50 a week, if they kept copying and sending the letters. The company took the money for the pens, but didn't seem to pay out much to its fast-growing army of workers. It was a precursor to modern multi-level marketing scams. Its letters briefly choked the mail system, and the company was declared a fraud by the government.

Some letters didn't ask for money at all, but just played on superstition, requiring the recipient to send out copies in order to earn a blessing and avoid a curse. These letters still circulate today, with ridiculous stories of people who threw away the letter and died hours later—although the victims somehow managed to include the story of their deaths in new versions of the letter.

Most letters tried to solicit money for a single business or organization. But around 1935, a con artist hit on a new and winning formula. It seems to have started in Denver, Colorado. Known as the "Send-a-Dime" letter, this new chain letter had a novel goal: to help the recipient make money. And it had an unusual feature. Instead of sending money to the person who started the letter, recipients sent it to earlier letter-writers.

The letter listed six names and addresses. All the recipient had to do was send a dime to the person at the top of the list. They then copied the letter and removed the top name. Each of the remaining names moved up one position, and the recipient's own name was added in the sixth place. The copied letter was then sent to five more people.

The letter explained that, if everyone followed the rules, the sender could expect to receive $1,562.50 (for the mathematically minded that's 5^6 dimes) in the mail.

The total is correct, but only the scheme's originators are likely to see that kind of money. The person who starts the scheme won't pay anyone and only needs 15,625 recruits to get their money. (They can make more money by ensuring that the next few names are also funnelled to them.) But by the time the letter has gone through six generations, it must reach nearly 250 million people for players to get paid. And for all those in position number nine to receive a payout, the letter will need to reach thirty billion enthusiastic recipients. Get breeding, people!

But petty mathematical impossibilities didn't worry the Send-a-Dime enthusiasts. They joined in droves. Out of the blue, the Denver post office faced a huge surge in the number of letters being sent. Their clerks were overloaded. They also received a flood of complaints from customers demanding to know why they hadn't yet received letters they were expecting.

Alarmed officials tried to work out what legal route they could use to block the letters, but while they debated the problem, the letter was spreading with amazing speed. It swept across the United States and into Canada.

A different variation took hold in the United Kingdom: it changed the dime to another small silver coin, a sixpence.

New variations quickly appeared. One asked for a 25-cent donation. Another asked for a dollar. Yet another asked for a $5 donation and required the money and message to be sent by telegram.

All these schemes offered rich rewards, especially if you were the person starting them or adjusting the wording so the people at the top of the list were all connected to you.

New laws eventually crushed the money-making chain letters, although the Send-a-Dime campaign may have inspired Roosevelt's March of Dimes campaign three years later. It wasn't a chain-letter—contributors simply mailed dimes to combat polio.

But other forms of chain letters exist to this day, spreading by mail, email and social media, offering blessings, recipes, kisses, poems and emojis. Chain letters still use the power of exponential growth to spread annoyance around the world.

A CHAIN FOR MY MOTORBIKE

In 1935, the chain-letter craze was in full swing, and people were quick to jump on to any new offering.

That summer, a cash-strapped telegram delivery boy in Ottawa, Ontario, was arrested for driving his motorcycle without a licence. According to the *Ottawa Citizen*, he pleaded guilty, and the judge fined him $10, plus $2 in costs. If he couldn't pay, he would go to jail.

He didn't have the money, but he asked the judge for a week's delay.

He quickly started a new chain letter. In one week, it brought in enough money that he was able to pay the fine on his next court appearance. Does that make him a con artist or an entrepreneur?

BUILDING THE PYRAMIDS

Chain letters and telegrams worked well, but then someone asked, "Why waste money sending letters and telegrams at all, when you could just talk to people in person?" A new scam was about to be born—the "Pyramid Scheme."

Early versions appeared after the heyday of the chain-letter craze. Ottawa, Ontario, historian James Powell described how one new system briefly captivated the Canadian capital in June 1935, coming hot on the heels of a city-wide obsession with chain letters.

The scheme's promise was: "Pay a dollar in, get ten dollars back." It sounded too good to be true, but North America was in the grip of the Great Depression, and people everywhere dreamed of being "in the money."

A story in the *Ottawa Evening Citizen* described the 900 percent returns. Their reporter visited the company's office, saw the lineups of hopeful people waiting to deposit a dollar and saw others receiving their $10 payout and paying it back in. Although the tone of the article was skeptical, it was good advertising for the business.

Of course, nothing comes for free, and the way "investors" earned their keep was by bringing in new blood. Names were entered on a list. When someone brought twelve people into the scheme, the person at the top of the list received $10, meaning organizers pocketed at least $2 on every payout.

The scheme was flexible in how it took your money. For those who couldn't afford a dollar, there was a 50-cent plan. It was half the price for a quarter of the return: it paid only $2.50. At the other extreme, people could sign up for a $10 plan, which promised a $100 return. In the midst of hard times, it sounded like easy money. The operators couldn't keep up with the demand.

The police and Crown counsel took a wary look at the offering. The organizers seemed to have been inspired by Charles Ponzi, whose 1920s stock market fraud was still a recent memory. They lured people in using the language of the stock market. Participants were called "investors," and the money went to "brokers." Nothing of value was made or sold, although some people certainly became broker. Beneath the investment veneer, it was just a chain letter without the letter.

The authorities didn't like the look of it, but systems like this weren't yet specifically prohibited by law, so they let it run. Copycat schemes soon appeared. Grocery stores used a similar system on their sales, giving an occasional payout to those who had paid to join a customer list. A hotel tried a scheme where bottles of beer were the currency: the person at the top of the list walked away with twenty-seven bottles.

The Canadian government made moves to update the law, banning chain letters and similarly structured schemes, but it was hardly necessary. The mathematics of the scheme limited its popularity more than the police could do. By the time officials moved to close down the "investment schemes," they were already running out of steam, and most "investors" walked away empty-handed.

But given time, people forget their bad experiences, and pyramids would be back in force.

THE PYRAMID CLUB

In 1949, a new get-rich-quick scheme appeared in California. It was called a pyramid club. It was a reinvention of the chain-letter epidemic of 1935. By then, chain letters that asked for money were illegal in most places, so this system didn't use the mail. This new variation presented itself as a social activity, and club members got together and paid over their money at a series of parties.

In a pyramid club, members paid money to people higher up the pyramid, while recruiting people to join at the bottom, which was continually growing. Like the chain letters before them, pyramid clubs became very popular and spread across North America in a matter of weeks.

As with the chain-letter craze, authorities tried to stop the clubs but weren't sure how to do it, and they faced pushback from members. Many people enjoyed the socializing and saw the clubs as harmless fun.

But the organizers had engineered a con. The pyramid didn't produce or sell anything. The people at the top made money only if they attracted large numbers of new members to the game. As with all such schemes, the system will quickly run out of the fresh humans it needs to feed it, so only the early bird gets the worm.

Pyramids are sometimes compared to Ponzi schemes, but one big difference is that the clients in a Ponzi scheme believe their money is being legitimately invested—only the organizers know it's a con that constantly "robs Peter to pay Paul." In most pyramid schemes, the organizers are upfront about the structure; they just keep quiet about the mathematical impossibilities.

What both systems have in common is that making money requires an exponential growth of new members. Eventually, it becomes impossible to sustain the growth.

The lack of sustainability was one problem with pyramid clubs, but there was an even bigger one: they were a magnet for con artists and racketeers. With thousands of dollars moving back and forth and very few records, it was easy to turn them into a more brazen scam.

Some cons were very simple. In February 1949, a California newspaper carried this terse report:

> *Firestone Park sheriff's deputies were looking today for a short, fat woman who collected pyramid friendship club 'membership fees' from three persons and disappeared.*

Other schemes were more complex.

One evening in February 1948, a smiling man and woman stepped onto a stage to be presented with $2,048 from a Los Angeles pyramid-club organizer. The onlookers clapped and dreamed of the day when they would be receiving their own payout.

Actually, no payouts were ever given. According to the *Los Angeles Times*, the organizer had pocketed all contributions and paid the couple $30 to play the role of the fictitious people at the top tier of the pyramid.

Unfortunately for the club owner, he had made a poor casting choice that night. When he took the couple to his office and tried to settle accounts, the man pulled a gun on him.

The couple were both undercover police officers. They arrested the pyramid-club organizer and confiscated the money he had collected but never paid out in the club's three weeks of existence—around $23,000, equivalent to around $280,000 today.

The pyramids built in 1949 were not as long-lasting as their Egyptian namesakes. The fad swept North America, but in just a few months, the pyramid clubs were falling apart, unable to sustain their growth.

Today, pure pyramid schemes are illegal in most places, but just as con artists invented pyramid clubs as a way to get around the restrictions on money-making chain letters, so new generations of scammers have found ways to reinvent pyramid schemes by disguising them in creative ways.

A common con is the "multi-level marketing" (MLM) scheme, which pretends to sell products to the public, but makes most of its money by getting "distributors" to recruit new "distributors," who pay for random merchandise. Pyramid-like schemes are also used to build cults and new religions.

It seems that each generation must learn the hard way. This joke from 1949 sums it up best.

Q. Why don't you join my pyramid?

A. Because it sphinx.

CHAPTER 13
S.O.B. STORIES

Playing for sympathy may be the oldest con there is. Children seem to do it instinctively, and many otherwise honest adults might claim an illness or injury as an excuse. But con artists take it to a whole new level.

SHHH–I'M READING

In 1962, the *Philadelphia Inquirer* reported on a woman who was working at home when the doorbell rang.

A youth stood at the door. His hair was a mess. His suit didn't fit. He gave the woman a card.

She read the text on it.

> *I am a deaf mute. This is the only way I have of earning a decent living for myself and my elderly father. Any subscriptions you would see fit to buy would help me make my way in the world without becoming dependent on public charity."*

The card was stapled to a subscription form for various magazines. The woman was moved and sympathetic. As she looked at the order form, she said quietly, without thinking, "You poor dear. How long have you been a deaf mute?"

"Oh, about eight years now," replied the salesman.

MIRACLE CURE

Most people would be sympathetic to a young person suffering with one type of cancer. How much sadder it is when they have three.

"Philippa" was a nineteen-year-old Iowa woman who had suffered a string of serious medical problems yet managed to stay upbeat and positive. She had acute lymphoblastic leukemia. Then she developed pancreatic cancer. She also had a "football-sized tumor wrapped around her spine."

According to *CBS News*, she posted about her difficult journey, offering insights and advice, and talked about her appearances as a guest speaker for various foundations. She also appeared on a podcast focused on pancreatic cancer. Her followers were moved by her stories and donated more than $37,000 to help her.

One of her secrets was staying positive, she told a local paper. "If you stay depressed and in a dark space, I feel like your body will never get better."

Philippa was philosophical about her condition. Talking to one newspaper, she said, "Of course, every day can't be sunshine and rainbows, but you can't just choose to be mad at the cancer. It just happens to people."

The only problem was, it hadn't happened to Philippa. She didn't have leukemia, she didn't have pancreatic cancer, and the only football-sized object wrapped around her spine was her self-absorbed head.

She posted pictures online, and some were seen by people with medical backgrounds. They were puzzled by what they saw: the medical equipment on her body was placed incorrectly, in what were described as "terrible life-threatening inaccuracies." It seemed that her hospital photos had been poorly faked in her own apartment. They contacted police, who subpoenaed medical records that revealed the truth.

In January 2023, Philippa was arrested for "theft by means of deception," and the collected donations were refunded. She later pleaded guilty to felony theft.

WHERE'S THE BABY?

In 2019, a Pennsylvania woman, "Iona," was excited to hear that a couple she knew, "Tina" and "Noah," were expecting a baby. The couple had lost a baby girl a few years earlier, so Iona wanted everything to go smoothly this time. She organized a baby shower for the couple, and friends brought gifts and donated money.

According to a report on *ABC News*, as the pregnancy reached the seven-month mark, Tina disappeared. She said she was on bed rest. Iona hoped for the best. Around the due date, she received a call. It was bad news. Tina had given birth, but the baby had died.

Iona was shocked and saddened. She asked what had happened. Tina said the baby had been born with fluid in his lungs. The hospital staff had given her the baby, saying he would be fine, but a few hours later the baby died.

Other odd details emerged. Tina had gone to the hospital alone—she hadn't wanted anyone to go with her. And, despite claiming to have had five hours with the baby, she had only taken two photos, neither of which looked like it was taken in a hospital.

The events sounded implausible to Iona, and her suspicions were aroused further when she saw a fundraising campaign to pay for the baby's funeral costs. The story gave touching details of how the tiny baby had grasped his parents' hands before dying. It was tragic . . . and yet, Iona didn't believe it. Was it possible her friends were carrying out a scam?

Iona phoned the funeral home to check. No, they hadn't had any dealings with the couple. She contacted police, who investigated the case. They discovered that there were no records of the baby's birth or death, although when they paid a call on Tina and Noah, they found a realistic plastic doll, styled like a newborn baby, which looked identical to one used in the fundraising campaign.

Friends and family were appalled and angry when the truth came out. The couple had made up the whole thing—there had never been a baby. And subsequent inquiries showed that their previous baby had also been a fraud. The family had been heartbroken, but the babies they were grieving for were both fictional.

The couple were found guilty of various theft charges and had to repay the money they had scammed.

GOODBYE, GENEROUS WORLD!

In 1859, a well-dressed, serious-looking young man walked into the Phillips House, a hotel in Dayton, Ohio. The clerk at the desk gave him a cheerful greeting, but the man's response remained dour. He asked for a room and signed the register in beautiful, flowing handwriting. His name was Albert Victor Lamartine.

The stranger went quietly to his room, but a short time later the clerk received a disturbing note.

"Dear sir, I am very unwell and do not expect to recover. Will you be so kind as to send for a minister to come to my room? I do not care of which denomination, so long as he is a true Christian, and a pious man. Yours respectfully, A.V. Lamartine."

The hotel staff were alarmed. They went to check on their patron. They found him collapsed. He was pale and weak. He admitted he had taken poison. The staff roused a doctor who happened to be staying at the hotel. He examined the sick man and noted his drowsy state, the blue tint to his lips, his clammy skin and his tiny pupils. This young man showed clear signs of an opium overdose. Lamartine nodded weakly at the diagnosis and produced an empty bottle of laudanum, a medicinal mix of opium and alcohol.

While the doctor did what he could for the patient, the staff discovered a letter on the table. It was written in Lamartine's flowing handwriting.

They read the letter. It was addressed to the "Unfeeling World."

"Call me not a self-murderer," it began, "for it is you that has driven me to this extremity. The public is my murderer, for it has denied me business, and without that I should be cast upon the world—a beggar. God forbid!"

The letter made his situation clear. He was a good man who had been reduced to poverty. He had too much dignity to ask for money. In his depressed state, he could see only one option.

"Quite out of funds, and no business. What am I to do? To beg? No, I am too spirited. To defraud my fellow man? No, my conscience will not permit me. Death, then, is a welcome expedient."

As they read on, they started to appreciate the gentle, poetic spirit in their midst.

"Yes, let me die and be forgotten. Like poor Byron, "I do not regret what I have done so much as what I might have done. I have been an easy-going, melancholy man—engrossed with books and not with money—'loving not man the less, but Nature more!'"

For a man who wanted to be forgotten, he was surprisingly eager to talk about his background.

"Virginia is my nativity—Cleveland my adopted home. As my name indicates, I am of French extraction. My family was good, and I tenderly raised. I am an orphan— few relations."

He gave instructions on his burial:

"Bury me here, and should I ever have a tomb, let this be my epitaph—'Far from home, in a land of strangers, he died—preferring death to dishonor!'"

The letter continued in the same self-pitying tone, dropping more literary references, and finally came to a close.

"I have had many warm friends, to whom I tender a last and final adieu! I have recommendations from the best of men, to whom I am grateful. As to death, I am not afraid to die. I never was calmer than now. I could write much more, but I will stop."

But he didn't forget to mention a mysterious love.

"One word, however—the last I shall ever write—'Agnes!'"

The writing may seem overwrought today, but the hotel staff who read the letter seem to have been deeply moved by this account of a man who was too noble and honest to flourish in this cruel world. They showed it to others around town, who were equally affected. What a shame that Agnes couldn't be here to help. And what a tragedy that this young man should die in their hotel.

But the doctor brought good news. Lamartine would not die. The dose of opium he had taken was large, but not fatal. With care and rest, he could be nursed back to health. Everyone was delighted. They cared for him and fed him. And now that they had learned of his financial troubles, they also raised money for him. When their patient was finally healthy again, they saw him off at the train station, presenting him with $25 and a ticket to Indianapolis. He took the gifts humbly and gratefully and left town.

Later, the people of Dayton learned that Lamartine had previously stayed at a hotel in Sandusky, Ohio, where he had also tried to poison himself with opium. The good people of Sandusky had nursed him back to health and given him $40 and a train ticket to Dayton.

LOOK WHO DIED

Con artists don't need to fake their own tragedies to profit from sympathy. Other people's can work just as well—even people who don't exist.

In early 2023, "Carly" saw a Facebook message from her friend "Dylan" that made her stomach drop.

"Look who just died in an accident. I know you were good friends. I'm so sorry."

Dylan didn't say in the message who had died, but she provided a link—presumably to a news story. Afraid to see which of her friends had died, Carly clicked on it.

Something must have been messed up with the link, because she suddenly found herself looking at the Facebook login screen. Carly hurriedly logged in again, typing her name and password. It didn't work. She tried get back to Facebook, but she couldn't get back into her account.

She picked up her mobile and called Dylan. "I got your Facebook message, but I couldn't see the link. Who died?"

"Nobody died," said Dylan. "My account has been hacked. I got a message about someone dying, and they took over my account. I think maybe you've been hacked, too, now."

Dylan was right. Carly was locked out of Facebook, but her friends started receiving the same "Look who died" message that she had read.

The "Look Who Died" scam exploits our natural concern for friends. When someone clicks the link, it takes them to a fake Facebook login page. If someone enters their login information, it is immediately used to log into their account and change the password.

Once the account is hacked, it can be used as a base for sending new phony messages. The hackers profit from the scheme because controlling the account also provides access to the user's information—birthday, email address, list of friends—which can be sold on the dark web and used for other scams.

A RIGHT ROYAL RIP-OFF

Cons playing on sympathy don't have to involve a person's own friends or relatives. Many royal family enthusiasts were upset by the death of Queen Elizabeth II in 2022. Her funeral was followed by a flood of different scams.

One of the first to be identified claimed to be from Microsoft and offered users the chance to post their message to the queen by logging into their Microsoft account. Once they entered their name and password, the hackers could use the account for their own purposes.

Investment projects offered a range of dubious crypto tokens named after the monarch and claiming to pay tribute to her.

Some sites offered commemorative coins, T-shirts and other memorabilia.

A number of fake sites popped up pretending to be the official Buckingham Palace site and offering to sell tickets to the funeral. ("Just enter your banking information here . . .")

Some fans of the royals couldn't believe the queen was dead. There was a scam for them, too. They received messages, supposedly from the queen, saying that the announcement of her death was false. The tone of the message was not entirely convincing.

"Hey, it's me Queen Elizabeth. I am not dead. Charles sent me to a deserted island, so he could be King. I don't have access to my royal money, so please cashapp me $300, so I can get back to the UK."

The queen's letters are usually signed "Elizabeth R." but this one ended in a less regal form. She just said, "Tea and biscuits" followed by a Union Jack emoji.

CHAPTER 14
WE'VE GOT YOU COVERED

Insurance policies can mean big money for beneficiaries. They can pay out in many ways—and there's a scam for every one of them.

LIFE UNSURE-ANCE

"Vanessa" was grieving the loss of her aunt, "April." Vanessa had been close to her aunt. When April died, she had written her obituary and helped organize the funeral. Now she was in the midst of dealing with the will.

When she received a phone call from someone wanting to talk to her about April, she assumed it was one of her aunt's old friends. But it turned out to be "Kyle," a representative of an insurance company. He asked Vanessa a few questions about her relationship to April and seemed satisfied with her answers.

"I don't know if you're aware of this," said Kyle, "but your aunt had a large insurance policy."

Vanessa had not known this.

Kyle explained some details of the policy, which was supposed to pay out a large sum in the event of April's death. As he talked, he displayed a detailed knowledge of April.

"There's one minor problem," said Kyle. "Your aunt was supposed to make a premium payment earlier in the year, but she missed it."

Vanessa explained that April had been unwell for some time. It had probably slipped her mind.

"I'm afraid we can't pay out the insurance until the final premium is paid. That can come from her estate, or if you want, you can pay it yourself."

Vanessa said she was happy to pay it herself. She gave her details over the phone.

"I'll be in touch soon with more information," said Kyle. Then he said goodbye.

The money came out of Vanessa's account, but she didn't hear back from Kyle, and no insurance cheque arrived. When she checked with the insurance company, they said they had no record of an insurance policy under her aunt's name. Kyle was a con artist.

She had been taken in by a bereavement scam—a con that targets the grieving relatives of someone who has died. The family are usually upset and have to deal with hundreds of unfamiliar details. It may be hard to think straight. And people who can't think straight are the con artist's favourite kind of people.

Scams often involve someone pretending to be from the funeral home wanting payment for services, vehicles or assorted charges. Asking for insurance money is another popular choice.

These cons are not always well prepared. In one case, a con artist asked for $45 for "an insurance thing." She couldn't offer any more details. That scam was not successful.

BAD GENES

Health insurance can be a rich field for modern scammers.

In April 2022, "Ralph" from Jacksonville Beach, Florida, received a call from a woman who said she represented his medical insurance company. According to *First Coast News*, the woman said she was going to send him a DNA test for medical screening.

"There's no charge," she said. "The cost is covered by Medicare."

It sounded fine to Ralph. He gave her some of his details—name, Medicare number, mailing address, and the name of his doctor.

A few days later, the test arrived. Ralph had done DNA tests before in the course of family tree research, so he had no difficulty with this one. He packaged up the sample and sent it off.

It was only later that Ralph realized he had been scammed into handing over his Medicare number to a stranger. He discovered that the DNA test had not been ordered by his doctor. The company would carry out the unnecessary test and submit the bill to Medicare using his number. If Medicare declined to pay it, the bill for the tests he had ordered for would come to him. In many cases, these costs can be around $10,000.

Some tests are given away at community "health fairs." A booth offers a coupon for free ice cream that comes with a prize. The lucky winner—everyone—gets a "free" health screening that includes genetic testing.

Profiting from this kind of test requires the collaboration of a medical lab that will pay kickbacks to telemarketers, as well as "brokers" who can foist the unsolicited tests on members of the public. It can be a profitable operation—if you can get away with it. One lab in Atlanta carried out this kind of business, working with a network of "patient brokers" who found patients to test and got telemedicine doctors to sign off on the tests, even though they had never had any interaction with the patient.

The company made more than $447 million this way, of which $21 million went to the company owner.

The fraud was eventually caught, and in 2022 the owner was convicted for defrauding Medicare of $447 million, as well as for a number of charges of conspiracy and fraud that carry long prison sentences.

DON'T LOOK AT ME—I'M DEAD

In 1982, the body of a drowned man was found in Manila Bay, in the Philippines. The body was unidentified for a couple of days, then someone came forward and said he recognized the man as his missing nephew, "Tony," who was visiting from California.

According to the *Los Angeles Times*, the body was cremated the next day, and back in California, Tony's wife "Mandy" filled out the forms to collect the insurance money on her husband's tragic death. But insurance company investigators were suspicious about aspects of the case. For example, someone had paid off a number of Tony's old traffic citations to make sure his record was clean. Why? Did his family feel his social responsibilities that keenly, or was someone anxious to make sure his car wasn't stopped in a random police check? The investigators decided to talk to friends and neighbours before writing a cheque.

They heard odd rumours. Some people thought they had seen the dead man at some of his old hangouts.

But they really hit paydirt when they talked to the couple's elderly neighbour, "Grace." It seems she watched local activities with the determination of a Gestapo officer.

Grace reported that she'd witnessed some strange activity at Tony and Mandy's place. She said that every morning, Mandy would go outside and look up and down the street to make sure nobody was watching, then a man would creep out of the house, get into the back of the car, and they'd drive away together. The man returned each night, under cover of darkness, although, apparently, no amount of darkness could foil Grace's eagle vision.

The insurance agents asked Grace if she could act as their lookout. It was the job she had waited for all her life. Three hours later, she phoned the police to report the return of the mysterious man. When they checked, they found the supposedly dead man at home and very much alive.

Tony and Mandy were both arrested for their clumsy fraud. As for the unfortunate drowned man, they knew nothing about him—they had just taken advantage of the discovery to work their insurance con.

HOW LOW CAN YOU SINK?

When you imagine what sorts of frauds occurred in ancient times, you might think of swindles involving goats, royal seals or curses. It's surprising to discover an ancient case that's all about marine insurance fraud.

Around 300 BCE, two Greek men who were interested in the shipping business came up with a plan to make a small fortune. A man named Hegestratos was the captain of a ship that was carrying a shipment of grain, as well as a number of paying passengers. A man named Zenothemis worked under him.

While they were still in port in Syracuse in Sicily, Hegestratos and Zenothemis each borrowed money from different local lenders. Each man told the lenders he was shipping grain to Athens and needed a high-interest loan to cover the cost of the cargo. The truth was that the grain belonged to a merchant in Athens who had already paid for the delivery. But when the money lenders checked on the ownership, each man vouched for the other. They received two sets of loans on a cargo that neither of them owned. The con had worked. The investors in Syracuse were taken in and were happy to put up the money.

One of the reasons the investors were so enthusiastic was that a loan for a ship's cargo could be an unusually good deal. The laws throughout most of the ancient world usually put strict limits on interest rates. If you charged more than, say, 12 percent, you were committing the crime of usury. But that was only for regular loans. A different set of rules applied if someone was lending money for goods sent by a sea voyage. After all, a ship faced the dangers of storms and rocks and pirates, so the ship and its cargo might easily be lost. Because lenders were taking big chances in putting up their money, it was only fair that they should earn bigger rewards—perhaps a 30 percent interest rate. The cost could be added to the sale price at the other end of the journey.

There was one catch for investors. The law said that they shared the risk with the ship owner. If the ship came in safely, they could collect their money. But if the ship sank, the loan was erased, even if the owner survived. These shipping loans were like a combination of banking and marine insurance.

So Hegestratos and Zenothemis intended to pull off a little insurance scam, using the Greek laws to cheat their lenders.

Their plan was sinister. They would sink the ship far from land and escape in the ship's boat. The rest of the crew and passengers would certainly drown, so when the two conspirators reached land, they could make up a plausible story about how the ship sank. They would still secretly hold the money from the investor's loans, but because the cargo it was supposed to have paid for had disappeared beneath the waves, they would not be under any obligation to repay it.

The ship and its passengers left Syracuse and in a couple of days, they were far out to sea, between Italy and Greece. Hegestratos made his move. After nightfall, he crept to the ship's hold and set to work making a hole in the bottom of the ship, while Zenothemis remained on the deck trying to keep the other crew and passengers occupied. Hegestratos tried to work quietly, but the sounds carried through the hull, and the passengers became alarmed. They ran below to investigate. When they saw Hegestratos trying to cut a hole, they ran at him. After a chase around the decks, Hegestratos jumped from the ship into the dark water, hoping to reach the ship's boat, which was being towed behind. He didn't make it. The ship and its boat sailed on, and the captain was drowned at sea.

The passengers and crew were shocked by what had happened. So was Zenothemis, who now found himself in a difficult position. If the ship successfully reached its destination, his creditors would be owed their money with hefty interest. They would soon discover that the cargo of grain wasn't his, and his fraud would be exposed.

But so far, none of the other passengers suspected that he'd conspired with Hegestratos to sink the ship, so Zenothemis pretended to be as horrified as they were about the captain's sabotage. His dead partner had done some damage to the hull, and water was coming in, so Zenothemis made the most of it.

"We've got to get out of here immediately. The ship is going to sink."

If he could persuade the others to abandon the vessel, it would sink on its own, and he would still succeed with his con.

Unfortunately for Zenothemis, a passenger named Protus didn't like that plan. Protus had been hired for the job of supercargo by the real owner of the grain. It was his duty to make sure that the cargo arrived safely, and he wasn't going to give up without a struggle. He offered the crew a generous reward if they could bring the ship safely to port. The incentive worked. To Zenothemis's dismay, the crew put in a heroic effort to save the ship. They bailed water and repaired the damage as well as they could. The ship eventually limped into a port on one of Greece's western islands.

In port, Zenothemis tried more tricks and persuasion, and went to court to prevent the ship from sailing on to Athens, claiming that it belonged to his friends in another city. None of his efforts worked. The ship sailed on, and Zenothemis sailed with it, still looking for a way to make the scam work.

His final ploy was to go to court in Athens, where he claimed that the captain who had tried to sink the ship was the legitimate owner of the grain and that he, Zenothemis, had previously lent the captain the money and was entitled to a refund.

The real owner of the grain was incensed. In his defense, he revealed all the facts about the murderous con that Zenothemis and Hegestratos had tried to pull off—which is the reason we know so much about this 2,300-year-old fraud today.

We only have the notes from the prosecution, so it's not clear how the case ended or what happened to Zenothemis. If he wasn't executed, we're guessing he may have gone on to a successful career in politics.

MOM-ME DEAREST

In 1990, a California man we'll call "Dean" learned that his mother had died in Japan. Unlike the others crooks in this section, Dean refused to collect on her insurance.

This was mostly because she was worth more alive than dead. He kept her death a secret from US authorities, forged her signature, and collected various government benefits.

The case is like a financial version of the film *Psycho*, where Anthony Perkins's character deals with the death of his domineering mother by becoming her. (We're sorry if that's a spoiler, but the film came out in 1960, so you had time.) Dean "became" his mother, carrying out financial transactions and forging her signature on documents. His version of his mother generously signed over her house to her dear son.

The most remarkable thing about the scam was how long he kept it going. It wasn't discovered until 2020, thirty years after the mother's death.

In 2023, *The Guardian* reported that Dean had collected more than $800,000 and would now have to sell his house and put the money toward repaying the money he had stolen.

On the plus side, the con didn't involve wearing the mother's wig and dresses. He also didn't stab Janet Leigh to death in the shower. (Again, you had time.)

CHAPTER 15
ROBBING PETER TO PAY PONZI

Ponzi schemes are the world's best-known financial scams—so infamous we couldn't avoid mentioning them twice before in this section. To recap, a Ponzi scheme is a fraud where a con artist takes the money from new investors and pays it out as fake profits to old ones.

The schemes were named for Charles Ponzi, but they didn't start with him and, unfortunately, they didn't end with him either.

DOUBLE YOUR MONEY IN NINETY DAYS

In 1919, a struggling businessman in Boston offered to mail a catalogue of business ideas. He would send the catalogue to anyone who sent return postage. He received one request from Spain. Included with the request was a yellow slip of paper—an International Reply Coupon (IRC). The businessman's name was Charles Ponzi, and when he received that coupon in the mail, it set off one of the most famous cons in history.

The International Reply Coupon is an odd item created to solve the problem of return postage.

Before the internet, many catalogues and products were sold by mail. A customer often had to include stamps so that the sender wouldn't have to pay the cost of mailing a reply—known as "return postage."

If someone in the U.S. mailed the request to a U.S. company, enclosing stamps for the return postage worked fine, but things weren't so easy if you wanted a reply from another country, say, if a customer in England wanted to send return postage to the U.S., or if someone in Spain wanted to send it to a seller in Germany. The person sending the request not only needed to find a source of foreign stamps, but they also had to know the foreign country's postal rates. This information wasn't so easy to obtain in pre-internet times. Every country had its own system of postal prices and weights, and the prices were subject to frequent change.

The postal services of the world discussed the problem and, in 1906, they came up with a neat solution: the IRC. It was a yellow slip of paper printed with blue text in multiple languages. All the participating countries honoured the coupon. Anyone could present it at a post office and exchange it for stamps to cover the minimum postage.

As Charles Ponzi examined the IRC he'd received, he noticed something curious. The amount his Spanish correspondent had spent on the coupon was 10 percent less than the cost of the stamps Ponzi could buy with it in the United States. In other countries, the difference was much greater. It meant that if someone were to buy these coupons in bulk and ship them back and forth between countries, they could exploit the difference in postal rates and make a lot of money.

Ponzi was excited about the new idea. He researched some postal rates, crunched a few numbers and liked what he saw. He put the system to the test. He sent American dollars to a relative in Italy, who converted them to Italian lire, then purchased IRCs with the money. The IRCs were mailed back to Ponzi, who took them to his local post office and exchanged them for US stamps worth twice what he had started with.

Ponzi figured that international trade in International Reply Coupons was a winner and set up a company to carry out the transactions. All he needed was the money to buy the coupons. He offered big returns to investors, promising to double their money in just ninety days.

The investors were intrigued, and some gave it a try. As word got around, more jumped aboard. Sure enough, Ponzi returned their money on time, with the promised profits.

In fact, Ponzi hadn't yet bought the IRCs that would create profits for the scheme; he was still working out some of the logistical problems, so he just paid off the early investors using the money coming in from the later ones to buy himself time and a good reputation to boot.

One problem he faced with his operation was how to increase the volume. It was one thing to send a few coupons back and forth between America and Italy, but exchanging thousands or millions of coupons was a different matter.

According to writer Dan Davies in his book *Lying for Money: How Legendary Frauds Reveal the Workings of the World,* Ponzi soon discovered that the problem he faced was impossible to solve. The people who ran the postal systems of the world were not fools; they had set up IRCs as a convenience for their customers but knew the system might be abused, so they had put safeguards in place limiting how many coupons a person could buy or exchange, and preventing them from using the coupons as a currency.

Ponzi should probably have admitted the scheme didn't work and refunded what money he could. Instead, he hid the truth and kept pretending that the scheme worked.

In the meantime, the number of new investors kept growing, and satisfied investors put their profits back into the scheme. Ponzi allowed customers to withdraw their money at any time, but if they pulled their money out early, they got no interest. Most were very happy with the money they were making and let their investment ride.

Ponzi was unable to pay everyone the money he owed, but he could keep kicking the can down the road, using money from the new investors to pay the returns or withdrawals of the current ones. If he played for time and convinced enough people to reinvest rather than take their profits and leave, he might come up with another scheme to cover the debts. Until then, all that mattered was that the number of investors kept growing.

Some people had their doubts about Ponzi. One writer in Boston suggested that the rapid profits Ponzi promised were impossible to deliver. He was right: to make the profits he claimed, Ponzi would have had to be trading more IRCs than were available in the world, and the quantities he would need to ship between America and Europe would have filled ocean liners. But Ponzi shut down the questions: he sued the writer for libel and won a huge sum in damages. Others who might have had doubts kept their mouths shut.

Ponzi hired sales agents and paid them generous commissions to find new investors. He opened offices in other cities. The number of investors went from hundreds to thousands to tens of thousands.

Ponzi was living like a king, and his company had millions in the bank, but the debts were mounting every day. He was trapped by his own success, and if things kept going as they were, a crash was inevitable and prison (or worse) would follow. He needed a way to turn his imaginary investments into real assets.

Ponzi used his bank deposits as a weapon. He demanded that one bank pay him all his deposits immediately, knowing full well that the bank didn't have sufficient cash on hand to do so. When the bank was unable to pay, he demanded that the directors sell him enough shares in the bank to make him the majority owner. They had no choice but to agree.

He tried the same thing with other banks and real estate companies. He even tried to buy surplus ships from the U.S. Navy. He may have thought that, if he could make himself powerful and important enough, he would be immune from prosecution.

If that was his plan, it didn't work. When the scheme started, he had rashly offered his first investor an option to buy a 50-percent share in the business. Now the investor sued him, demanding his share. The court case was minor, but it brought to light some of Charles Ponzi's previous history, including a string of minor frauds in Canada.

The revelations made the public uneasy, and some wondered if his other promises could be relied on. Investigators took a closer look at his business model and started asking for paperwork. Exactly how many IRCs had Ponzi purchased and what profits had he made on them? The answer to both questions appeared to be: almost none. His office was raided by regulators. They found IRCs, but their total value was $61.

Charles Ponzi turned himself in. His company collapsed, taking down five banks with it. He seemed to have few regrets. Later in life, he described his scheme as "the best show that was ever staged in their territory since the landing of the Pilgrims! It was easily worth fifteen million bucks to watch me put the thing over."

He was convicted of mail fraud and received a relatively light sentence of five years. He was released after his third year, but to his surprise, he immediately faced new charges of larceny that sent him back to prison on a seven- to nine-year sentence. He appealed, and while he was out on bail, he escaped.

As a fugitive, he would probably have been wise to keep a low profile. Instead, almost unbelievably, he took advantage of his freedom to set up a new shady business, cashing in on the Florida real estate boom. After creating the Ponzi scheme that Ponzi schemes are named after, Charles Ponzi participated in another scam cliché: literally "selling swamp land in Florida."

He was soon caught and convicted again. Ponzi was finally released in 1934, but after he defrauded so many people out of so much money, officials weren't done with him. Ponzi was an Italian citizen and had never become a naturalized American, so he was declared an undesirable alien and deported to his birthplace. The man who had built a con based on International Reply Coupons ended up being stamped "return to sender."

MADOFF WITH THEIR MONEY

Bernie Madoff operated a Ponzi scheme that was not only the largest in history, but also one of the longest-running. One ex-employee said the fraudulent activities of Madoff's company went back to the 1970s. In total, the scheme lost its clients nearly $65 billion.

Madoff didn't offer huge profits like his predecessor Charles Ponzi. Instead, he promised steady, reliable returns and on paper he delivered them. But the reports he gave to clients were fictional. He decided how much he would claim to deliver, then used a computer program to search stock prices and calculate retroactively what stocks would have had to be bought and sold in order to generate the desired numbers. The reports appeared to show supernatural timing on his trades: he often sold shares at their highest price and bought them at their lowest. In fact, he had bought and sold nothing. He just kept moving money around, skimming some for himself and keeping a portion aside in case clients wanted to withdraw their money.

Some clients, the lucky ones, walked away, taking their large profits with them—all taken from their fellow investors. However, most clients were happy to leave their money with him and watched their accounts grow ever larger.

Many stock market experts were concerned about Madoff's business: the consistency of his profits, around 10 percent, year in and year out, defied stock market logic and smelled like a Ponzi scheme, although without the sky-high rates Ponzi schemes usually offer. Madoff's restraint in the profits he offered was one of his smarter criminal choices and allowed him to keep his scheme going for longer than many other Ponzis. His performance was impressive, but plausible to most people. But some experts had serious doubts.

One man, Harry Markopolos, analyzed Madoff's business and concluded that it didn't add up. He noted that Madoff's profits came from the use of stock options. It was possible to make money that way, but to do it on the scale that Madoff claimed would mean buying more stock options than actually existed. It was just like Charles Ponzi's claims that he made millions selling international reply coupons. In both cases, there weren't enough items circulating to explain the profits.

Markopolos repeatedly warned the U.S. Securities and Exchange

Commission that Madoff's business must be fraudulent, but their people failed to uncover the glaring problems.

Later, after he was convicted, Madoff would express his contempt for how the investigations had been conducted. He complained that one investigator acted tough and asked questions "like Lieutenant Columbo" but focused on irrelevant details, while never investigating the areas that would have made the Ponzi scheme obvious. For example, the investigators scoured corporate emails for subtle clues, but didn't look to see whether Madoff's company had actually made the trades his reports claimed.

It all came crashing down with the 2008 stock market. Many of his investors scrambled to cash in their investments, and Madoff had no way to pay them. He knew the game was up. He was arrested and charged with securities fraud.

His clients included many American charities, and the case drew extra attention because of the number of big names from entertainment who were affected, such as Steven Spielberg, John Malkovich, Zsa Zsa Gabor and Larry King.

In court, he pleaded guilty and was given the maximum sentence—150 years in prison—although he only served twelve years before going to that great Ponzi scheme in the sky.

TAKE THE MONEY AND JUMP

Melissa Caddick was a successful Australian financial adviser. She used her skills and qualifications to invest for her family and friends, getting excellent returns on their money. As for her own investments, she was living the dream. She owned two houses in Sydney and lived a life of luxury, buying the finest designer clothes, expensive cars, artwork and jewelry.

But in 2020, Melissa went missing. The forty-nine-year-old's disappearance made headlines in Australia and became one of the biggest missing persons cases in years. According to reports on *BBC News*, she had left the house early in the morning, leaving her phone at home. Her family said they assumed she had gone for a run, but she never came back.

Around the same time, police were investigating her. Melissa's life was a fraud. She had faked her qualifications, and her investing skills were nothing more than a giant Ponzi scheme: she took her clients' money, somewhere in the region of $30 million, spent it, and gave fraudulent reports of how well their investments were doing.

Some people speculated that, when investigators started closing in, she killed herself, jumping from the cliffs near her home in the Sydney suburb of Dover Heights. Others said she ran away. Some wondered if it was an insurance scam (her insurance covered suicide) or if she was murdered by her husband or an angry investor.

Police suspected she had escaped and gone into hiding, and most of their investigations pursued this line.

But three months later, a disembodied foot in an expensive running shoe washed up on a beach several hundred miles away. It was plausible that ocean currents could have carried remains that far, and indeed a DNA analysis showed that the foot was that of Melissa Caddick. Given the state of the foot, examiners couldn't tell what had happened—murder? suicide? shark attack?—but Melissa Caddick was officially declared dead.

Even that didn't entirely put the matter to rest. As one crime expert grimly commented, "You can survive without a foot."

FORTUNE TELLER TO FORTUNE TAKER

Ponzi schemes may go by that name now, but one American woman ran the same scheme years before Charles Ponzi was born.

In the 1870s, Sarah Howe was living in Boston. She had been working as a fortune teller, but wanted to make money on a bigger scale, so in 1879, Howe opened an unusual bank in Boston. The Ladies' Deposit Company purported to be an institution set up to help women.

Clients had to meet a set of criteria. They needed to be single women who did not own their own home (most would have been renters). They also had to be "unprotected," meaning that their money wasn't controlled by a father, brother or guardian. Deposits had to be between $200 and $1,000.

The bank didn't advertise and only accepted new clients on the recommendation of existing members. But the most unusual thing was the interest rate: 8 percent per month.

Howe seemed a kindly figure. She had one-on-one meetings with some of her depositors, lending a sympathetic ear and offering morale-boosting compliments. She said the bank was funded by Quakers who wanted to support women in need.

In fact, her bank was a Ponzi scheme, and targeting single, unprotected women who were not too wealthy may have been Howe's way of keeping banks and financial experts at a safe distance and making prosecution less likely. Although Howe had been a vulnerable single woman herself, she preyed on this group, drawing heavily from her depositors' funds to buy herself a nice house and expensive decorations.

The press became curious about how her bank could possibly pay the promised rates. The term *Ponzi scheme* had not yet been invented, but some suspected that she was paying interest using the money from new depositors, and if that was true, they knew it was just a matter of time before it all came crashing down.

The crash came the following year, in 1880. A series of newspaper articles declared her bank a fraud. Depositors lined up to withdraw their money. When the bank couldn't pay, Howe was arrested. Investigators discovered that the Quaker charity supporting the bank was a fiction. She was sent to jail for three years.

It didn't deter her. When she was released, she tried the same scheme again and then a third time in Chicago. When those banks were also closed down, she gave up on the Ponzi business and went back to fortune-telling.

THE "520-PERCENT" MAN

Early in 1889, a man named William Miller, a prominent member of a Brooklyn church, started an investment business. His offer was simple enough for anyone to understand.

"Give me $10. I will give you $1 next week and every week, until you decide to withdraw the principal."

Maria Konnikova's 2016 book *The Confidence Game: Why We Fall for It ... Every Time* describes Miller's business in detail.

Miller claimed he had access to reliable inside information on stocks. It meant that a $10 investment, left with Miller for a year, would earn $52. To put it another way, he was offering simple interest at the astonishing rate of 520 percent.

A few people took the chance. They weren't disappointed. They received their payments, every week, right on time. Word spread fast about this incredible deal, and new clients joined the plan. Growth was explosive. Miller renamed his business. Henceforth, his investment business would operate as the Franklin Syndicate. He took steps to incorporate it.

Dealing with small depositors was becoming a nuisance, so Miller raised the minimum deposit to $50. He assured prospective clients that "our business is honest, safe, legitimate, and profitable."

Many people didn't believe the claims could be real, but Miller pointed to all the other famous investors who had started small and become millionaires in a short time. Those others proved such growth was possible. And he, Miller, knew the secret to it. Of course, he couldn't share it. They just needed to believe.

Miller advertised heavily, and word spread more widely about the investment genius people were now calling "the 520-percent man." Hundreds—then thousands—of people, signed up with his investment company.

In eight months, Miller's business grew from zero to $1.2 million.

But then came trouble. Miller's attempts to incorporate had led to questions about the company. Investigators discovered that nobody knew anything about Miller's business. It had a fancy office now, but no officers and no board of directors. An article in the *New York Times* expressed doubt about the legitimacy of the business. The headline told readers what to do next: "Desert Miller's Company."

Miller read the headline and took the advice himself. He left town and escaped to Canada.

Concerned investors crowded around his office, wanting their money back, but the building was now occupied by police, and there was no money to give out. Many hoped the closure was just temporary and that the Franklin Syndicate would reopen soon.

Miller's business was another Ponzi scheme before Ponzi's Ponzi scheme. He had made only one stock market investment, which had gone very badly. Aside from that, all the payouts came from the money new clients threw his way.

Once the fraud was revealed, everyone started looking for Miller. A few months after his disappearance, he was arrested in Montreal and brought back to face charges in New York. He was found guilty and sentenced to ten years in Sing Sing.

As for the money, Miller had taken care of that before he left for Canada. He figured that, if he was caught, all the money would be taken from him. He was also concerned about his wife, who was left behind in New York, so he made a deal with his lawyer, a man named Robert Ammon. The lawyer would look after the money (attorney-client privilege would keep it safe from investigations), and Miller could get it back later. In the meantime, the lawyer would ensure that Miller's wife was well taken care of.

Ammon sent the wife $5 a week and kept most of the rest. Miller had conned his clients, and now Ammon was conning Miller.

But the crooked deal ended badly for Ammon. Miller told authorities that Ammon had his money, then testified against the lawyer. Miller's clients ended up getting a portion of their money back. In gratitude for Miller's cooperation, the authorities released him from prison early, and it was Ammon's turn to go to Sing Sing.

Miller was done with fraud after that. He changed his name and spent the next ten years running a grocery store.

CHAPTER 16
HIGH-TECH CONS

Whenever a new technology comes along, it brings new opportunities for the public, for businesses and for the con artist.

CHEAT CODE

We think of codes and passwords as modern phenomena, but they have been around a long time. A century ago, important messages were sent by telegraph, tapped out a letter at a time using Morse Code, but other codes were layered on top of it.

Telegrams were expensive (you paid by the word) and not very secure—the message would be seen by telegraph operators, deliverers and anyone who was able to listen in on the message, which could be many people if those dots and dashes were sent using radio.

Many companies protected their sensitive information by using their own secret book of telegraph codes, which replaced frequently used words or phrases with other common words. For example, the word *Jar* might mean "We received your message sent today," while *Jasper* might mean "Please ship the following products."

The codes were meaningless to any outsider who intercepted them, but the real recipient could look up each word in a code book and translate the coded message into regular English. The codes made the message more secure and also cut costs by making it shorter.

In 1914, a few months before the start of the World War I, the *Birmingham Daily Mail* reported a fraud using telegraphic codes.

Cook's travel agency office in Brussels received a telegram from Nottingham in England. The message used the firm's private code. When decoded, it gave instructions for the firm to pay £50 to a man who was going to call on the office. The next day, the man turned up and identified himself, and the clerks paid him the money.

A few days later, the Cook's office in Birmingham, England, received a telegram from the Brussels office. Again, it used the company's code, and instructed Birmingham to pay £50 to a man named Bush. And the next day Mr. Bush showed up, identified himself, and received the money.

The Birmingham office sent a message back to Brussels, letting them know that Mr. Bush had been paid, as they had requested. "But we didn't make that request!" said the Brussels office. Company officials realized that they had been the victims of fraud. They contacted the Birmingham police and provided a description of the man who had appeared in the Birmingham and Brussels offices. It was clear that the man knew how the company operated and had access to the code book. Investigators guessed it was an employee—or, more likely, ex-employee.

Sure enough, the description matched that of a man who had been fired by the company. The police now used the telegraph against the criminal, sending his description to all seaports in the United Kingdom. It paid off: they discovered that a man matching the description had sailed from Glasgow to New York. The British government sent a telegraphic message to their American counterparts. When the criminal arrived at Ellis Island, New York, he faced arrest and deportation back to England. The wonders of telegraphic technology.

DELIBERATE MISTAKES

The first telegraph systems didn't use wires or Morse Code. Most used towers with giant semaphore arms on the sides. Messages were sent a letter at a time. The operator set the arms at a certain angle to indicate a letter or number.

The "optical telegraph" towers were spaced miles apart, within sight of each other, with observers watching nearby towers using a telescope. When they saw a signal coming from the closest tower in the chain, they would pass it on to the next one. It sounds clumsy, but a message could be sent hundreds of miles in a few minutes—much faster than a messenger on horseback could carry it.

France was a leader in this technology. It had a network of towers spanning the country, operated by the military. Information about troop movements could cross the country in less than an hour, but commercial information, like stock market prices, was still sent by horse. If stock prices increased in Paris, it would usually be five days before the news reached Bordeaux by stagecoach, 360 miles away. Once the news reached that city, the Bordeaux market would inevitably see the same kind of increase.

Some traders tried to get an advantage over others by sending a message using a fast rider or sending messages with pigeons, but it was still slow. If investors were able to send a message by telegraph from Paris to Bordeaux ahead of the messengers, their colleagues would know the stock market movements days before other traders and could clean up. But how could this be done when the military didn't allow such messages?

In 1834, two brothers, Francois and Joseph Blanc, who traded stocks in Bordeaux, came up with a solution to transmit stock information by military telegraph.

They realized that telegraph operators sometimes made mistakes. When an error occurred, the sender sent a subsequent message, "erasing" the previous character and replacing it with the correct one. Both the error and the correction would be sent down the line.

The brothers' idea was to send an "error," then correct it. They might send a *U* character if the Paris market went up dramatically, a *D* if it suddenly dropped, and an *N* if it showed no large changes. In practice, the messages had to be longer than this, to prevent a genuine mistake from being interpreted as a stock market message.

If they bribed operators at the beginning and end of the line, they could send a series of deliberate mistakes inside the regular military communications. The operator at the end could note the key mistakes and reveal the hidden message to the traders, but the errors would be removed from the military message and no officials would be the wiser.

There was one problem. At certain key stations, an official would decode the entire message, correct any mistakes, then send the cleaned-up message on a letter at a time. This added a delay, but stripped out the errors and corrections that had accumulated along the line. One of these stations was in Tours, partway between Paris and Bordeaux. Any hidden message from the brothers would have to be inserted at Tours after, since their deliberate errors would be automatically removed when the message was retransmitted.

The brothers bribed a telegraph operator at Tours to insert the deliberate mistakes. A colleague in Paris brought the message to Tours on horseback.

Another accomplice, a former operator who lived within sight of a telegraph station close to the end of the line, transcribed the messages, noted the errors and passed them on to the brothers. They received word from the Paris stock exchange days before other traders and continued using the system for two years before it was discovered.

In 1836, the brothers and their associates were put on trial. Those who had taken bribes were in trouble, but it was hard to figure out what charge to lay against the brothers. After all, they hadn't committed any fraud, and the information they had sent wasn't secret—it just arrived faster than normal. And although they had made use of telegraph towers which were normally used by the military, there was no law on the books that made this a crime. In the end, the brothers escaped punishment.

They were ahead of their time. Today, traders around the world make money by sending stock information on the fastest possible networks. Being able to trade a billionth of a second faster than others can mean big money, and the competition is so intense that even an edge of a trillionth or a quadrillionth of a second makes a difference. Today, as in 1830s France, there's no law against it.

MOBILE PHONY

Mobile phone use has soared in India. Areas that had poor phone access until quite recently are suddenly connected with fast new systems, and new phone towers are popping up across the subcontinent.

"Vijay," a businessman in Mumbai, received a message from an executive at a local mobile phone company. The executive, "Subash," explained that the use of mobile phones was exploding, and they were looking for land where they could install a mobile phone tower.

"I don't want to sell my property," said Vijay.

"You don't have to," said Subash. "We can install the tower on your terrace. It won't be in the way, and we will pay you a monthly rent for use of the location."

"Rent?" said Vijay. This was intriguing. "How much?" he asked.

Subash considered the location of Vijay's property. He offered 45,000 rupees per month—roughly $550.

It sounded like a good deal to Vijay—a modest but steady income just for owning land.

A little later, Subash contacted Vijay with good news. The company had examined the site using a satellite survey, and it had been approved as a location for a mobile phone tower. He told Vijay that he would be receiving his first payment in a few days. In addition, he would receive an advance deposit of 15 million rupees—more than $18,000. Vijay certainly wasn't going to object. This deal was getting better all the time.

"We will send it as soon as we have completed the registration process," said Subash. "It's the usual thing: fill out some details, pay the registration fee..."

"Fee? How much is the fee?" asked Vijay.

"Not much," said Subash. "Just 125,000 rupees."

That was the equivalent of $1,500. But, as Vijay considered it, it would be covered by three months' rent, and in a few days he would receive many times that amount for his initial deposit. He agreed and sent the money.

There were more formalities to go through. He needed to provide ownership papers for his property, which he did. A series of minor expenses followed: taxes on his future earnings and a number of government fees.

The money was adding up, and Vijay still hadn't received the initial payment he had been promised, so he tried to cancel the deal.

Vijay said the ministry had approved the use of his site. If Subash cancelled now, he would face a 20-percent fine. So he stuck with it, paying the various fees and borrowing to do so, until he happened to mention it to a friend, who advised him to go to the police.

There was no phone company and no rent. The whole deal was a classic "mobile tower scam"—a common scam across India. In his pursuit of a steady $550-per-month rent, Vijay ended up losing the equivalent of more than $180,000 to the scammers.

NETWORKING NOT WORKING

Today, most people have access to some form of high-speed internet, delivered over digital phone lines, cable, or using mobile phone networks.

In the 1990s, it was different. Connecting computers together meant using a modem. Phone lines were designed for transmitting the human voice, and the modem had to turn the computer's data into audible tones that could be sent the same way. It worked, and engineers kept finding ingenious ways to push the boundaries and tweak more speed out of the connection, but it was still much slower than the networks found in offices, which used thick, coaxial cables.

Everyone was talking about the future of media, how the internet would be used to transmit television and movies to people's homes. Companies like Blockbuster Video and CNN took a keen interest in the idea: Why rent videotapes if you can send movies instantly to your customers' homes? The problem was that, in most homes, the only way to connect to the internet was through old-fashioned phone lines and a modem. When users downloaded a large image, it would appear slowly, line by line. Downloading a music video might take hours. The system was too slow for movies.

A Florida inventor we'll call "Jackson" had a solution. He had invented a device that would send data over regular phone lines at amazing speeds—a thousand times faster than the modems of the day. People were skeptical, but he put on a demonstration. Using just old-fashioned telephone lines, he transmitted high-quality video from one computer to another computer half a mile away. The engineers who witnessed the feat were astonished. How was this possible?

Jackson said his technology was secret, but it was based on low-energy physics.

Investors threw money at Jackson to buy into his revolutionary technology. He was collecting millions. It took a while to deliver the prototype devices, but Jackson had excuses. Some prototypes had been destroyed by lightning strikes or fire or floods.

Investors did a little digging and investigated the warehouse where Jackson kept some of his gear. They discovered that the ordinary power strips Jackson's computers had been plugged into contained not only electrical cable, but also coaxial network cable. And when they searched outside, they discovered more coaxial cable going into a river and emerging half a mile away. Suddenly the truth became clear.

The reason the two computers used in the demonstration were able to connect at office-network speeds was that they were connected by an office-network network.

The investors sued the inventor for misrepresenting his invention. But Jackson had an excuse. He claimed he had been in a car accident some months earlier and suffered amnesia, forgetting some of the technical details that made his remarkable device work. He admitted he had been forced to simulate the demonstration. But he would get it all working again, just as soon as he had reverse-engineered the working units.

The investors faced a choice. They could accept that they'd been scammed out of millions or they could believe an implausible story and keep putting money in with the promise of billions in the future. In an impressive display of cognitive dissonance, many kept playing, and the con kept going for years, delivering nothing to its investors but disappointment.

ATTORN-E

In 2023, a man sued the Colombian airline Avianca. He claimed that, four years earlier, he had been on a flight from El Salvador to New York and a metal serving cart hit his knee.

The airline said that there was a two-year statute of limitations on passenger injuries on international flights. That time limit had expired on the case.

"Not so," replied the man's lawyers. The time limit could be extended under certain conditions. In their submission, they drew attention to such important cases as "Shaboon v. EgyptAir," "Varghese v. China Southern Airlines," "Martinez v. Delta Air Lines," and "Zicherman v. Korean Air Lines Co. Ltd."

The judge was not familiar with the cases, and neither were the airline's lawyers, who specialized in aviation law. When they looked up the cases, they were unable to find them. That was because the cases didn't exist.

One of the man's lawyers, who seems to have been pressed for time, had turned to ChatGPT for a legal opinion.

ChatGPT is an artificial intelligence (AI) chatbot. Ask it a question and it will quickly provide a reply. It is an astonishing technology, but its work is definitely the product of artificial intelligence, not the real kind. Although the chatbot draws from a vast pool of online information, it doesn't understand the question or care about the answer. It analyzes countless millions of documents written by real people and looks at what words typically follow each other and how sentences are strung together to provide a block of text that resembles the sort of answer a person might give.

The lawyer didn't understand ChatGPT's limitations and asked the chatbot to generate his legal submission. He then passed it on to the lawyer in the courtroom, who signed off on it, believing it had been properly researched.

Not only were the cases invented, the arguments in the document were legal gibberish. The judge did some checking of his own and found that some of the references involved real cases but had no connection to aviation law.

The judge asked the plaintiff's lawyers if the cases they had used were real. The lawyers confirmed that they were—they had checked.

Unfortunately for them, their method of checking didn't involve looking up the cases in legal references. Instead they had just asked ChatGPT if the cases were real. The chatbot doubled down on its fabrications, saying, "The cases I provided are real and can be found in reputable legal databases."

The case against the airline was dismissed, and the lawyers were fined $5,000 each.

ChatGPT may not be much good as a lawyer, but it makes an impressive con artist.

CHAPTER 17
ROMANCE AND MARRIAGE SCAMS

L ove is a powerful force and it makes people do the craziest things. Con artists know that, and it's the reason some of them will cruelly exploit other people's feelings of love to satisfy their own feelings of greed.

But success in crime is as fickle as success in love, and things don't always go the scammer's way.

THE NOT-SO-GOOD DOCTOR

Mary Trapp was a widow living in Leavenworth, Kansas, in 1876. She was an attractive woman with two children and a large property.

One day, she met a man she hadn't seen in the town before. He introduced himself as Dr. John Stark. He said he was based in Kansas City, where he ran the Surgical and Medical Institute, but he had come to Leavenworth to do some work. His institute had an excellent reputation, and although he had only been in Leavenworth for a few weeks, a steady stream of patients had been to see him.

The doctor was an imposter. The real Dr. John Stark was still in Kansas City, running his medical business and occasionally dealing with complaints from patients who had seen the false doctor.

The fake doctor was charmed by Trapp. When he wasn't dealing with patients, he gave her all his attention. Then he proposed marriage. To sweeten the deal, he offered her a share in the Kansas City Surgical and Medical Institute.

Trapp accepted his proposal, and they planned to get married the following week.

One of Trapp's friends, Mrs. Jollie, heard about the wedding. She was delighted at the match and spoke highly of Dr. Stark, who was an old acquaintance of hers. She said to Trapp, "Ask him to call on me."

Trapp passed Mrs. Jollie's invitation on to her fiancé. He pretended to be delighted. "Yes, I would love to pay a call on dear Mrs. Jollie."

His bluff to Trapp made sense, but what seems incomprehensible is that the imposter followed through on his promise and actually paid a social visit to Mrs. Jollie. What was he thinking? Did he imagine Mrs. Jollie had forgotten what her friend looked like? Did he believe his impression of the real doctor was good enough to fool her? Was he delusional and convinced he was actually Dr. Stark?

Whatever he thought, he did indeed pay a brief call on Mrs. Jollie at her house. The woman welcomed him, and they talked pleasantly. Soon he left, probably feeling very pleased with his latest triumph.

But Mrs. Jollie hadn't been fooled for a minute. The moment she set eyes on him, she knew the man was not her old friend. She stayed calm and played along.

When the false doctor had gone, Mrs. Jollie visited Mary Trapp and told her that her Dr. Stark was an imposter. The two women then contacted the real Dr. Stark in Kansas City and told him what was going on.

The real Dr. Stark hurried to Leavenworth and met the widow. When the fake doctor came to call, the two men met, and the real doctor kept his identity a secret. He was amused to hear the imposter describe his good work in Kansas City. Finally, the real doctor said, "You are a damned fraud. I am Dr. Stark, of Kansas City."

The imposter said, "Is that so? I am really pleased to know you, doctor," then made a run for it.

The real doctor chased his doppelgänger and nearly caught him. The fake pulled a pistol. The real doctor responded by picking up a large rock. It was not the response the imposter expected, and he took off again.

The real doctor kept up the chase, shouting "Stop! Thief!" An old-fashioned hue-and-cry followed, with more than fifty people pursuing the criminal. But despite the pursuers' numeric advantage, the imposter managed to escape the town without being caught.

According to coverage in the *Kansas City Times*, the real Dr. Stark returned to the house of Mary Trapp to tell her that the imposter had escaped. She was grateful that the fraud had been exposed. As for the real doctor, "his bachelor heart warmed at her kind and courteous attentions." The two made plans to see each other again.

YOU REMIND ME OF SOMEONE

A woman in Florida, "Cheryl," received a message on Instagram from an attractive-looking man, "Dave." According to *WTVJ-TV* in Miami, they exchanged a few messages, then his tone quickly became very romantic. Within a day, Dave told Cheryl he loved her. He said she was the woman of his dreams. He said he wanted to marry her. It was a little rushed, but it was flattering.

Then, without wasting much more time on the romance angle, Dave switched tracks. He said he needed $6,500 for his mother's surgery.

Now all the lavish compliments made sense to Cheryl. She wasn't falling for it. She told Dave she knew he was a liar. She wasn't going to marry him, and she wasn't going to send him any money.

Dave didn't take it well. He turned mean. He said he could access her phone and download her pictures. He threatened to create Photoshopped nude photos of Cheryl and post them on the internet. He threatened to hurt her children. If she didn't send the money, she was in for a world of pain. "You have two days to comply."

Cheryl was shocked and frightened, but when she thought about it, she figured Dave was probably bluffing. She lived in a gated community, and the school her kids attended had good security.

Then there was the man's awkward use of English: "The doctors demand a sum of 6500$ to conduct a surgery of which I was not having the money." Not only had he put the dollar sign in the wrong place, he seemed to have no clue how much surgery cost in the United States. He probably didn't live in the U.S. He probably wasn't even on the same continent. So Cheryl ignored the threats. She was right: Dave's threats were empty, and nothing bad happened to her or her children.

Later, though, she was scrolling on Facebook and was surprised to see Dave's handsome face under the profile of a man named "Marcus." He warned people that criminals had used pictures from his account to create fake identities.

Cheryl wrote to Marcus and told him about her unpleasant run-in with one of the scammers. He was sympathetic. He had heard from others—women who had lost thousands of dollars and gone into debt. He wasn't responsible, but he felt bad that his face was being used to cheat people.

Cheryl and Marcus lived in the same part of Florida. They decided to meet to share their stories and raise awareness about how the scammers operated. Maybe they could help other women avoid being conned. Cheryl found that Marcus's photos really did him justice—he was a pleasant, attractive guy. He was equally drawn to Cheryl. They hit it off, and before long they were a couple.

A fake romance had led to a real one.

CRYPTIC MESSAGES

"Viktor" was an immigrant to the United Kingdom from Eastern Europe and was trying to build a good life in his new home. Viktor held down two jobs, often working an eighty-hour week. When he wasn't employed at a kitchen assistant in a hotel, he made pizzas at a local restaurant.

He was single, in his early thirties, and he dreamed of having a wife, a family and a house of his own. Over the past few years, he had managed to save £42,000—perhaps a quarter of what he needed to buy a modest house in the town.

He met a woman online, "Gemma." Her profile picture was attractive, and when they started chatting online, she had a personality to match. They seemed to hit it off. She took a lively interest in Viktor's ideas, interests and ambitions. He told her about his birthplace—a town in Moldova, not far from the Ukraine border. His parents were still there, but they were having a hard time: his father had suffered a stroke and needed a wheelchair. She was sympathetic.

Gemma asked what Viktor's long-term goals were. He said he wanted to find a partner, buy a house, start a family—and eventually bring his parents over to live with him, so they'd be well looked after. That might have scared off some women, but Gemma seemed to appreciate Viktor's concern for his parents. In fact, she had an idea of how she might help him.

Gemma told Viktor about her Uncle "Bryce." He was a financial genius. He worked at a big trading company, where he was a cryptocurrency expert, and he knew how to turn a small amount of money into a much larger one. She was sure he could help Viktor and wanted to put the two men in touch with each other.

Viktor agreed and the two men talked on the phone. Uncle Bryce said he didn't normally work with clients like Viktor, but since his niece was interested in a relationship with him, he would help him out. Uncle Bryce admired Viktor's work ethic but didn't think much of his investment skills. He told him he could earn a much better rate of return with cryptocurrencies.

Viktor was nervous, but Uncle Bryce assured him he could start small and see how things progressed. Uncle Bryce and his assistant set up an account for Viktor, and he transferred a small amount to it using cryptocurrency. Everything worked smoothly, so a few days later Viktor moved the bulk of his money over. But when he tried to move some back again, it didn't work. The money seemed to be gone.

He tried to contact Uncle Bryce but couldn't reach him or his assistant. Worse, Gemma's account had also vanished.

Viktor realized with horror that the whole thing was a scam. He had never met Gemma face to face. Was that beautiful online photo really her? Did Gemma even exist? With a terrible sinking feeling, Viktor knew the answer. Gemma was a fiction—a way of luring him in so the scammers could take his money.

He lost £42,000 through the scam. Because the money had been moved by a fast bank transfer to the fraudulent account, the bank was not responsible for the loss any more than if he'd taken out cash and given it to a swindler. The bank representatives suggested he take up the issue with the cryptocurrency exchange. The police were sympathetic, but they offered little hope of retrieving the lost money.

Viktor's dreams of a house, a family, a life in England with his parents were all gone or pushed years into the future. But unlike many scam victims, he decided to talk to the newspapers about his experience. At least he might help someone else avoid the hustle that had fooled him.

Viktor's story is an example of the classic "romance scam." The relationship remains online and progresses quickly. The wooer talks about marriage, even though the two haven't met face to face. This sort of behaviour might have been common for Renaissance royalty, but it's strange for regular people in the twenty-first century. Of course, there's always some plausible reason why the love interest can't meet the victim yet—the person might claim to be working overseas, on a ship or an oil rig or for a charity in Africa.

A subcategory of the scam is known by the cruel name "pig butchering." Prospective victims are "fattened up" over months in preparation for a big "butchering." They believe they are in a close, loving relationship. When the victim fully trusts the scammer, they are persuaded to invest in a phony cryptocurrency scheme—a convenient way for criminals to receive payments anonymously. Their losses can be enormous.

One Philadelphia woman was taken in by this scam. According to a story in the *Philadelphia Inquirer*, "Anita" worked in a good job at a big tech company.

She was divorced and wanted to find a new partner. She found "Yves" on the Hinge dating site. He claimed to be a French wine trader who now lived in the city. His photos looked good, he was healthy and fit, and he seemed charmed by Anita. In fact, Yves was so impressed by her that, shortly after they began corresponding, he removed his profile from the dating site where she'd met him. From now on, he said, he wanted to focus on his relationship with her.

Yves gave various excuses for not being able to meet Anita in person. As a wine trader, he was often travelling. Anita understood—she travelled quite a bit, too. But they made plans to meet.

Yves shared some of his dreams with Anita. His wine business was going well, but he wanted to be financially independent. He had had a lot of success trading cryptocurrency and he encouraged her to try it. She downloaded the app he recommended and invested a little money. In minutes, she saw it increase by 25 percent and she was able to withdraw the money and pocket the profits.

Anita made a few more investments, again seeing good returns, and exchanged loving messages with Yves. Unfortunately, their plans to meet kept falling through. He had to cancel the first date to attend an unexpected business meeting. They rescheduled, but he couldn't make it because he had to care for a sick uncle.

They had a few brief exchanges on video chat, but although his online profile was handsome, he was shy about showing his face on camera, so he showed her his dog instead.

Yves encouraged Anita to make bigger profits in the crypto market. He said he would lend her $150,000 if she could transfer her other assets to the account. She liquidated her company pension account and all her other investments and transferred the money to the cryptocurrency app. Yves's money showed up there, too. The account's value increased. A few weeks later, her money had doubled.

Well pleased with her investment, she decided to withdraw the cash, but the withdrawal wouldn't go through. She received a notification that she had to submit more money to pay the 10 percent "personal tax" on her profits.

This seemed weird. *What was this tax? Why wouldn't it be subtracted from the payout?* Alarm bells were going off, and when Anita did more digging, she discovered that the pictures of Yves had been lifted from the profile of a German fitness guru. Suddenly, she understood why she had never been able to meet her new boyfriend, and why he had been so camera-shy on the video calls. The app had been part of the scam, allowing the criminals to show her a huge return in her investment, while they took out her money and spent it.

HE'S SO UNUSUAL

Agnes Ottaway lived at Albion House, a boarding house at Port Moly-neux, a few miles from the southern tip of New Zealand's South Island. Her family owned the property, and, as a single woman in her early thirties, she lived with them there.

One day, in 1909, a new guest arrived. His name was Percival Red-wood, and he caught her eye immediately. He was sensitive, kind and charming.

The local women were charmed by this pipe-smoking bachelor. He was nearly fifty years old, but he was definitely a catch. He had good manners and a good job, by all accounts. He was a talented pianist. And it was said that his family had money, too. They were wealthy sheep farmers, and his uncle was an archbishop.

He was certainly generous with his spending. When one girl mentioned that she liked apples, he arranged for a box to be sent to her. He seemed delighted by many of the unmarried ladies, and they all wondered if he would propose marriage to one of them. He chose Agnes Ottaway.

Ottaway's mother received a letter from Redwood's mother. She said her son had £1,500 of his own, and she was going to give him the same amount again so the couple could buy a house. Another letter arrived at Albion House: it came from the Auckland Drainage Board. The secretary of the board was retiring, and they wanted to give the job to Redwood, at a salary of £7 a week—a healthy wage in those days.

Locals said it was just as well he had money of his own, because Percival Redwood was spending and borrowing heavily. He bought jewelry and tickets for a honeymoon trip to Melbourne. Redwood made other purchases around town on credit. He borrowed money from the local solicitor. He didn't have the money now, but it would all be sorted out soon, when his rich family arrived in town.

In April 1909, the wedding day arrived, but none of Redwood's relatives showed up. The locals who had counted on being repaid for purchases and loans were becoming concerned. Percival Redwood said he couldn't understand his family's absence. Then he realized what had happened: "My sister is getting married at the same time! My family must have gone to her wedding rather than mine." Redwood's brother was supposed to be best man, but Redwood asked a local man, an engineer, to stand in.

The couple had their wedding ceremony in the drawing room of Albion House. A letter had arrived in the meantime, and it confirmed Redwood's suspicions. His sister was to be married on the very same day. She and her husband would be leaving for America immediately, so the family felt they should attend that wedding. They promised to visit Redwood and his new wife in the next couple of weeks. Of course, that would delay the couple's departure for their honeymoon in Australia.

It was a strange set of circumstances, and it became stranger on the wedding night. Percival Redwood stayed up late playing piano. When he finally went to bed, he didn't join his wife, but instead shared a room with the best man. He didn't undress for bed, just pulled pajamas over his day clothes.

It got stranger still. Percival Redwood was actually a woman. Her name was Amy Bock, and she was one of the most notorious con artists in New Zealand history. She had been scamming people for decades.

She was born in Tasmania in 1859. Her mother had mental health issues and believed she was Lady Macbeth. The mother was sent to a mental asylum, where she later died.

Bock was a smart, popular girl, but she started on her criminal path very young and seemed to do it more for the challenge than the profit. As a girl, she purchased books on her father's account, then gave them away. Her father confronted her about the problem, but she kept on doing it.

As a young woman, she became a schoolteacher at a rural school. She faked illnesses to get days off. Teachers were paid by the number of students they taught, so she faked attendance records pretending to have more students. She racked up debts, then found excuses to avoid paying them back, including posing as her sister and claiming that Amy Bock was dead.

She constantly invented stories about the money she was about to receive so she could buy on credit. Bock often backed up her story with letters and documents she'd written herself. She worked in different households and found ways to get money from them.

Bock spent money as quickly as she stole it, but the items she bought were often strange. On one occasion, she visited all the undertakers in town and ordered coffins, which were all sent to the same family. She claimed she had inherited her mother's mental illness, but some skeptics thought the weird purchases were part of her cover and she was faking mental illness to get sympathy if she was caught for the more profitable crimes.

She moved to New Zealand and bought as much as she could on credit, until she was convicted of fraud. When she was released from a month in prison, she went back to buying on credit. She got another job as a teacher, scammed more money, and used it to buy boots for the students.

She had used many aliases: Amy Maud Bock, Amy Chanel, Amy Shannon, Amy Vallance, Amy Skevington. But of all her scams and false identities, her role as Mr. Percival Redwood was the most audacious. A few weeks before she arrived at Albion House, she had used the same identity at another lodging house in the city of Dunedin, New Zealand. When she arrived there, the owner's ten-year-old daughter opened the door and went running to her mother, saying, "There is a woman at the door dressed in man's clothes." But nobody listened to the kid, and they treated "Mr. Redwood" as the man he claimed to be. Percival Redwood told them his wallet, containing more than £300, had fallen into the sea, and he now needed to pay a diver £40 to retrieve it. A trusting local woman paid him the money. Redwood took it and left town.

But Bock had pushed her luck and her stories too far at Albion House. Some of the locals made inquiries to the police, who were familiar with Amy Bock and her MO. When one of the detectives, Henry Hunt, saw a photograph of "Percival Redwood," he recognized Bock immediately.

Bock was never a violent criminal. When Detective Hunt showed up at Albion House, she accepted her fate. She said, "If you have anything to do, do it as quietly as possible so as not to disturb the house."

The detective said, "You are Amy Bock. I arrest you on a charge of fraud."

She said, "I see you know all. Yes, I will tell you all about it and will plead guilty at the proper time."

The court case was a huge news story in New Zealand. An auction was held and members of the public bid for items from the scandalous wedding. Bock was sentenced to two years in prison, with hard labour, and declared a habitual criminal. When she was released, she had a few more minor run-ins with the law, but never went to prison again. She died in 1947, at the age of eighty-four, and this con artist remains an unusual New Zealand folk hero.

MILLIONAIRE ACTORS IN NEED

A woman in Spain joined an online Brad Pitt fan group in 2022. The actor paid a visit to the group's forum and struck up a conversation with her. Their correspondence blossomed into an online relationship. He sent her pictures of himself on the red carpet, with affectionate notes. He expressed his love for her and even talked about coming to Spain and making a movie with her.

In the meantime, though, he seemed to have a string of financial troubles and kept asking her for loans. She had sent a total of nearly $190,000 before she began to suspect that perhaps her Brad Pitt was an imposter.

It seems most actors are expensive to maintain. The hard thing for the scammer is coming up with a reason why a multimillionaire actor needs thousands of dollars from his fans.

A recently widowed woman in Texas, "Sabrina," received a private message from Leonardo DiCaprio. According to the *Daily Beast*, she didn't believe it was really the famous actor at first. She should have listened to her instincts, because, of course, she was being conned, but the fake DiCaprio love-bombed her with affectionate messages, and she started to enjoy the correspondence.

Their friendship grew. He talked about the places he was visiting and the films he was working on—the details were always correct.

As time went on, "Leo" told Sabrina he loved her. He also confided in her that he was a virtual slave of the Church of Scientology. All his money—hundreds of millions of dollars—was under their control, and all his financial people were church members, so he needed money to escape their grip. The only problem with this story was that DiCaprio has never been associated with Scientology.

Sabrina started sending money to some of his trusted associates. She contacted the FBI, but only to get their help in freeing DiCaprio. In total, she ended up being scammed out of more than $800,000 before she realized she was being conned.

But most fake Hollywood lovers are more vague about why a rich celebrity needs money.

In 2019, Hollywood actor "Jason Statham" convinced another British woman to send him a large sum. The exact amount in that case is unknown, but she said it was in the range of "hundreds of thousands of pounds." His reason was that he "needed help with some financial difficulties."

In 2022, a British woman paid $10,000 to "Nicholas Cage," who said he would be visiting her in the United Kingdom soon and asked her to keep the relationship "on the low down." He said he needed the money "for tax reasons."

In Kyoto, Japan, a successful manga artist named Chikae Ide was taken in by a fake Mark Ruffalo. The woman ended up falling in love with her correspondent and sent him half a million dollars over three years. He gave many reasons for needing money: "I missed my flight," "I'm having trouble cashing my performance fees," "I have injured my foot." Part of this long-running scam involved him sending Ide what was supposedly millions of dollars in cash coated in black dye. (We'll return to the "black money" scam later.)

Ide was an intelligent woman, and the fake actor's tricks and excuses were ridiculous, but the relationship met an emotional need, and it was only in hindsight that she realized how obvious the scam was. She turned her experiences into a graphic novel titled *Poison Love* to warn other women who might face a similar con.

KTLA-TV News reported on a Los Angeles woman, "Yona," who received regular messages from "Keanu Reeves," who repeatedly declared his love for her. After he had established her net worth, he asked her for $400,000 so he could make a documentary. Yona didn't send him any money—she knew it was a scam. Even so, she kept up the correspondence. She said: "It was very flattering."

CALL IT A DOWRY

In India, romance scams are often carried out on marriage websites rather than dating websites.

Around 2022, a woman we'll call "Anika" from Bangalore, in the southwestern region of India, was reviewing the eligible bachelors on a marriage website and found a promising profile. "Darsh" was a nice-looking man and a doctor. The two connected, and Anika found him charming.

They married. But soon after the wedding, he disappeared. Also missing were Anika's money and all her gold jewelry.

She contacted the police, who managed to track down Darsh. He had cars, gold, money and many mobile phones. It turned out that Darsh was a fraud who usually posed as a professional man: he had been a doctor, an engineer and a civil contractor. But his real profession was marrying middle-aged women, stealing from them, and running away.

Unhelpfully, police advised women to be more careful when using marriage websites.

A RELIABLE MAN

Another Indian man, Ramesh Kumar Swain, married even more women—twenty-seven at last count. All the women had good jobs, and were well-educated and highly intelligent. One was a chartered accountant, one was a doctor, two were lawyers, one at India's Supreme Court and one at the Delhi high court, and one was an assistant commandant of the border police.

Swain had no qualms about having several wives simultaneously. He kept three apartments in one city and would travel back and forth between women, each of whom imagined she was his one-and-only.

He claimed to be a professor who also held an important government job as deputy director-general in the health ministry. He used his job to explain his frequent absences, claiming that he had to travel across the country to carry out an urgent inspection of a medical college.

One of the wives, a teacher, finally figured out what was going on and reported him to police. A squad went to arrest him, tracking his rented car. They imagined that a man who had been so successful in attracting and defrauding women would be movie-star handsome. But when they stopped his vehicle and he emerged, they were surprised. He was in his mid-sixties and looked his age. He was a small man, only 5'2" tall, with a figure the *Hindustan Times* described as "portly." When the police interrogated him, they found him to be poorly educated. He had at best a high-school education, but had somehow managed to fool people into believing he was a professor.

How did he do it? It was partly the pressure Indian women feel to get married. In Indian society, even successful single women often feel stigmatized, and these women were looking for love and affection, which he seemed to provide.

One of the wives said he was a good listener and a gentleman. Ironically, a big part of his attraction for her was that he claimed he had never been married before. She wasn't looking for a genius or a movie star—she wanted someone unpretentious and reliable, and that was what he seemed to be.

But as soon as he tied the knot, he would start tapping his wife's income to find the next wife, robbing Petra to pay Paula.

He seems to have viewed women only as a resource. When police looked at his mobile phone, they found his "wives" were listed by city rather than name: "wife Bangalore," "wife Guwahati," "wife Bhilai." And others were identified by their job: "wife teacher," "wife doctor." Future prospects were labelled in a similar way: "to be wife Dhenkanal," "to be wife Jagatsinghpur." It seemed as if he couldn't bother to keep track of their given names.

His marriage scams were not his only crime. He had used more than one hundred forged credit cards to defraud banks and also ran a scheme where he charged people to get their children non-existent places in medical programs.

As of this writing, he is in prison awaiting trial on a range of serious charges.

CHAPTER 18
TOO GOOD TO BE FALSE?

O f all the cons ever, there must be one that is the biggest and most audacious. Some famous scams have made many "Top 10" lists, but many are not all they seem.

What are the ultimate cons ... and did they really happen?

COUNT YOUR MONEY

"Count" Victor Lustig was one of the most devious con men in American history, and many people consider him a supervillain among con artists.

The con starts with his identity. He wasn't really a count, and his real name probably wasn't Lustig. In fact, his background is a mystery, but he was certainly smart and slippery.

He was a suave figure who spoke five languages and travelled in a chauffeured limousine. He was said to be skilled in cheating women out of their money using romance scams—then known as "the marriage racket."

Lustig sometimes operated from Europe, posing under various false identities. He seems to have had success making fraudulent business deals with wealthy American travellers. The suckers' resistance was lower when they were dealing with a fellow American in a foreign country.

Despite his cultivated image, he was a dangerous man, suspected of involvement in some prominent killings. Although he was often arrested, he rarely spent long in jail.

But "Count" Lustig made most of his money from—literally—making money. The phony kind. He really put the "count" in "counterfeiting."

In his early years, one of Lustig's favourite cons was known as the "Green Goods" swindle. That meant selling counterfeit money.

In one clever version of the scam, buyers were offered notes of very high quality, and the mark was shown a suitcase filled with bundles of money. They might pay $600 for a case containing $10,000 in "green goods."

The reason the counterfeit money looked so good was that it wasn't counterfeit. The perfect bills were merely real currency, and the money in the case consisted of bundles of green paper sandwiched between two real bills. The buyer was usually an out-of-towner who had been lured to the city for the swindle. After he had paid real cash for the suitcase, the cases were switched, and the sucker took the train home holding a suitcase full of newspaper. When victims have been conned in this way, they are not likely to complain to the police. Even if they did, the con man couldn't be accused of counterfeiting, because all the money involved was genuine.

Perhaps it was this scam that made Lustig interested in producing counterfeit bills that really were as good as the "fake counterfeit" (i.e., real) bills he used in his cons.

In the 1920s, he teamed up with William Watts, a New Jersey pharmacist. Watts did photoengraving on the side and used his talents and his knowledge of chemicals and photography to produce flawless fake bottle labels and government revenue stamps—all very useful for bootleggers.

Lustig persuaded Watts to try his hand at high-grade counterfeit currency. Watts rose to the challenge, and while he steadily refined his technique, Lustig quietly built a network of hundreds of criminals who could pass the fake money and exchange it for the real thing. Each "passer" was a self-employed crook: they bought the fake bills for 20 percent of their face value, then went out to spend it.

As a counterfeiter, Lustig was behind cons every day, always looking for new ways to convert counterfeit bills to the real stuff.

In the early '30s, one group of big spenders—probably working for Lustig—turned up at a Saratoga, New York, racetrack and started betting on favourites. It was a scam: they were spending fake bills and (if they won) getting back real ones. The bookmakers who accepted the bets were ruined.

Lustig's group passed millions of dollars in counterfeit currency, and as their skills improved, it's reported they were producing as much as three-quarters of the counterfeit bills in circulation. The forger Watts was a quiet and reclusive figure, but he had become one of the most skilled counterfeiters in the country.

When the Secret Service examined his fake money in 1933, they were astonished at its quality. The printing was perfect to the naked eye and just as perfect under a magnifying glass. The Watts-Lustig notes were described as "dangerously good." The only sign that this was not real money was the paper—it lacked the tiny red-and-green threads that run through genuine currency. But even this had been cleverly simulated by printing a pattern of tiny red-and-green lines. Only a skilled expert would spot these bills as phony. And by the following year, Lustig and his team had found a way to add real silk threads to their currency. "Lustig money" became a serious threat to the US economy.

Lustig was careful to stay at arm's length from the counterfeit operation that became his biggest source of income. He never carried counterfeit money, and most of his agents were "small fish" who didn't meet him in person. Many of the passers were arrested, but they were quickly replaced.

But the more successful Lustig became, the more the authorities wanted to bring him in. Eventually they caught up with him. In 1935, both he and Watts were imprisoned. The authorities also seized the printing plates used in his operation.

Over the years, Lustig was known to have used at least sixty-four different names, including Robert V. Miller, Bert Lausting, Robert Lamar, Charles Gromer, Edward Baker, George Shobel . . . the list goes on. One newspaper from the day quipped that prison might be a pleasant break for the con artist—he would only have to remember his convict number.

Lustig was sentenced to twenty years in Alcatraz and he was still a convict when he died twelve years later.

THE RUMANIAN BOX

One of Lustig's favourite cons in the 1920s and '30s was selling a machine known as "the Rumanian box," which was supposed to print perfect counterfeit bills.

Using various aliases, he sold these machines to people who wanted to break into the counterfeiting racket.

The device was a large box with some kind of mechanism inside and was supposed to use a chemical process to copy bills. Just insert your blank paper, and after the machine had run for a while, a perfect $100 bill emerged at the other end. When the bill was ready, Lustig invited his client to take the money to the bank and deposit it. The teller would invariably examine the money carefully, then accept it as the real thing.

That's because the money *was* the real thing. His mysterious machine was an updated version of the "Green Goods" swindle, which had become overworked by the 1920s.

Lustig advised his victims that the machine worked very slowly—it took hours to make each bill. It didn't matter. His customers saw the opportunities in a machine that spit out unlimited amounts of cash, even if it was slow. They paid his high asking price.

Customers might have paid hundreds for a suitcase of counterfeit money, but they paid tens of thousands for the fake counterfeiting machine.

Once Lustig had his money, he disappeared. The machine had been pre-loaded with a real bill or two, but it wouldn't produce any more, and by the time the victim realized they'd been swindled, Lustig was long gone. As with the "Green Goods" swindle, most people were reluctant to go to the police with the complaint that their counterfeiting machine didn't work as promised.

However, it's said that in Texas, one of Lustig's customers did complain, and the con man was caught and jailed by a local sheriff, one Que R. Miller from Foard County. From his cell, Lustig used all his smooth-talking powers on his captor and persuaded him that he should also buy one of the money-making machines. Miller was excited by the idea. The crooked sheriff released Lustig and used embezzled money to buy a machine—perhaps figuring he could easily print out the money and repay it before its absence was noticed.

The sheriff's machine didn't work any better than those sold to the earlier victims, and he caught up with Lustig to settle the score. Lustig persuaded the sheriff that he had used the machine incorrectly and talked him into paying more money for an attachment that would improve the process.

Que R. Miller later became involved in distributing $100 bills for Lustig. In 1936, in what feels like a Hollywood cliché, the corrupt southern sheriff was convicted of passing fake banknotes and sentenced to ten years in the Atlanta Penitentiary, where we're guessing he uttered futile curses against the criminal who had outsmarted him. "Dagnabbit! I'll get that son of a gun!"

EIFFEL FOR IT

The most famous legend about Lustig was that time he sold the Eiffel Tower for scrap.

Twice.

The story goes that an ambitious French businessman named André Poisson had moved to Paris with dreams of joining the business elite, but climbing the social ladder was harder than he expected. He had plenty of money, but the snooty Parisians looked down their noses at "provincials." It didn't help that his business was an unglamorous one—scrap metal.

One day in 1925, an interesting opportunity fell into his lap. Poisson was selected as one of a small group of dealers to be part of a confidential meeting. A few days later, he walked into the Hotel de Crillon, one of the city's more luxurious hotels. He and the other guests were treated to an excellent meal accompanied by fine wine. They wondered what this meeting was all about.

Finally, their host identified himself. "I am Victor Lustig, the deputy director-general for the Ministry of Post and Telegraph." Lustig needed his guests to help him solve a problem.

The problem was the Eiffel Tower. It had been built for the 1889 World's Fair. The tower was then the tallest human-made structure in the world, but it was never meant to be permanent. The original specifications were for a tower that was easy to dismantle, and the Eiffel Tower had been scheduled to come down years earlier, back in 1909. But it remained standing, and now Paris was stuck with the expense of maintaining and painting this enormous structure.

All the people at the table were familiar with the debate about the tower. Although it was a landmark, it was a divisive one. Some locals loved it, but many artists, architects and intellectuals hated the way this mass of metal girders dominated the Paris skyline, giving the city an industrial feel. Newspaper articles discussed the problem. People were talking seriously about tearing it down.

So when the Eiffel Tower was mentioned in the meeting, the metal dealers finally knew the reason they had been called together that day. The government wanted to demolish the Eiffel Tower and sell it for scrap.

The deputy director-general explained that the plan was strictly confidential. The bidding process needed to be quick and discreet to avoid a public outcry.

Lustig took the VIPs to inspect the tower. Poisson enjoyed being part of this privileged group. He watched as Lustig flashed his ID, allowing the scrap metal dealers to cut through the crowds. Lustig pointed out the team of workers who were scraping the rust and the peeling paint—in 1925 the tower was a sickly yellow-brown. He explained that the workers were part of the demolition team who would soon be dismantling the tower. Poisson looked at it all in wonder and thought of the money he would make from the steel all around him—all seven thousand tons of it.

Poisson was excited. Disposing of a structure of this size seemed like an incredible opportunity. The government just wanted to be rid of the metal, so this steel was a steal. If he could win this job, he would not only make a fortune, he would also have something to brag about to the Parisian elite. "Removing the old Eiffel Tower? Yes, I helped with that." It was the kind of deal that made a person famous. It was the kind of deal that opened doors.

But then the doubts set in. Did Poisson, a businessman from the provinces, really have a shot at the contract? What were the chances that a Parisian official would give the steel to him? The bureaucrat had probably already chosen some old schoolfriend as a buyer. Poisson was a rank outsider. If he wanted a chance of winning this deal, he couldn't rely on a fair contest—he had to use some underhanded methods.

When the group presentation was over, Poisson arranged a one-on-one meeting with the deputy director-general and pumped him for information. The official talked about the difficulties of the job—it was too much work for too little pay. Poisson thought he could see what the bureaucrat was hinting at. He was asking for a bribe. That wasn't unusual in turn-of-the-century Paris. Poisson knew the ways of the big city now and he was ready to play ball. He offered Lustig 20,000 francs for the scrap metal and another 50,000 francs as a bribe. In modern money, it was the equivalent of about a million dollars. Poisson knew the bribe would cut into his profits, but it was worth it to get this prestigious deal.

The deputy director-general was receptive to the offer. He made it clear that, if Poisson could get the payment to him, the Eiffel Tower contract was his.

Poisson made the payment to Lustig and went home satisfied. He had outplayed the Paris industrialists at their own corrupt games. Now he just had to wait for the money to come rolling in.

But no contract came through.

Poisson tried to follow up, but he discovered that Lustig had left town just hours after being paid. He also discovered that nobody in the government knew this man Lustig, who had claimed to be deputy director-general. Moreover, although there had been well-publicized problems with the Eiffel Tower, other officials claimed there was no plan to tear it down. In fact, the workers Poisson had seen scraping at the rust were there to repaint the tower.

Poisson realized he'd been conned. He considered going to the police, but then he had second thoughts. What would he say? That he'd been tricked into buying the Eiffel Tower? That the official he had tried to bribe was a swindler? The police would laugh at him, and so would the society elites Poisson had tried so hard to impress. No, the story had to stay buried. Poisson swallowed his pride and his enormous losses and kept quiet about the whole thing.

I FELL FOR IT ONCE, EIFFEL FOR IT TWICE

It's said that Lustig fled Paris as soon as he had received Poisson's money. He travelled to Austria and waited there, checking the newspapers every day for an article about his Eiffel Tower con. But no news item appeared. Lustig had an idea of what had happened: he guessed that André Poisson had been too embarrassed to report the scam.

Now Lustig had a new idea. Since he had managed to get away with the scam, he could freely repeat it. A few months later, he returned to Paris, sent out a new set of invitations to a new group of scrap-metal merchants, and got a second payout.

Unfortunately, his second victim complained to the police, and Lustig was forced to flee to the United States.

IS THE FAKERY REALLY TRUE?

There's no question that Victor Lustig was a major con man and counterfeiter. In the 1930s, he was a criminal celebrity whose counterfeiting ring was so successful it actually shook confidence in the American dollar—a shadowy figure who evaded the law with his intelligence and cunning. Exaggerated stories tend to accumulate around such figures.

The money-making machine was real. At least one victim went to the police in New York in the 1920s, after losing $43,000 to the swindle.

But the tale of Lustig selling the Eiffel Tower for scrap? It would be an astonishing con if it were true, but we have our doubts. The story doesn't seem to make its first appearance until 1961, in a book titled *The Man Who Sold the Eiffel Tower* by James F. Johnson, "as told to" Floyd Miller.

According to the book's foreword, it is the memoir of a former Secret Service agent who spent years tracking Lustig, talked with him at length, then spent more years verifying the extraordinary tales he had heard.

Despite the agent's claimed efforts, some details of this story are clearly wrong. For example, Lustig was said to have been assisted in Paris by another con artist, an American named "Dapper Dan" Collins, under the alias Monsieur Dante.

Collins was a real associate of Lustig, but he went by "Dapper Don," not "Dapper Dan." It seems a small mistake, but "Dapper Don" Collins was a notorious criminal in his day and his name should have been well-known to police. We also wonder why Lustig scammed only one scrap-metal dealer from his meetings, when he could have targeted each of them simultaneously.

The second victim Eiffel Tower buyer is supposed to have complained to the police. If the report happened, the astonishing story didn't seem to reach the newspapers of the day. In fact, no reports of this con emerged until the book came out, nearly forty years after Lustig died.

The writer, Floyd Miller, was mostly an author of hard-boiled crime novels. His book about the Eiffel Tower scam was written in a novelistic style, with detailed scenes and conversations that are clearly imagined. The book was very successful, and the claim that Lustig "sold the Eiffel Tower twice" has become one of the best-known facts about him, but there are many reasons to doubt it.

Con artists create aliases and false stories. Is this a case where a writer has done the same?

PSST! WANNA BUY A BRIDGE?

There's a famous line used to address a gullible individual: "If you believe that, I have a bridge to sell you." Selling the bridge is said to have its origins in one of the grandest and most famous cons of all time, in which audacious New York criminals "sold" the Brooklyn Bridge to tourists and recent immigrants.

The Brooklyn Bridge is a suspension bridge over the East River connecting Manhattan to Brooklyn. When it opened in 1883, it was one of the wonders of the modern world. In those days, New York had a population of just over a million. There was not yet an Empire State Building or Chrysler Building. Tourists made a point of visiting the bridge. But did anyone really try to buy it?

The con man most associated with selling the bridge to naive visitors is George C. Parker, who is said to have sold the bridge twice a week to a parade of gullible suckers. Some writers have claimed that it was such a common and successful scam that the authorities at Ellis Island had to hand out pamphlets advising newcomers that major New York structures were not for sale.

The buyers, who were mostly recent immigrants to the United States, were told that they could make an income by setting up toll booths and collecting money from people who wanted to cross. Of course, once they tried to make some money from their purchase and set up their own toll booths, the police arrested them.

When he wasn't selling the Brooklyn Bridge, Parker sold other New York real estate.

He is also said to have sold Grant's Tomb (claiming to be a descendant of Grant), the Statue of Liberty and the Metropolitan Museum of Art.

Others who sold the bridge include Joseph "Yellow Kid" Weil, Reed C. Waddell and the Gondorf Brothers, Charles and Fred. It was said that the Gondorf brothers timed their sales to avoid police patrols. Once the officers were out of sight, they hung up a "For Sale" sign and raked in the cash.

Their victims were said to be rich-but-dumb "Westerners" or immigrants fresh off the boat who took the "land of opportunity" line a little too literally.

Tales of the bridge scam are well-known and widely repeated, but so are many urban legends. Was this scam real? Considering how many con artists are supposed to have sold the bridge, it's surprising that there don't seem to be any contemporary news reports of anyone buying it.

All the con artists associated with selling the bridge are real people, but none were ever prosecuted for selling the Brooklyn bridge, and most were specialists in more ordinary and more profitable scams.

As for the toll booths that naive buyers tried to set up on the famous bridge: if it happened, the newspapers took very little interest in it, which is surprising considering what a newsworthy story it would have been. Most reports about the scam were written many years later, in the 1940s.

The popularity of the tale may reflect the opinions New Yorkers had about the new immigrants who were flooding into the city.

The earliest news story we could find about an actual Brooklyn bridge con comes from 1928, when the *Brooklyn Daily Eagle* reported the arrest of a sixty-eight-year-old man then going under the name of William McCloundy. He went by many other aliases, too, including "IOU"

O'Brien, "Warden" James Kennedy and "Captain" George C. Parker, the fake captain of an ocean liner.

He was later booked under the name George Parker, so that's the name we'll use.

Parker had been pulled in after trying to sell some lots in Brooklyn to a man named Max Schmeyer, lots that Parker didn't own. The police caught up with Parker as he was measuring a backyard with a tape measure. With refreshing candor, Parker said that if the police hadn't interrupted his work, he would have been able to sell the property for $17,000. But the con man was wanted for a different, and rather petty crime—he had tricked a woman out of $150 after giving her a worthless cheque.

Once he was in custody, Parker talked very freely to the police, and he seems to have spent some time explaining his past accomplishments to the amazed officers, who then shared the information with the press.

He claimed that, back in 1885 (other reports said 1901), he met a wealthy businessman from the West. He posed as a big businessman himself and was so successful in charming him that he was able to sell him the Brooklyn Bridge for $50,000. Parker said he was later caught and convicted for the crime and spent more than two years in Sing Sing.

When he came out of prison, Parker claimed, he sold other New York real estate, again focusing on rich visitors from the American West. City Hall Park seemed a prime location, so in 1911, Parker said he divided it into imaginary lots and sold them for a total of $25,000. He said that one group of buyers was ready to start digging a foundation for their new building when Mayor Seth Low put a stop to it. The police were sent looking for Parker but were unable to find him.

Parker claimed he committed other crimes, too, often against figures connected to law enforcement. He said he tricked the widow of a former police inspector out of a $5,000 ring, which he said he was taking for repair.

Jails didn't hold this criminal genius for long. He boasted of one prison escape where he used a pointed stick to remove a large stone from the prison wall, then climbed through the opening and ran to freedom. On New Year's Eve, he was arrested and taken to jail by a new sheriff. The sheriff left his fur coat and hat in the office. Parker put them on, pulled the collar around his neck, and walked out, waving greetings to the officers, who wished the sheriff "Happy New Year."

His criminal claims were related to events in the late 1800s. Strangely, none of the claims seemed to be on his official police record, which listed small-time forgery, impersonating a police officer and passing dud cheques.

Parker was convicted for passing a worthless $150 cheque. It was a far cry from selling the Brooklyn Bridge for $50,000. As a multiple offender, he was given a life sentence. It's said that he was a popular figure in Sing Sing for the stories he told.

But are the old con man's stories true? If you believe they are, then I have a bridge to sell you.

THE REAL BROOKLYN BRIDGE CON

Most people have heard the questionable stories about people who tried to sell the Brooklyn Bridge, but a much more expensive, dangerous and undoubtedly real con was involved in its construction, and it affects the bridge to this day.

The bridge's two huge suspension towers and thick cables support a span more than a quarter of a mile long. The main span of the bridge was so high that the masts of ships could pass under it with ease.

The bridge's designer, John A. Roebling, was an enthusiastic proponent of using cable—he called it "metal rope"—to build a suspension bridge. It was a novel method in those days—earlier suspension bridges had been held up by chains, but steel cables were much lighter and less expensive. The new bridge would require enormous quantities of steel cable, and it had to be strong enough to support the structure's colossal weight.

Several companies bid on the contract to supply the cable. The lowest bid came from a company owned by Joseph Lloyd Haigh, who had connections to one of the bridge trustees. Roebling didn't like Haigh—he seemed shifty—but nobody could beat his price, and Haigh got the contract.

Roebling's instincts were accurate. Haigh was a con artist through and through, and while he made shady deals for the bridge cable, he also juggled a series of romantic scandals that would have shocked his business partners. Haigh was a married man, but he had sent his wife to live in the country with the kids—he claimed it was for the sake of her health—then pretended he was a New York bachelor and attended a local church and Sunday School, where he paid special attention to the women. The church ladies considered him a "catch," and he charmed an attractive eighteen-year-old. The couple even set a wedding day. But the bride's brother-in-law and father learned that Haigh was already married. They were scandalized and confronted him at gunpoint.

Haigh weaseled out of it: "It is all a mistake, I assure you. I have a married cousin who has the same name as my own. You have confused me with him."

The father put his gun away and vowed he would get to the bottom of the matter. He later discovered that there had been no mistake. There was no cousin! The man who wanted to marry his daughter was the same man who had a wife in the country. The wedding plans were cancelled, but by then, Haigh had escaped with his life.

After a period of lying low, Haigh went back to being a bachelor again. He was renting a room in the Lower East Side of Manhattan, where the landlord's daughter caught his eye. He started romancing her. Fortunately for her, another tenant knew about Haigh's recent history and warned the daughter and her parents, and that relationship ended, too.

Not to be deterred, Haigh began yet another relationship with a young woman. He had divorced his first wife by then—at least, that's what he told his new girlfriend—and the two were married. According to a newspaper report, the first wife watched from a window as the happy couple emerged from the church.

He continued claiming to be a bachelor and married a third time. By then, he had two children by his first wife and several more by the second. One of his friends asked Haigh why he behaved this way. He said, "I do not know, I am sure, but I believe that Satan must have captured me."

This, then, was the man who was entrusted with producing high-quality steel cables to support the world's largest suspension bridge. Providing a good product was not high on his list of priorities. His only goal was to make as much money from the deal as possible.

Haigh's company produced the wire and had it spun into cables. The cables were then tested. The cable had been cheaply made from the wrong kind of steel, and most samples failed the tests. The cable that didn't meet the specifications was stored in a large shed, while the few batches of good wire were taken by truck to the bridge yard, where they were used in the construction.

It was a costly, inefficient process as far as Haigh was concerned. But he found a simple way to increase sales. After each coil of cable was accepted and signed off, Haigh's people loaded it onto their truck, then swung around to the shed and swapped it with the bad stuff.

The defective cables were used on the bridge. One cable snapped, and debris tumbled into the river. Two men were killed in the accident, and public confidence in the bridge was shaken. Bridge designer John A. Roebling couldn't explain it. Then an administrator noticed discrepancies in the amount of rejected cable being stored. The engineers realized they had been duped and given inferior cable. Unfortunately, large amounts of Haigh's work had already been strung across the river and would be very difficult to replace.

Haigh's cut-rate cables had earned him $300,000 in profits, but the cables only had half the strength specified. Fortunately, Roebling had gone out of his way to make sure that the bridge wouldn't be toppled in a windstorm. He had over-engineered it, making it far stronger than was necessary. Even with the inferior cable, the bridge was safe, and it was made even safer with a minor redesign to add more cables and more strength. But Haigh's low-quality material remains in the bridge to this day.

Exposing Haigh's fraud would have been terrible publicity for the bridge, so the builders hushed it up for a while. Haigh was not criminally charged. He wasn't even fired from his job. Instead, he was required to pay for higher-quality wire, which was produced by Roebling's own company.

The bridge opened with a publicity stunt. The circus showman P.T. Barnum marched twenty-one elephants and seventeen camels across, including his most famous elephant, the enormous Jumbo. Any lingering doubts the public might have about the strength of the bridge were dispelled.

Haigh had—mostly—escaped scot-free with a $300,000 swindle. He should have stopped there, but he seems to have approached his commercial affairs the same way he approached his love affairs: he couldn't resist moving on to the next scam. It proved to be his undoing.

In 1880, about three years after the business with the faulty cable, Haigh was caught forging a bank draft. Investigators discovered that he had been doing this for a while, using various forged documents to cheat the banks out of tens of thousands of dollars. Most of the losses came from a New York institution named the Grocers Bank, which went out of business because of the crime.

Haigh was caught and charged with forgery. He was sentenced to four years' hard labour at Sing Sing. Soon after his release, he was in trouble again, but the scale of his crimes was pitiful. Ironically, after serving time for defrauding the Grocers Bank, he was arrested for stealing an 8-cent loaf of bread from a New York grocer.

So, if anyone does offer to sell you the Brooklyn Bridge, ask them to replace the cables first.

WOULD YOU LIKE IT WRAPPED?

One of Ireland's most notorious con artists was Michael Dennis Corrigan.

He came from County Cork in Ireland, but he operated in London, England, in the 1930s and '40s, speaking in an upper-class English accent and walking with what people described as a "military bearing."

His manner impressed people, and he managed to carry off some audacious scams. It's said he sold London Bridge to American tourists on several occasions (What were they planning to do with it?). He is also said to have sold the Tower of London (which holds the Crown Jewels).

One of his favourite scams was to persuade people to put down a deposit on an impressive home he was selling in the heart of London. In fact, the huge house, at 145 Piccadilly, was a royal residence and had been the childhood home of Queen Elizabeth II.

Were these cons real? He claimed they were, but he claimed a lot of things. That's what con artists do. It is often hard to separate fact from fiction.

Corrigan likely made most of his money from less exciting business cons. Posing as a representative of Mexico, he is said to have sold imaginary oil concessions.

Corrigan's undoing was a deal he made to sell arms to the government of China. He shipped hundreds of crates, and the documentation that went with the shipment said the crates contained machine tools valued at £9,000. The actual content was doubly fraudulent. It was not the weapons the Chinese were expecting, but worthless junk—old car tires and stones from a demolished church.

However, the crates were intercepted and opened by the authorities before they ever reached China.

Corrigan had defrauded the Chinese, but the Chinese embassy, probably wanting to avoid a diplomatic incident, denied that it had been trying to buy weapons, so Corrigan was safe from them.

However, the police had another way to get him. The documents said the shipment was worth £9,000, but it was clearly worthless, so they charged him with making a false declaration on the customs form. It was just the beginning of a string of charges against the con artist. A French arms dealer said Corrigan had paid him not to be a witness at the trial. More charges followed, and Corrigan, who was now nearly sixty, knew he was likely to spend the rest of his life in prison. He hanged himself in his cell.

THE CACIQUE OF POYAIS

Gregor MacGregor is Scotland's most famous con artist, and he might just take the prize for the biggest con of all time. In this case, there is no doubt that it happened for real.

He didn't persuade people to buy a bridge or a building. He sold them an entire fictional country.

MacGregor was born into a family that was comfortably off, and they had the money to give him a good education. After university in Edinburgh, he joined the British Army as an officer. The way you did that in the 1800s was to buy a commission, and MacGregor's family did that for Gregor. At the age of sixteen, he found himself a smartly dressed ensign in an English infantry regiment.

MacGregor's military career started well enough. He was quickly promoted to lieutenant. He also attracted the attention of a woman named Maria Bowater, whom he married when he was eighteen. Her father was an admiral, and her well-connected family also included two generals, a member of parliament and plenty of money. It would normally have taken seven years for MacGregor to get his next promotion, but he could now afford to buy his way up the ranks. He purchased himself the rank of captain.

MacGregor had joined the 57th Regiment of Foot (the term for an infantry regiment in those days), but he was more interested in ranks, uniforms and medals than in military drills. He soon got tired of the British Army and quit, getting a refund on the money he paid for the rank upgrades. He was lucky in his timing. Soon afterwards, the 57th Regiment of Foot were sent to fight Napoleon and became famous for holding their ground in a battle where nearly 60 percent of the officers were killed.

When MacGregor's wealthy wife unexpectedly died, he found himself strapped for cash again. He enjoyed the high life and looked for other ways to climb further up the social ranks. Around that time, many of Spain's American colonies were rebelling again their rulers, and Britain was supportive of the rebels. MacGregor thought that joining the fight might be a smart move.

MacGregor offered his services to the Spanish rebels, dropping the name of his former regiment—"Yes, I was an officer in the 57th Foot"—and letting them assume that he was one of the heroic survivors of their famous battle.

The rebels were delighted to accept him into their ranks and made MacGregor a colonel, putting him in charge of a cavalry regiment. His performance was a mixed bag—some officers thought he was a phony—but he looked good and had some military successes. On the basis of those successes, he was soon promoted to the rank of general.

One of his missions involved capturing Florida, which was still a Spanish colony. He rounded up mercenaries in the United States and managed to capture Amelia Island, where he declared a new Republic of the Floridas. He didn't get much support from the islanders, and when he told his troops they weren't allowed to loot local properties, he didn't get much support from his army either. He didn't have enough troops or weapons to invade the mainland of Florida, and he eventually had to leave the island.

After a few other military failures, MacGregor found himself at the Mosquito Coast. The area runs along the Caribbean coast of Nicaragua and Honduras, and was named not for the biting insect (although there were plenty of those), but for the Miskito people, who were descendants of Indigenous people and Africans who had been enslaved, then shipwrecked. The Miskito people had been an egalitarian society, but the British had gone out of their way to recognize them as a kingdom and to declare some individuals royalty. If the Miskito were a kingdom, the British could establish treaties and alliances with the locals for their "protection." It was a cynical move that put the British in charge and blocked Spain from colonizing the area.

MacGregor spent some time with George Frederic Augustus I, who was the nominal king of the Miskito. MacGregor made a deal with the king, giving him rum and jewelry in exchange for around eight million acres of land. The king had several rivals more powerful than he was, and it may have seemed a good move to befriend someone who was supposed to be a great military figure.

All around him, MacGregor saw South American soldiers declaring new republics and setting themselves up as heroic rulers, giving their followers newly invented honours and titles. Now that he owned an area of land the size of a small country, why shouldn't he do the same?

MacGregor returned to England and began a huge confidence trick. He named his land Poyais and claimed that the Miskito king had made him the prince, or "Cacique," of it.

The British public were impressed by MacGregor, the Cacique of Poyais. He became a popular figure in London society. MacGregor described the land in glowing terms. It was a thriving society with a democratic government, aristocrats and a flag. (The flag was a green cross, which MacGregor had previously used for his short-lived Republic of the Floridas.) All it needed was colonists and investors, and naturally, they should be British.

MacGregor published a book, *A Sketch of the Mosquito Shore*, describing his kingdom. It sounded like a paradise on Earth. The soil was unbelievably fertile. The climate was healthy and well-suited to Europeans. Farmers could grow sugar, tobacco or corn. The kingdom's capital, St. Joseph, was a beautiful coastal town with a population of twenty thousand people who loved Britain and its culture. The city's wide streets were lined with mansions and stone buildings with tall columns, including a bank, an opera house and a theatre. He described the cathedral, with its domed roof. Then there were the rivers, where, it was said, people sometimes found nuggets of gold.

The book's author was supposedly one Thomas Strangeways, captain in the First Native Poyer Regiment. Actually, MacGregor had written it himself, and it was a work of fiction from start to finish. Still, the "Little Britain" he presented was appealing. MacGregor began selling land in his kingdom. People could buy an acre for 2 shillings and threepence—the equivalent of around $200 today. At those prices, you didn't need to be an aristocrat to own land. Buyers snapped up the offering.

MacGregor increased the price of the land, then he increased it again. Even at 4 shillings per acre, the land sold well.

The land sales alone would have been enough to make MacGregor enormously wealthy, but he wanted profits on a quicker timeline. He announced a sale of Poyaisian government bonds. A £100 bond offered an interest rate of 6 percent, which was twice what British government bonds paid. The bonds were also sold at a discount, and investors could buy with only 15 percent down, paying the remainder the following year. With everything guaranteed by the gold-rich (albeit imaginary) government of Poyais, it seemed like a fine investment.

MacGregor's kingdom also needed British settlers. They had to be "industrious and honest, none others shall be admitted among us." The search for colonists helped establish the reality of the country in the public imagination.

For his settlers, MacGregor went to the land of his forefathers—Scotland. It was part of the United Kingdom by now, but when Scotland was an independent country, it had tried to occupy parts of Central and South America. In the late 1600s, Scotland had launched the Darien Scheme, which involved establishing a colony called New Caledonia in what is now Panama. More than two thousand Scottish farmers tried to build a life there. The colony failed badly, and most inhabitants died from malaria and other diseases. Scotland's South American colony was a disaster and a national humiliation. MacGregor claimed that he was descended from one of those brave Scottish settlers. But now, under his leadership, Scotland had a chance to do things properly.

Several hundred Scottish settlers signed up, including farmers, soldiers and skilled craft workers. They bought land and exchanged their British currency for "Poyais dollars," thoughtfully printed by

MacGregor. The "Cacique of Poyais" was familiar with the idea of buying military ranks, and he sold commissions in the Poyaisian army to the sons of colonists. A cobbler was given the title Official Shoemaker in Poyais.

When the colonists arrived at the Mosquito Coast, they found a land that looked beautiful from a distance, but became steadily worse as they approached. It was lush and green, but there was no opera house, no cathedral, no streets and no town. The soil was sandy, and the water was salty. They faced torrential rains and landslides, as well as mosquitoes and disease. The Official Shoemaker shot himself. It was like a replay of the terrible Darien Scheme.

The colonists met the king. He told them there was no such kingdom as Poyais, and that he had taken back the land he gave to MacGregor. They could stay if they wished, as his subjects, or leave. Most chose to leave. Out of around 250 settlers, only fifty had survived.

Investors were also hit hard. News that the country of Poyais was imaginary played a part in a huge stock market crash in 1825. Seventy banks failed, and the Bank of England was saved only by loans of gold and silver from its French counterpart.

MacGregor was not prosecuted in Britain. Sensing trouble, he had quietly left England while the surviving settlers were on their way back to England, and he relocated to France. There, he tried to sell the French on the same scam and even rounded up some settlers, but before they could leave, they were stopped by the authorities. MacGregor was tried for fraud, but the prosecution had a hard time getting hold of the papers they needed as evidence. He was found not guilty.

MacGregor made a few more attempts to keep his Poyais scam going, but without much success. He spent the last years of his life in Venezuela, where people still believed he was a great military leader.

MacGregor carried out what might be the biggest and most audacious con in history and somehow managed to escape any punishment.

CHAPTER 19
THE IMPOSTERS

W e're all intrigued by imposters. They move among us like secret agents, masters of disguise, slipping on new identities as smoothly as ordinary people might change a coat.

At least, that's the theory. It doesn't always work in practice.

IT TOLLS FOR THEE

Tom Bell was born in the early 1700s. He came from a good family. His father was a shipowner, and Tom, who was a quick learner, received an excellent education, learning both Latin and Greek. After school, he attended Harvard. But he couldn't stay out of trouble. He stole letters and told lies. Finally, he was kicked out of Harvard for stealing another student's chocolate cake.

Despite his criminal nature, he had the background and education to pass himself off as a gentleman, and that's what he did, travelling from one city to another under a series of false identities.

In 1739, Benjamin Franklin was visited by a young schoolmaster who called himself William Lloyd. Franklin was impressed by the man, who spoke excellent Latin and Greek. When his guest left, Franklin discovered that he was missing an expensive shirt and handkerchief. The visitor was almost certainly Tom Bell.

He often pretended to be the son of some well-known administrator. With the right name, you could make yourself at home in somebody's house or buy on credit, then disappear with the goods.

When things became too hot for Tom Bell in America, he travelled to the Caribbean and carried out the same scams there. In Barbados, he claimed to be Gilbert Burnet, the son of the former governor of Massachusetts. His petty crimes brought calamity on others. He was invited to a Jewish family wedding, where he tried to steal the gifts. The family caught him and beat him. He then gave a distorted account of the assault to the wider Christian community, who responded by destroying the synagogue.

Bell returned to America. In New Jersey, a stranger mistook him for a Presbyterian minister, Rev. John Rowland. Bell decided to exploit the similarity in appearance and travelled to the next town, where he pretended to be the famous minister. A local family welcomed him and gave him a place to stay. He went with the family to preach at their church. On the way, Bell claimed he had left his sermon behind. He returned to the house, stole their valuables and rode away on one of their horses. Later, when the real Rev. Rowland visited New Jersey, he was arrested for horse-stealing, and it took some time to convince authorities it was a look-alike who'd done it.

When he was between jobs, Bell used his classical education to get work as a schoolmaster, but he didn't stick at it long before he was back to some form of criminal activity—swindling or counterfeiting.

He became so notorious that newspapers announced his movements to warn the public that he might be in town. Bell was frequently recognized by former victims and would spend time in jail.

Finally, he gave up on America and went to Jamaica, where he began a new career as a pirate. He was first mate on a ship that attacked a Spanish schooner. It didn't go well. Bell and the ship's captain were caught and sentenced to death. Bell killed himself before he could be hanged.

A US STEAL

In 1904, the Citizens National Bank in the little city of Oberlin, Ohio, received a special visitor. Her name was Mrs. Cassie Chadwick, she lived in Cleveland, about thirty miles away, and she was married to a wealthy doctor. But those who had their finger on society's pulse knew she was more than that—she was the illegitimate daughter of Andrew Carnegie, founder of U.S. Steel and (adjusting for inflation) one of the wealthiest Americans in history.

It explained some of Mrs. Chadwick's spending habits. She was a woman who liked to spend money. She sent her friends lavish tokens of her affection—items like pianos and cars. But to her, a few thousand dollars here and there were nothing—a drop in the bucket.

The president of the bank, Mr. C.T. Beckwith, made sure he dealt with Mrs. Chadwick personally. She confided in him about her parentage, and it confirmed everything he had heard. Her father was Andrew Carnegie, and he was so racked with guilt about her illegitimacy that he constantly sent her money. Swearing the banker to secrecy—she did not want to embarrass her dear father—she showed him papers and stocks worth nearly $14 million. She promised she would let the bank handle all her affairs soon. In the meantime, she wanted Beckwith and the bank's chief cashier to receive $10,000 a year for their trouble in looking after her business.

The banker accepted the offer. He told Mrs. Chadwick that he would keep her secrets and that her credit was good at his bank—he would make sure of that. The loans carried a high interest rate and were profitable for the bank. She was good for it. She could borrow what she liked.

And borrow she did. She borrowed and she kept borrowing, and Beckwith kept lending. She spent a fortune on jewelry, fine clothes, gifts and many other luxuries. The debt grew higher and higher. Chadwick owed the bank $240,000—a vast sum in those days, and several times more than the small bank had available to lend. Beckwith made creative adjustments to the bank's paperwork so the money would keep flowing to Mrs. Chadwick and topped up the funds with more than $100,000 of his own money.

The bank president knew that if he could keep Mrs. Chadwick happy now, he would have a very wealthy friend in the future. Having a customer like her in his small-town bank was an incredible stroke of luck.

Beckwith might not have felt so lucky if he had known more about Cassie Chadwick's background.

Her real name was Elizabeth Bigley. She had been born in 1857 in rural Ontario. Her father was a rail worker, but Bigley aspired to the high life and used fraud to get it. When she was twenty-one, she forged a letter from a lawyer in London which stated that she had been bequeathed $1,800. She showed the letter to get credit from local stores and buy what she liked. But that scam couldn't last forever. Eventually, one of the merchants wanted payment and, when Bigley couldn't pay, she was arrested.

Fraud was a serious charge, but Bigley's behaviour during the trial was strange—she made faces at the witnesses. The jury thought she must be insane, and she was acquitted.

For some years, she wandered around, using various aliases. Sometimes she rented rooms, then made a few dollars by hawking the furniture. But that was no way for a lady to live, so she changed her identity. She pretended to be the heiress to an Irish estate. In this persona, she married a Cleveland doctor. The marriage quickly ended when he saw how much she had spent on wedding gifts for herself. Bigley adopted a new identity and spent time as a fake clairvoyant, topping up her income by passing forged financial notes. That crime got her sent to prison for a few years.

When she came out, she ran a brothel. But she pretended she came from a wealthy New York family and became romantically involved with another Cleveland doctor, Leroy Chadwick. When Dr. Chadwick found out about the brothel and confronted Bigley, she fainted. She claimed she had no idea her decent boarding house was being used for such purposes. Dr. Chadwick believed her, and the couple were married.

The doctor was comfortably off, but not wealthy enough for Mrs. Chadwick. Her wealthier neighbours didn't take to her—she tried too hard to win their affection with gifts. She had "made it," but only as the wife of a respected doctor. She would never be accepted into high society.

That's when Bigley came up with her biggest con. She asked one of her husband's lawyer friends, a man named Dillon, to take her to Andrew Carnegie's house in New York, where she had some business to conduct. He saw her go inside.

When she emerged, she "accidentally" dropped a document. Dillon saw it. It was a promissory note for $2 million, signed by Andrew Carnegie. When Dillon asked what it was all about, Mrs. Chadwick revealed that she was Carnegie's illegitimate daughter.

Dillon naturally assumed she had gone into the house for a private meeting with "Daddy." In fact, she had only made an appointment with the housekeeper, claiming she wanted to check the references of a former servant.

Mrs. Chadwick carefully dropped word of her dark past in all the right places, and soon it was a well-known secret that she was heir to an enormous fortune. Banks all over Ohio lined up to lend her money.

C.T. Beckwith, president of the Citizens National Bank in Oberlin, was one of her suckers and had bet the most on his client's credentials. Mrs. Chadwick lived very well on the money from the banks for several years. It seems like a high-risk strategy, but it's possible she was waiting for Carnegie's death, at which point she could make a claim on his estate.

But that didn't happen. Another banker, who had also lent money to Cassie Chadwick, learned that she had taken on huge new loans. He sued to get his bank's money from her. Andrew Carnegie heard of the case and denied any connection to Chadwick. The banks looked inside a package which they had been assured contained Mrs. Chadwick's millions in stocks and bonds. It actually contained a stack of low-value stocks and a forged trust certificate.

The banks lost enormous sums. The little bank in Oberlin went out of business. The president and his chief cashier were charged for their involvement. They had honestly believed Mrs. Chadwick's story, but they had conspired to lend her money she should not have received. The cashier went to prison for five years, but for Beckwith, the stress was too much—he died before the trial.

Cassie Chadwick's own trial was a media sensation. All of America wanted to know how an ordinary woman could swindle banks out of millions. She was found guilty and sentenced to fourteen years in prison. Her health declined rapidly once she was behind bars, and she died in less than two years.

Her "father," Andrew Carnegie, lived another eighteen years. He used much of it spending his vast fortune on philanthropic work.

PROSE AND CONS

One con artist spent years tricking big-name authors out of their manuscripts. Publishers and authors knew this was going on, but nobody knew who was behind it or what they were up to.

Like many "phishing" scammers, the con artist created hundreds of domain names resembling those of real businesses, so "randomhouse" in a domain name might be written as the visually similar "randornhouse." The scammer exclusively focused on publishing.

Pretending to be an editor or literary agent, and using an email address from his fake publisher, the con artist would contact the author and ask for a draft of an as-yet unpublished novel. The emails were convincing and used the language expected of someone in the publishing business, and many authors sent the requested manuscript before they realized they'd been tricked.

He targeted many big names, including Sally Rooney, Ian McEwan and Margaret Atwood.

The profit motive for the scam was hard to figure out. In some cases, the early release of the book might have been costly for publishers, but the material never appeared online, and the con artist never made any blackmail demands.

Some people speculated he was a corporate spy. Others thought he was working for Hollywood, getting advance information on books that might make good films.

The truth finally emerged in 2022, when the FBI arrested a twenty-nine-year-old man who had held a low-level job at publisher Simon & Schuster. He admitted to the fraud, but it seemed that his actions came more from an obsession than a desire for profit. He said he saw people at his workplace sharing manuscripts and wanted to feel like he, too, was a real publishing professional. According to a report in *The Guardian*, he had collected around a thousand manuscripts because he wanted to be "one of the fewest to cherish them before anyone else."

He was charged with wire fraud, which can carry a sentence of up to twenty years in prison. He didn't get prison time other than the time he had already served, but he had to pay $88,000 to one publisher to cover their legal costs. Because he was not a US citizen, he was ordered to be deported from the United States.

TWO-FACED POLITICIANS

Between 2015 and 2017, a number of super-wealthy individuals received video calls from Jean-Yves Le Drian, who was then the French defense minister.

Peering grimly over his glasses, the elderly minister explained that he had come to them with a problem. Two French journalists had been taken hostage by Middle Eastern extremists in Syria.

It was the policy of the French government not to pay ransoms, but if the ransoms weren't paid, the journalists would be killed.

Le Drian thought his wealthy contacts might be able to provide discreet help behind the scenes and save the lives of the journalists. He wanted them to send money privately and anonymously to the kidnappers so the journalists could be released.

He gave them details of a Chinese bank where the money could be wired.

The caller was fake. He was later discovered to be a French-Israeli con artist in his early fifties, sitting in a mock-up of the minister's office. He wore a silicone mask to make him appear like a bald man in his seventies. The mask would have been detectable up close, but the caller kept his distance from the camera and made sure the video quality and lighting was imperfect. Under those conditions, the appearance of the mask was good enough.

The con artist and his team contacted more than 150 prominent individuals: company CEOs, church leaders, presidents, prime ministers and kings. In most cases, they were either suspicious or chose not to hand over their money. But the con didn't have to work often to be profitable. A handful of donations netted the scammers around $60 million.

The con artists may have chosen the minister because he was an important figure, but not someone very well-known by the public. However, one of their targets was a multimillionaire in the wine business. He knew the minister quite well, but was completely taken in by the performance. That is, until the fake Le Drian made a mistake: he addressed the businessman with the formal French "vous." As a friend, he should have used the more casual "tu."

In 2017, authorities eventually tracked down the gang to a hideout in Ukraine. The seven members were arrested as they planned their next scam. The details of that con are unknown, but judging by the photos on their mobile phones, it involved using a mask of Prince Albert II of Monaco.

Most of the gang received prison sentences. The leader, who had played the role of the minister, went to prison for seven years, and also had to pay a 2-million euro fine.

I THINK AI KNOW YOU

In the old TV series *Mission Impossible*, agents routinely impersonated people using rubber masks. It works well in TV and film because, until the mask is dramatically peeled off, the agent who wears it is played by the same actor who plays the person being impersonated.

When rubber masks are used in real life, as they were in the Le Drian impersonation, the silicone prosthetics are not so easy to work with. They often don't look good up close, and even when they're not coming unstuck, they give the face an unnaturally rigid appearance. Then there's the problem of imitating a person's voice—it's very difficult to get that right.

But advances in computer technology offer new options to the modern con artist. For example, we've seen scams where criminals target adults with fake messages from their children and grandchildren. These can be made more effective with a little help from AI.

In 2023, "Lynn" in Pittsburgh got a call from her adult daughter. She was sobbing. She said she had been in a car accident and her nose was broken. A police officer then came on the line. It seemed Lynn needed to transfer money to help her daughter.

In the meantime, Lynn called and sent a series of texts to her daughter to find out how she was doing.

Eventually she got a response. The daughter said, "I don't know why you keep calling me. I'm in a conference." Although the tone was irritated, Lynn was hugely relieved—it meant that the car accident was a fiction.

When Lynn talked to *KDKA News* in Pittsburgh, she said that the sound of her daughter's voice had been completely convincing. It's likely that the criminals took samples of the daughter's voice from social media posts and used them to create a customized message.

‖‖‖‖‖‖‖‖‖‖

The con artists targeting Lynn failed in their attempt, but others have been more successful. In August 2019, the *Wall Street Journal* reported on a case where con artists tricked the CEO of a UK energy company. "Charles" received a phone call from "Friedrich," the head of the parent company in Germany. Charles recognized his boss's distinctive voice, and when Friedrich said he needed Charles to make an urgent transfer of nearly $250,000 to a Hungarian bank account, Charles did as he was told.

Friedrich called back to say that the parent company would reimburse the UK company. No reimbursement arrived, so when he phoned again asking for another transfer, Charles become suspicious and didn't send the money, but the first payment was unrecoverable.

However, the ultimate in digital fakery involves using AI to simulate both the voice and the appearance of a caller.

In early 2023, "Yichen," a business executive at a technology company in the Chinese city of Fuzhou, received a video call from his friend "Jiang."

According to *China Daily*, Jiang said he was bidding on a big project in another city. He needed to make a large payment, but he couldn't do it from his own account. He asked if Yichen could help him. He would move money to Yichen's corporate account, and Yichen would send the payment on Jiang's behalf.

It was a little unorthodox, but Yichen trusted his friend and was willing to help. Jiang gave him the banking information, and Yichen made the transfer in two transactions—the total was about $600,000. Then Jiang sent a screenshot of his own bank transfer voucher to show that he had refunded the money Yichen had sent.

A short while later, Yichen called Jiang to verify some of the details of the money transfers.

"What money transfers?" asked Jiang.

"The money transfers you asked me to make on that video call."

"Video call? I didn't make a video call."

The calls were part of a con. It's believed that Yichen was talking to an AI-generated simulation of his friend. Yichen recognized his friend's voice and face and was taken in.

Yichen quickly contacted police, who discovered that the money had gone to a bank in Mongolia. There was time to reverse one of the transactions, but a large chunk of the money was gone.

As of this writing, computerized face-fakery is still rare, but it seems inevitable that it will become a growth area in the world of frauds. It works much better than a rubber mask.

UNREAL ESTATE FEES

It's slightly disappointing to learn that the most lucrative impersonations are not exciting or daring. They often involve pretending to be an anonymous bureaucrat and catching the right people at just the right time.

A mother and daughter in Colorado wanted to buy a townhome. In March 2023, they found a place they liked and put in an offer for just under $200,000. The sellers accepted the offer, and a closing date was set.

According to Denver's *KDVR-TV* news, a representative from the title company emailed "Jenny," the mother, with a "polite reminder" that the funds needed to be transferred in the next forty-eight hours.

Jenny had the money ready. She replied that she would call back in an hour.

"I'll be doing another closing then," the rep emailed back. "But there's no need to call. Just send the money. I'll give you the information you need."

Jenny took down the instructions and did as she was asked. The transaction went smoothly. It was another step completed in the purchase of her house.

On the closing day, Jenny and her daughter went to the title company to complete the paperwork. There were reams of paper to sign. Once it was all done, the staff member asked about the money.

"Yes, we sent it," said Jenny.

The woman was puzzled. She checked. "No, we didn't receive anything."

Jenny was overcome by horror as she realized that the person she had emailed was not connected to the title company, and neither was the bank account where she had transferred $200,000—her entire life savings.

This type of scam is called a "business email compromise." The scammer had hacked an email account to read the emails going back and forth, and inserted themselves into the process at a critical time. The hackers' emails seemed completely convincing: the rep said they were from the correct company, the emails (copied from real ones) looked the same, and they knew the amount to be transferred. But when the money was sent, it went straight to an account controlled by the criminals.

As of this writing, the police and the FBI are still investigating the crime, but unless they get a break in the case, there is not much Jenny can do to get her money back. Her mistake was understandable—she was dealing with an unfamiliar process—but for someone familiar with this kind of scam, sending money based solely on emailed instructions was dangerous, and the email request "Don't phone me" was a red flag.

CHAPTER 20
CHUMP CHANGE

Many successful cons dispense with cheques, computers, disguises and other ingenious plans. They're all about the money.

QUICK-CHANGE ARTISTS

In 2020, a middle-aged man we'll call "Fergus" walked into a well-known "big box" store. This was peak COVID-19, and he was wearing a polka-dot face mask. Fergus wasn't buying much today. He put a couple of small items on the counter, and the young cashier, "Elsie," scanned them. The total was $6.25. Fergus pulled out his wallet and realized he only had a $100 bill.

"I'm so sorry, this is all I have."

"No problem," said Elsie.

He handed her the bill, and she started to make change, while Fergus explained.

"See, I figured I had another thirty-five in there: a twenty and a five. And also a couple of ones. So one-thirty-seven. But then, I realized I'd spent $12 on lunch . . ."

Elsie nodded and smiled, although it was difficult keeping track of his number-filled conversation while she was counting bills and coins.

She handed back the change for his hundred, then suddenly, Fergus made a discovery. "Well, I'll be. I had a five in my pocket all along. Now where are those quarters?"

In a moment, Fergus had triumphantly put the exact change for the purchase into Elsie's hand: "$6 and 25 cents! There you go, all that fuss for nothing! So, if you would just give me back my hundred."

"Uh . . . sure."

Elsie handed back the hundred and closed the till.

"You have a nice day now," said Fergus, leaving the store.

A minute later, Elsie realized that she had accidentally given Fergus not only $93.75 in change, but also the hundred he had given her in the first place. She looked out in the parking lot, but he was nowhere to be seen.

The miscount was no accident. The *Central New Jersey Home News* reported that "Fergus" had gone from store to store making small purchases with a $100 bill. He was good at confusing inexperienced cashiers and usually left the store with more than $90 in change he wasn't owed.

The "Quick-change" scam is a classic con where the artist keeps money moving back and forth until the cashier can't keep track of how much is owed.

In a perfect world, the cashier would cancel one transaction before starting another, but instead the con artist talks to the cashier while the till is open, offering helpful suggestions on how to make change and handing over money, so the cashier must mentally keep track of the bills going back and forth.

Some quick-change specialists operate as a team. One fiddles around adding bills and coins to the purchase, while the other interrupts with confusing questions.

One thing that works in the criminal's favour is that cashiers are often unable to describe the con artist—all their attention was on the money.

If the cashier spots the error, the con artist can claim it was an honest mistake. Even so, the scam has risks. A team of two Chicago quick-change operators worked their way across Iowa in 1985, getting money from many of the stores and diners they visited. They were about to make a nice profit from buying two cups of coffee, when the cashier realized what was going on and grabbed the con artist, getting the money back. A second botched operation led to a business owner noting the car's licence, and police caught and arrested the team.

Quick-change cons can involve sleight of hand, as well as confusing language. One trick is to hold up a bill of one denomination, then palm it and hand a lower-value bill to the cashier. This works best in countries like the United States, where all bills are the same colour. It would be harder to do in Australia or England, where bills are not only different colours, but also different sizes.

Sometimes, the quick-change con is carried out by the merchant rather than the customer. Someone buying a $15 item hands over a $20 bill and asks for change. The merchant palms the $20 and holds up a $5 bill. "Change? You still owe me $10." The embarrassed customer may believe they have made a mistake and will pay another $10, apologizing as they do so.

MONEY ON THE LINE

Years ago, young criminals used to get a discount for phone booths, vending machines and pinball by using a coin with a hole drilled through it, attached to a length of fishing line. After the coin had been popped into the slot, the criminal could pull it back up using the fishing line.

Recently, in the United Kingdom, a team of four criminals, aged from mid-thirties to late fifties, carried out a more modern version of the same scam using banknotes.

British betting shops use digital terminals that accept cash. The criminals inserted laminated £20 and £50 banknotes into slots. The banknotes were connected to plastic leads. Once the machine had registered the payment, they pulled the money out again, then casually placed their next bet.

To a casual onlooker, they were just regular customers using the betting machines. Their con was to appear ordinary and unremarkable as they casually robbed the business.

There was no guarantee their bets would win, but that was okay—if they lost, it cost them nothing but time. However, if a bet paid off, the gang received real money from the machine.

Over two months, this barefaced scam cheated the betting shops out of more than £660,000. The shops soon noticed the discrepancies between the machine's reported take and the actual cash inside it. When police reviewed security footage, they saw the same men, wearing the same clothing and baseball caps at each location.

The police identified a group of suspects and when they arrested them, they also found a bag with the matching clothing and baseball caps.

The scammers knew they were caught. In court, they all pleaded guilty to conspiracy to commit fraud and received jail terms ranging from nine months to more than four years, as well as a lifetime ban from betting shops.

HALF-CROWN BIBB

In England in the late 1700s, locals were entertained by a con artist known as "Half-Crown Bibb." Bibb had worked as an engraver but then lost his job, so now he supported himself and his heavy drinking by "borrowing" money from everyone he met, usually a half-crown coin (worth two shillings and sixpence—or one-eighth of a pound).

Someone at the time calculated that Bibb must have been earning £2,000 a year from his requests. If true, it would have been enough money to live as a gentleman. He is said to have been the inspiration for a swindler named "Jeremy Diddler" in a popular comedy play at the time.

On one occasion, Bibb approached a writer for money. The writer was a successful man, so Bibb doubled his usual rate and asked for the loan of a crown (that is five shillings or sixty pence—equivalent to about $25 today). The writer said he didn't have that much change on him, but he did have three shillings and a sixpence.

Bibb accepted the money with thanks, but before saying goodbye, he said to the writer, "Remember, I intended to borrow a crown, so you still owe me eighteen pence."

THEY WEREN'T COUNTERFEIT

In early 1896, a well-dressed man entered G.S. Rosenberg's, a store in Louisville, Kentucky, and asked to buy a collar button. The button was 10 cents, and the man only had a $10 bill. That was a large bill in those days, equivalent to about $360 today. The clerk said he couldn't make change for a $10 bill, and the man left the store without making a purchase.

Later, the man returned and bought a tie, and was served by the same clerk. The purchase completed, the man was about to leave when a thought seemed to occur to him.

"I came here earlier, and you wouldn't make change for a ten. Did you think the bill was counterfeit?"

"No, not at all," said the clerk.

"Good, good," said the man. "Even so, it's a good idea for a clerk to be able to identify a counterfeit bill." He leaned closer as if to share something confidential. "I know a good method. If you want, I can show you."

"Yes, I would like that very much," said the clerk.

The customer asked for a couple of bills, which the clerk took from the register: a $5 bill and a $2 bill (about $250 today), and handed them to him. The customer took a nickel from his pocket, moistened both sides, and placed it between the two bills.

"We're going to squeeze them together," he said, as he constructed this money sandwich. "After a while, the nickel should make an impression on the bills, but if they're counterfeit, there won't be any impression."

He folded the bills together into a square around the nickel, then put wrapping paper around the little package and tied it tightly together.

"It takes a while to work," he said, "so I'm going to step out and get a drink, but I'll be back in a few minutes, then we'll open the package and see if the bills are good."

The customer departed, leaving the package on the counter. The clerk waited, but after half an hour, the man still hadn't come back. The clerk suddenly became suspicious. He opened the package. It contained a nickel, but no bills. The customer had palmed them while he wrapped the package.

BLACK MONEY

In 2003, a seventy-three-year-old Florida man, a retired electronics expert, travelled to the Middle East to pick up a suitcase full of bills. "Gus" had paid more than $300,000 for the case, but the contents were worth far more—the bills inside totalled more than $21 million.

Arriving in Dubai, he met his contact, "Azif," who took him to an ordinary-looking house. Inside, armed guards protected a windowless room. There, Gus saw the grey metal case holding his money—bundles of $100 bills. Azif opened the case so Gus could inspect his purchase. But there didn't appear to be any money inside—just stacks of black paper.

Gus was puzzled. What was going on?

Azif explained that the money was dyed to protect against theft. The dye was easily removed.

A chemist entered the room wearing rubber gloves, carrying a dish and a small bottle of solution. He put the dish on the table and poured the solution into the dish, then took three of the black bills and dunked them in the liquid. The black coating dissolved, exposing three $100 bills.

Gus examined the bills. They were the real thing. All that remained was to wash the rest of the money and take his cash home. But there was a problem with that. It seemed the chemist had just used the last of the high-security cleaning solution. They could get more, but it would cost money—close to $300,000.

Gus paid it.

He had fallen victim to the "Black Money" scam, which you might recall from the story of the manga artist who was courted by a fake Mark Ruffalo. There was no actual cash—or very little. Con artists present their mark with a stash of black construction paper cut to the size of currency. A few bills are real money, coated black. These can be "randomly" selected from the case or switched using sleight of hand.

The real bills are typically coated in a waterproof layer of glue, then painted with a dark brown iodine solution. When the iodine-coated bills are washed in the right solution (ground-up vitamin C will do the trick), the iodine becomes transparent, and the money is revealed. Of course, the rest of the black paper is worthless.

A man in Stamford, Connecticut, lost more than $400,000 to the same scam. In this case, the con artists told "Milton" they needed money to remove the dye from millions of dollars of cash from Sierra Leone. They explained to Milton that the US government had dyed the bills to prevent them from falling into the hands of terrorists.

Milton had the cash at his house (he didn't trust banks but did trust smugglers from Sierra Leone). The con artists demonstrated the cleaning process at a hotel room, then claimed that if Milton combined his cash with their black money, it would speed up the process. He was left with black paper and no money.

A man arrested with black money in South Africa turned out to be the victim. Even the real money he had been given was counterfeit. The expensive chemical he'd bought for removing the dye was actually a raspberry fruit-drink powder.

Con artists may give different explanations for why the money is black. It may be a security measure against theft, or it may have been stained in a heist or as part of a government process to destroy the money.

The scam doesn't always go smoothly. Two crooks in Rhode Island took their mark to a hotel room to demonstrate how the bills could be washed clean. They arrived with suitcases full of black paper. For their chemical demonstration, they used ammonia, which they boiled. The fumes it created set off the fire alarm, and the con artists ran from the scene leaving the chemicals and suitcases behind. It was a lucky escape for the man they had intended to con.

The Black Money scam is sometimes used on its own or it may be the final stage of a longer scam. In Gus's case, the black bills were the last step in a classic Nigerian Prince type of scam involving funds that were supposed to belong to a dead German businessman.

Gus had spent the past year negotiating this deal. Gus was already having trouble staying on top of his expenses, but he paid fake fees to allow millions of dollars to be moved from one foreign bank to another. To raise the money, he mortgaged his house and borrowed money against the value of his cars. The way Gus saw it, the money he spent was an investment, and the payoff from it would solve all his financial problems for good.

Gus's son, who knew about the deal, told him not to do it and insisted it was all a scam. Gus got the same advice from the police. Gus felt differently, and seeing the "money" in front of him in a suitcase was the proof he needed. He kept borrowing to pay for chemical treatments until he was unable to get any more money.

The scam left him penniless, but even so he was luckier than some of the victims, who never returned from their overseas trip.

CHAPTER 21
BAD COMPANY

Some of the biggest scams involve corporations. Sometimes they're the victims, and sometimes they're the con artist.

WHERE THE VOLK IS MY CAR?

The Volkswagen emissions scandal, "Dieselgate," has brought the company some embarrassing headlines in recent years, but the origins of the company and its most famous car were mired in an even bigger scandal, which deceived hundreds of thousands of German citizens.

In 1933, after Hitler became chancellor, he convinced Germans that he could provide them with a better standard of living. Cars were luxury items in those days, but he promised a driving lifestyle for everyone. Germany was already building a set of the multi-lane highways—the Autobahn—but Hitler needed inexpensive cars for these new roads. He wanted to promote a German car for the German "folk"—although in Nazi Germany, the term "Volk" implied a white "master race" descended from Vikings. "Volkswagen" is basically German for "folks-wagon"—a car for "the People."

Hitler brought in Ferdinand Porsche as a designer, and he came up with a design—although some say he just stole it from the work of the Hungarian inventor Béla Barényi.

The car wasn't called the "Beetle" or the "Volkswagen" at first. One of the Nazi slogans was "Strength through joy"—"Kraft durch Freude" or "KdF." The new car was named the "KdF-wagen"—the "Strength-through-Joy-wagon." Not too catchy, is it?

But the little car looked good for its day, and Hitler was later photographed in a convertible model given to him for his birthday. The vehicle was sold at the bargain price of 990 Reichsmarks—very inexpensive for a car in those days and, by some estimates, about half what the car cost to produce—but even that bargain-basement price was five months' salary for a factory worker and far beyond what most Germans could afford. That was one barrier to owning the car. The second problem was that the factory that would make the cars hadn't actually been built yet.

But the Nazis had an answer for both issues. They launched a program allowing average Germans to buy the new car by paying into the scheme ahead of time. The company would use the money to build the factories, then the factories would build the vehicles. Prospective buyers were issued a "savings booklet" allowing them to pay for the car gradually. The booklet had space for fifty green or red stamps, each decorated with the design of the car.

A single stamp cost 5 marks—just about manageable for most people, if they cut back on their groceries. The kids could join in, too. They could put their coins in a tin savings box, which counted their small change on a dial and opened a door when they had put in enough to buy a 5 Reichsmark stamp.

According to the rules, buyers had to keep paying into the program or lose everything they'd contributed so far. It gave consumers a strong incentive to keep investing.

Families needed to purchase two hundred stamps to buy the car, so filling four of the savings booklets would do it . . . almost. Because there were some extra costs. If Germans wanted a convertible like the one owned by their mustached leader, it cost an extra twelve stamps. Then there was a delivery charge—another twelve stamps . . . unless they wanted to collect the car from the factory . . . once they finished building it. Finally, there was the insurance charge. That was another forty stamps, and it was compulsory. So in fact, the average buyer had to fill out at least five booklets to pay for their vehicle.

But once that was done, after roughly three years of saving, the family could be the proud owner of their very own Strength-through-Joy-wagon.

Not quite.

Around seven hundred thousand people signed up for the car savings program. By the end of the Second World War, nearly half had paid off the full amount of a car. It was a bad investment. The number of people who received a car was—zero. Only a handful of Beetles were produced, and none of these went to the people who had bought the stamps. But even though nobody had got a car, people kept paying in, not wanting to lose their "sunk costs."

A factory was constructed in KdF-stadt—Strength-through-Joy City. The metropolis didn't contain as much joy as you might imagine: the factory used mostly forced labour to produce military vehicles for the war.

Although the car was associated with Hitler, Volkswagen production didn't start until after the war, when Hitler was dead.

The Allied occupation forces discovered the factory and some prototype cars, and a British major, Ivan Hirst, decided to get it up and running. He figured it would keep the German workers gainfully employed, and the factory could produce the little cars for the use of the occupying forces and Allied workers. Soon, the vehicles were rolling off the production lines at the rate of a thousand every month.

KdF became Volkswagen, and the Beetle became a symbol for a new Germany. The car remained in production, with fairly minor redesigns, until 2003.

The people who had saved stamps felt cheated by the whole thing. In 1950, they sued Volkswagen. The case moved slowly through the German courts. Finally, after twelve years, they won their case—although it was a small victory. They were awarded a 12 percent discount on the price of a new Beetle. Wanting to put the whole stamp business behind them, Volkswagen pointed out that, as a company that had basically been created by the Allies after the war, it wasn't the same one that had offered the car-savings scam. The people who had conned the German "folk" were the Nazis.

INVESTMENT BANKS OF THE MISSISSIPPI

Some people will go to extremes to get their share of a hot new thing. And sometimes the hot new thing is a share. In 1719, everyone wanted to buy shares in the Mississippi Company, and they were hard to get hold of.

During this period, one wealthy French lady sat in her carriage, riding back and forth through the streets of Paris, waiting for the right moment for her coach driver to crash the vehicle.

She hoped to win the sympathy of a man named John Law, a Scottish banker living in Paris who had authority to sell the shares, and she thought a carriage crash might do the trick. She patrolled the city for three days, then she spotted Mr. Law. She called to her coach driver, who promptly drove into a post, upsetting the carriage.

Her timing was perfect. John Law was shocked by the accident and ran to the scene, helping the lady from her carriage. He took her to a nearby hotel to recover.

"Are you all right?" he asked? "Would you like tea?"

She said, "I am too shaken."

"Brandy?"

"I don't think I could manage it."

"Is there anything I can get for you?"

She perked up. "Yes—I'd like to buy shares in the Mississippi Company."

The company had been John Law's initiative. In 1719, France controlled a big chunk of what is now the United States, as well as various islands in the Caribbean. Law had come to France to get away from a manslaughter charge in Britain. As well as a banker, he was a gambler and a ladies' man who had killed a man in a duel over a lady.

But once he was settled in France, he found many financial opportunities. In particular, Law had the idea of combining all the country's trading operations under one huge monopoly.

The new "Mississippi Company" would control all of France's North American trade. The company would get money from taxes on North American settlers, as well as from all the resources found in the area, which included beaver furs and huge amounts of gold. Best of all, the public were allowed to buy shares. John Law promised massive profits on each share: 120 percent per year.

With profits like these, everybody in France wanted in on the action. There were nowhere near enough shares to meet the demand. Aristocrats lined up for hours outside Law's house in the hope of catching a glimpse of the great man so they could beg to buy shares.

Many people used underhanded methods to get to Law. The carriage crash was one of the more extreme strategies. It's said that Law was amused by the lady's guile and sold her the shares she wanted.

Another woman, named Madame de Boucha, tried a different ruse. She tracked Law to the house where he was having dinner, then shouted "Fire!" The diners jumped to their feet in alarm and ran for the exits. Madame de Boucha ran forward, hoping to catch Law. Unfortunately for her, he spotted her running toward the supposed fire, realized it was a trick, and ran the other way to hide from her.

Law's servants were frequently offered bribes by aristocrats and rich merchants who wanted access to their master. Law's own coach driver became so wealthy that he quit his job. He offered his former boss two other coach drivers to replace him. Law chose one, and the former coach driver hired the other.

The shares soared in value, and anyone who had been fortunate to buy at the original price became rich.

The desperation to purchase shares caused many French buyers to become con artists. But all their small cons were eclipsed by a much bigger con. John Law had greatly exaggerated the wealth of the Mississippi Company. The territory wasn't producing the huge amounts of gold he had claimed.

Charles Mackay wrote about the scandal in his classic 1852 book *Memoirs of Extraordinary Popular Delusions and the Madness of Crowds*. The way he saw it, Law was an unwitting "confidence man." He said that Law "did not see that confidence, like mistrust, could be increased almost ad infinitum, and that hope was as extravagant as fear."

Once the truth came out, and people realized the stocks would never pay the profits they'd been promised, their value dropped like a rock. Those who had bought at the peak were ruined. The French public was furious. John Law fled France and relocated to Italy. He had been the cause of the problem and he was also one of the victims—he had invested his own money in the Mississippi Company and lost it all. He died a poor man.

THE OLD SHELL GAME

Many corporate cons are an attempt to make products look better than they actually are. But in the Netherlands in 1973, executives in the egg industry turned that rule on its head.

The Dutch Egg Board was worried about sales; demand for eggs was falling. It didn't make sense—the industry had gone out of its way to improve the way eggs were delivered to its customers. Modern eggs were all factory-cleaned and were presented in colourful plastic boxes, which protected them from damage.

But when the board carried out a consumer survey, they discovered that cleanliness was exactly the problem. People were sick of living in a world that seemed to be racing too fast into the future. Many consumers had grown up buying farm eggs, which were often imperfect. The new packaging and ultra-clean eggs seemed unnatural, part of a sterile, antiseptic world with too much plastic and industrialization.

The egg-producers had to make their eggs more natural, so they did it with a harmless con: they took the freshly cleaned eggs and carefully added bits of dirt and the occasional feather, restoring that farm-fresh look.

UNFRIENDED

Facebook and Google are often used by con artists to reach potential victims, but sometimes the giant companies become targets themselves.

Between 2013 and 2015, a Lithuanian man sent invoices to these huge companies for supplying them with computer hardware. He used the name of a Taiwanese computer company that both Facebook and Google had legitimate dealings with. His invoices and paperwork looked like the real thing, but he arranged for the payments to be sent to accounts he controlled personally, then laundered the money through a series of international banks.

In total, he managed to scam more than $120 million from the two companies.

Accountants finally realized what was going on, and in 2017, he was extradited to the United States to face charges of wire fraud. In a New York court, he was sentenced to five years in prison.

The companies said they had since recouped most of the lost money—and had convincing-looking paperwork to prove it.

CHAPTER 22
ANIMAL SCAMS

You may harden your heart to the plight of an unfortunate human, but who doesn't love a cute animal?

There are some terrible cons out there: people who steal your dog, then try to claim the reward on finding it, or crooks who show up as animal-control officers and say they will take your dog away unless you pay a fine on the spot.

But some animal scams are much stranger, while others are downright . . . beastly.

RABBIT BABIES

We'll tell you upfront that this story isn't as cute as the title suggests. Some cons aren't pretty, and this one is gruesome.

In September 1726, a woman named Mary Toft living in Surrey, England, suffered a miscarriage. While she was recovering, another woman suggested she might turn her loss into a profit. "If you do what I tell you, you'll make such a good living that you'll never need money again."

Later, a local doctor was called to Toft's house and was amazed to find she was giving birth to rabbits. All were dead, and most were in pieces, but he carefully collected them. Toft said she had given birth to other animal parts, too—pieces of a cat and parts of an eel.

The doctor couldn't explain it and he wrote to other medical authorities about the astonishing event.

Toft had probably planned to make some money as a celebrity, charging pennies to meet her and look at the rabbits she claimed she had produced. But the story quickly became much bigger than she anticipated.

The King of England, George I, heard about the case and was fascinated. He sent two of his courtiers to investigate.

One was the royal surgeon, Nathaniel St André. He was a Swiss-born gentleman who, after unsuccessful stints as a language teacher and fencing instructor, had turned to the field of surgery. Here he had more luck and was appointed surgeon to the royal household in England. Many critics said he'd only reached this high post because he spoke German, like King George I and his courtiers.

St André wanted to improve his scientific reputation, and this case of rabbit births might give him the chance. He hurried to see the woman and was amazed and delighted when she gave birth to more rabbit parts a few hours after his arrival.

He asked Toft how this had come about. She said she had been pregnant when she was in a field with a group of other women, and they had startled a rabbit from its hiding place. Toft and the other women chased the rabbit, trying to catch it, but it escaped. The event left Toft with a strange desire for rabbit. The yearning for rabbit made her ill, and she had a miscarriage. Since then, she could not stop thinking about rabbits, and she had given birth to a number of them, one a day for several days running.

St André took careful notes for a book he would be writing on the case. He had Toft moved to London, where he could control access to her and show her off to other medical experts. Toft didn't like all this medical attention, but the surgeon assured her that the king was interested in her case, and she would be given a royal pension to support her all her life.

Toft put on a good show. She convulsed impressively as she produced more rabbit parts, then lapsed into unconsciousness.

Two hundred years earlier, the event would have been explained as witchcraft, but this was a more advanced age. One expert on women's medicine, Dr. John Maubray, believed that women could sometimes become spontaneously pregnant and give birth to a mouselike creature known as a "sooterkin." He also believed that pregnant women shouldn't play with apes, dogs, squirrels and other animals, because the animal traits would be transferred to their unborn children. He examined Toft. Her case proved all his theories. She had obsessed over rabbits, and her body was now producing them.

Mary Toft was a sensation. People all over London were talking about her.

But not all the doctors were convinced. One examined the rabbit parts and discovered that the animals seemed to have been cut up with a knife, and their stomach contents showed they had previously eaten straw and grain.

A politician, Thomas Onslow, investigated the movements of Toft's family. He discovered that, in the days before the announcement, her husband had purchased rabbits.

Another doctor, Richard Manningham, heard that Toft had tried to bribe one of the porters to bring some pieces of rabbit to her room. The doctor confronted Toft and threatened surgery to uncover the truth. This was too much for her. She confessed that she had placed the animal parts inside herself so she could expel them later—a dangerous trick that could have led to a deadly infection.

News of the hoax spread fast.

Mary Toft was sent to prison, then released and sent home.

The medical community was mocked for being so credulous, and the careers of some of the more gullible doctors were ruined. The ambitious Nathaniel St André was one of the victims. The king was livid that

St André had made him look foolish and he turned the surgeon away from his court.

St André lived to the age of ninety-six, but died in poverty. It's reported that, after the business with Mary Toft, he never again ate rabbit.

I FOUND YOUR DOG

A Denver man, "Ron," owned a little dog just a year old. In April 2021, a visiting relative left the gate open. The dog seized the opportunity and made a dash for freedom. The relative chased the dog, but the puppy was fast. Soon it was out of sight.

The family searched the neighbourhood for the dog, but there was no sign of it. They asked everyone in the neighbourhood if they'd seen the puppy. They put up ads and posted on social media.

The next day, they got a response from someone who had seen their post on Craigslist. A man named "Felix" messaged Ron. He said he had found the lost dog and would be happy to return it. Ron was relieved. He asked for Felix's address—he'd be right over.

"Not so fast," said Felix. "I need to make sure you are the real owner of the dog, not someone pretending to be the owner."

That sounded a little paranoid to Ron—after all, Felix had contacted him through Craigslist. It would be hard to intercept that message. But Ron figured the guy was just being careful—his heart was in the right place.

Felix sent Ron a verification code. He asked Ron to tell him what it was. That would prove Ron's identity.

Ron checked his messages. A new one had appeared. It contained the wording, "134324 is your Google verification code. Don't share this with anyone."

Felix asked for the code. Ron replied, "It says don't share this with anyone. So I'm not going to tell you that."

Felix said he would send another code. A second message appeared—same wording, but a different code.

Again, Ron refused to tell Felix the code. Felix said he wouldn't hand the dog over unless Ron could prove his identity. He asked him questions about his family and friends and requested their phone numbers.

Ron realized that he was being deceived. He guessed—correctly—that Felix didn't have his dog and was playing some criminal game of his own.

We don't have any information about whether Ron eventually found his dog, but he can be proud of himself for dodging a cruel and very effective scam targeting people who have lost pets. Victims are often in an emotional state and may not be thinking about computer security. The scammer tries to use the victim's Google account to take control of their Google Voice account, which they can do if the victim reveals the secret code provided by Google. Once the scammer has the one-time code, they can make changes to the victim's Google account and create a phone number connected to the victim's. That number is then used to scam other people.

A DIFFERENT KIND OF PIGEON DROP

"Sanjay" from Mumbai found an injured bird. He wanted to help the creature but wasn't sure who to call, so he searched on Google and found a local animal-welfare organization that could help. According to the *Times of India*, he called the toll-free number and the person at the other end took his information and guided him through a registration process. There was a nominal registration fee of 1 rupee—a little more than 1 cent. He went through the process of paying this fee through Gpay. He received a confirmation message from Bird Emergency Rescue.

Later, a man phoned from the organization to let Sanjay know that the bird rescue team was on its way. He waited for an hour with the injured bird, but no team showed up. In the afternoon, he received a message from his bank. Nearly 100,000 rupees (about twelve hundred US dollars) had been removed from his bank account.

PUPPY MOTEL

Many scammers prey on animal lovers, but they don't usually wait for them to call in with news of an injured mammal or bird.

A common scam for a fake rescue organization is to post a picture of an injured animal, requesting donations. They may claim that the animal is scheduled to be euthanized unless they can collect enough money for treatment.

In reality, there is no animal: the scammers have reused an old photograph and made up a compelling sob story.

Many fake rescue organizations are a front for selling dogs from "puppy mills" or animals that have been stolen. If buyers don't bother to check into the background of the organization, confirm its charitable status, or visit the facilities, they can be easily taken in.

In 2018, *Associated Press* reported on a California woman who ran a fake rescue organization offering "rescue dogs" for adoption. Between 2014 and 2017, more than a hundred families paid $450 to adopt a puppy, thinking their money was going to an animal shelter. Their contributions kept the scam going.

The woman lived in a motel room, surrounded by dogs. She didn't care for the puppies, and most of the animals were seriously ill, with viral or parasitic infections. Around thirty dogs were so sick that they died soon after being adopted.

Police raided the motel room, where they found another thirteen dogs ready for sale. They arrested the woman and took the dogs to safety. She was sentenced to four months in prison for animal cruelty.

WE STILL DON'T HAVE A PUPPY

Other adoptions offer animals that don't exist. In 2019, *Global News* reported on a Nova Scotia couple, "Sheila" and "Marc," who lived in a pretty rural area not far from Halifax. They answered the doorbell one day to find a stranger at the door.

"I've come about adopting the puppy."

Sheila didn't know what the person was talking about. After a few apologies, she assumed they must just have the wrong address, but some weeks later a different visitor came to the door asking for a puppy.

Sheila and Marc soon realized something strange was going on. The next few times it happened, they had a longer conversation with their visitors. It turned out that all their callers had been taken in by the same scam, which offered a cute puppy to a loving home.

The pictures were different in each case—sometimes a chihuahua, sometimes a corgi, sometimes a Jack Russell—but all were cute.

Each time, the con artist gave a different email and a different phone number, but for some reason he always gave the same address—Sheila and Marc's home.

The con artist built up a rapport with each victim. He gave a variety of reasons he needed to give up the dog: a sick family member, a long-distance move. The dog was "free," but the scammer wanted $500 for shipping. Evidently, some potential victims had the bright idea of driving to his house and picking up their new pet in person.

One visitor drove from Toronto—an eighteen-hour journey. Another made a twenty-hour trip from Newfoundland that included hundreds of dollars for a ferry ride.

In each case, the couple had to give them the bad news that they'd been scammed.

You might wonder why the con artist provided a home address at all. But it added credibility to his posts, and he may have figured that most people wouldn't bother driving to rural Nova Scotia when they could just have the dog shipped to them.

Sheila and Marc received about a dozen visitors in total, but these were likely the tip of the iceberg—there were probably many more anonymous victims who sent the money for shipment and lost it all.

NOT MY MONKEY

Many animal-themed cons were all about gaining ownership of an ape. It wasn't even a real ape, just a cartoon picture of one.

The *Bored Ape Yacht Club* is a collection of cartoon images, each showing a bored ape in various outfits and poses. Each image is attached to a unique cryptocurrency-like token called a non-fungible token (NFT), so owning one is rather like having the only copy of a rare baseball card.

The price of one of the cartoon-monkey NFT has been as high $3.4 million. To put this in perspective, the same money could buy you a van Dyck, a van Gogh or a Picasso. Then again, those paintings won't show a bored simian with gold fur, a turtleneck and a wacky propeller cap.

When that kind of money is changing hands, it's no surprise that con artists are hard at work to take a cut.

One French website lured users by offering to animate their ape pictures. Owners who signed on were tricked into revealing the password details for their digital wallets.

A Moroccan con artist created a fake marketplace website. Victims who thought they were selling their tokens were actually giving them away for free.

Some have claimed that the ape token is itself a con, where sellers conspire with celebrities to pump up the price. Class action suits are in progress. But it all poses the question: "What *is* the correct price for a cartoon ape?"

We would tell you more about the many computer-based cartoon ape scams, but we're not crypto enthusiasts and, like the ape, we're bored.

THE APE PRINCE

About a thousand years ago, people also invested in an ape. It happened in the Turkish city of Harran around the year 1216 and was witnessed and recorded by a writer named Al-Jawbari.

It all began in the city's large mosque, on one of the Islamic holy days. A well-dressed Indian slave entered and laid down an ornate carpet. Some onlookers were a little curious about who the visitor might be. Judging by the carpet, they figured it must be someone wealthy and important.

A short time later, they found out, as the mystery figure made his way toward the mosque. The worshipper was an ape. He was dressed in the finest clothes and anointed with expensive perfumes. He sat astride a mule, on a saddle decorated in gold. A group of servants and slaves accompanied the ape. One slave carried a prayer mat.

As they passed the astonished crowds, the ape made the traditional salaams at the citizens, touching his forehead and bowing.

Some people in the crowd asked the slaves what was going on. Why were they serving an ape?

"He's not actually an ape," came the reply. "He is a prince, the son of one of the greatest kings of India. He is under a terrible spell."

The news spread through the crowd. Doubtless many people were skeptical, but whether they believed the story or not, they were interested to see how this played out. As the ape's company made its way to the mosque, they were followed by fascinated onlookers. When the ape reached the mosque, one of the slaves placed a prayer mat on the expensive carpet that had recently been laid down. The ape dismounted and did the things expected of a good Muslim: washing, cleaning his teeth and bowing in thanks. He then took out prayer beads and seemed to use them to recite prayers.

One of the slaves then addressed the crowd. He told them to be thankful for their good health, because the creature they saw before them had lost everything.

"This ape was once a prince—handsome, kind and devout. He was heir to the most powerful kingdom in India."

The slave explained that the prince was married to a princess. But scheming courtiers had spread a false rumour that the prince was in love with one of his slave boys. Outrageous!

The prince had denied the rumours, of course, but the princess didn't believe him. She left the palace, making the excuse that she wanted to visit her parents. Once she arrived at her father's home, she did not return, and she cast a spell on her husband to punish him, turning him into an ape.

You might think the prince's family would stand behind him, but no! When his father saw what his son had become, he was disgusted. He cast him out of the palace and banished him from the kingdom. The prince had only his small band of loyal servants to accompany him.

As the crowd listened to this story, the ape held a handkerchief to his face, apparently weeping at his sad fate.

The slave said that because the princess had departed in a hurry, she had left many of her prized possessions at the palace. Her treasure was worth a hundred thousand gold pieces. Later, she regretted the loss of this fortune. She offered a deal. If she was compensated for that amount, she would restore the prince to his human form.

And that was why the crowd saw an ape before them now. The slave explained that the prince had toured the world looking for help. The other kings of India had all contributed to the prince's fund. The sum of ninety thousand gold pieces had now been raised and sent to the princess. But there was still another ten thousand gold pieces to go if this young man was to be restored. "On this holy day, in this holy place,

who will show kindness to this unfortunate Muslim prince, who has lost everything?"

Many of the people who heard this speech were convinced and moved by it. A large sum was donated by the townsfolk. To the writer Al-Jawbari, it was clear that the ape was merely an animal trained for the scam. He was amazed at the scene before his eyes: an ape dressed in outlandish clothes, surrounded by con artists, being showered with gold by the gullible population.

Perhaps that crazy procession is a good symbol for the madness than underlies all cons.

We don't seem to have learned much in a thousand years. Today, sophisticated people pay millions for a cartoon of a bored ape in crazy clothes, while others scheme to steal it from them.

At least the citizens of Harran got to see a real ape.

POSTSCRIPT

Con artists are cunning and devious, but they are not geniuses. And while the methods they use are frequently surprising at first glance, the practitioners are not particularly creative. As we've seen, many con artists don't innovate, but merely repeat or rework the same tired techniques.

The wild cons in this book have worked for centuries, and the same cons, or variants of them, will probably keep on working far into the future.

That could be a depressing thought. And yet perhaps our susceptibility to cons and scams reveals something admirable about us.

Because the attributes the con artist exploits as human "weaknesses" are also our best and most appealing qualities—our willingness to trust others, our desire to offer help and assistance, our readiness to believe in a positive vision, and our determination to chase grand dreams that seem impossible.

The shady world of the con can't exist without the bright light of the human spirit, and the victims of scams are often those in whom the human spirit shines most brightly. If the world's wildest cons work, it is only because they are shadows of the much wilder aspirations that lift us to our greatest heights.

ACKNOWLEDGMENTS

A special thanks to Lachina McKenzie, who did a wonderful job researching and checking many of the stories in this collection.